COMPARING RELIGIOUS TRADITIONS

Judaism, Christianity, Islam,
Hinduism, and Buddhism on

THE LIFE OF VIRTUE

What Do We Owe Ourselves?

Edited by
JACOB NEUSNER
Bard College

With essays by

BRUCE CHILTON
Bard College

CHARLES HALLISEY
Harvard University

BRIAN K. SMITH
University of California, Riverside

TAMARA SONN
College of William and Mary

WADSWORTH
 ™
THOMSON LEARNING

Australia • Canada • Mexico • Singapore • Spain • United Kingdom • United States

Religion Editor: Peter Adams
Assistant Editor: Kara Kindstrom
Editorial Assistant: Mark Andrews
Marketing Manager: Dave Garrison
Print Buyer: Robert King
Permissions Editor: Joohee Lee
Production Service: Matrix Productions

Text Designer: Karen Thomas
Copy Editor: Jan McDearmon
Cover Designer: Bill Stanton
Cover Image: PhotoDisc
Compositor: R&S Book Composition
Cover and Text Printer: Webcom, Limited

Printed in Canada

1 2 3 4 5 6 7 04 03 02 01

For permission to use material from this text, contact us by Web: www.thomsonrights.com
Fax: 1-800-730-2215   Phone: 1-800-730-2214

Wadsworth/Thomson Learning
10 Davis Drive
Belmont, CA 94002-3098
USA

For more information about our products, contact us:
Thomson Learning Academic Resource Center
1-800-423-0563
http://www.wadsworth.com

International Headquarters
Thomson Learning
International Division
290 Harbor Drive, 2nd Floor
Stamford, CT 06902-7477
USA

UK/Europe/Middle East/ South Africa
Thomson Learning
Berkshire House
168-173 High Holborn
London WC1V 7AA
United Kingdom

Asia
Thomson Learning
60 Albert Street, #15-01
Albert Complex
Singapore 189969

Canada
Nelson Thomson Learning
1120 Birchmount Road
Toronto, Ontario M1K 5G4
Canada

Library of Congress Cataloging-in-Publication Data
The life of virtue: what do we owe ourselves?/edited by Jacob Neusner; with essays by Bruce Chilton . . . [et al.]
    p.   cm. (comparing religious traditions)
    ISBN 0-534-53057-5
    1. Religious ethics. 2. Virtue.   I. Title: At head of Title: Christianity, Judaism, Islam, Hinduism, and Buddhism on the life of virtue.   II. Neusner, Jacob, 1932– III. Chilton, Bruce.   IV. Series.
BJ1188.L54   2000
291.5—dc21   00-034976

This book is printed on acid-free recycled paper.

Contents

◦⋖⋗◦

Preface

Religions not only answer public questions about society, politics, and economics; they also guide individuals in their private lives, as people work their way through life from birth to death. So to make sense of the world in which we live, we compare and contrast the choices religions make. To understand the lives people lead, therefore, we study about the religions they profess and practice together. Here we experiment with what it takes to compare religions. That is because, in our view, to know only one religion is to understand no religion. Comparison alone affords perspective, a clear picture of the choices people make and the settings in which they make them. Each religion forms a coherent whole, the parts of which fit together within a particular rationality. When, as here, we compare the parts of one with the parts of another religious tradition, we gain perspective on the whole of each of those traditions. And since we take up what is to all of us a program of familiar human issues—family, work, and virtue—we deal with what is accessible to us all out of our life's experiences.

To identify the difficulty of comparing religious traditions, take the social order first of all. Religions shape economics, politics, and public policy. In economics, the science of the rational disposition of scarce resources, religions variously define what they mean by "scarce resources." Moreover, they form their own diverse definitions and distinctive conceptions of what we deem "rational," as a comparison between Christian and Buddhist philosophy makes clear. But even where religions concur, the agreement masks difference. Context is everything. Islam and Judaism and Christianity each impose its own prohibition upon usury. But each draws its own conclusions from that prohibition. When we look closely, we see that the comparison yields mostly contrasts.

So too, in politics each frames a doctrine of how religion relates to the state, that is, to the institutions that legitimately exercise violence. They may concur that the state should realize God's purpose. But they do not form a unified consensus upon the consequences of that conviction. For instance, Hinduism and Buddhism may appear to be in agreement in their uneasiness about the use of force by government, and both dream of a nonviolent state based on moral order. But they do not agree on what these dreams say about actual, less-than-perfect governments.

As to the requirements of the good and the just society formed by the faithful, all three frame a theory of "the mystical body of Christ," or "the Jewish People" (meaning the contemporary continuators of the Israel of which Scripture speaks), or "the ummah" or "community of Islam," a theory rich in implications for the social order. So even where religions appear to resemble one another, they turn out to differ.

The distinctions make a difference not only in intangible ways but to the everyday world, because religion shapes public affairs, not only personal proclivities. We may well form an intense, personal relationship with God. That begins in a private moment of encounter. But commonly, the personal preference spills over into public policy. That is why, when we study about religions, comparing and contrasting their positions on a common program, we deal with facts, not only feelings; culture, not only conscience. In two different traditions originating in India, for example, Hinduism and Buddhism, there is an apparent agreement that the ultimate religious goal consists of freedom or liberation from a world of repeated death and rebirth. But because of different conceptions of the true nature of the self in these two traditions, they have not only conceived of the religious goal differently but have also put forward different religious paths leading to the goal—paths that entail different social, economic, and even political consequences.

Whether religions concur or differ on matters of public policy, how we are to interpret their points of intersection is not always clear. People can say the same thing for different reasons, and they can mean different things by the same statement—and so is the case with religions. For understanding a given chapter in the story a religion tells depends on knowing what came before and what will happen next. Indeed, everything in the end makes sense only in the proper context. Hence, even at points of confluence, how are we to compare and contrast the social, political, and economic conceptions of the great religious traditions, when each body of thought focuses upon distinctive historical experience, a very particular context of public life? Therefore what looks alike—affirmations in common—may upon closer examination prove quite different, and difference may well obscure the meaning of points of concurrence.

That is because the work of comparing religions in their public dimensions involves many complications. When we wish to compare one religion with another, doctrines or practices concerning public life pertain to situations we may find alien or beyond all comprehending. What one religion deems weighty another ignores altogether. Church order preoccupies Christians, but structures that transcend the local circumstance of Judaism do not precipitate equivalent conflict. Judaism precipitates debates on "who is a Jew," or "who, and what, is Israel," meaning, we recall, the holy people of which Scripture speaks. But Catholics do not endlessly debate on who is a Catholic. Religions do not select their issues from a single menu; each frames its system in its own distinctive structure, and a common category formation does not accommodate them all. One may compare it to how they serve dim sum in a Chinese restaurant: different food comes on different carts.

So even if they say the same thing, the shared language does not yield the same consequences. That is why it is difficult for purposes of comparison and contrast to set side by side (to give one example) (1) Christian thinking about Church-state relations with (2) Islamic thinking about the same matter and (3) Judaic doctrines, beginning with the Hebrew Scriptures, about God's stake in holy Israel's public life. Christian doctrines of politics emerge from a long history of Western institutions of church and state and their relationships, and Islamic ones from a quite different history altogether, one of rapid expansion in a remarkably brief period. Judaic doctrines take account of political experiences, such as defeat and political disempowerment, that Islam in its formative age never knew. So if Judaism, Christianity, and Islam concur on valuing peace, as they do, or on assigning to the state responsibilities for the moral ordering of society, as they do, that does not mean they concur on much that matters. Even when religions talk about the same things and come to comparable conclusions, the differences in context make it difficult to find a level plane for the purposes of comparing and contrasting what different traditions say about the same matter. A negative example serves. Buddhist emphasis on monasticism and the rejection of family life prevents us from seeing how much South Asian Buddhists share with Hindus in the ethics of family life.

Given the variables and imponderables that religions draw in their wake, we may wonder whether the work of comparison and contrast in the end demands more than it is worth. Out of despair or sheer incredulity, some may retreat into a latitudinarian tolerance, dismissing religions as all right or all wrong—and who cares? For from such an attitude, all rationality fails. We may incline to give up trying to make sense of the world shaped by religions and the affect upon the world of religion. But these choices prove impractical. Religions make a large difference in their social settings, whether Islam in North Africa, the Middle East, India and Pakistan, and Indonesia and Malaysia; or Christianity in Europe and the Western hemisphere; or Hinduism in India; or Buddhism in Southeastern Asia, China, and Japan; or Judaism on its own in the State of Israel and in the Diaspora—and in its influence upon its continuators, Christianity and Islam. So however tentative our effort to understand the difference religion makes, we cannot desist from trying. For to make sense of the religiously and culturally diverse world in which we live, we need to find generalizations, traits of religion that emerge through the comparison and contrast of religions.

What makes comparison and contrast so urgent? The theory of the matter is simple. These form essential modes of thought when we try to generalize on the basis of a set of cases. If we need to make sense of many things, it is often by looking for what they have in common, the traits of the whole that govern the parts. In the present context, that means to try to generalize about *religion* out of the study of *religions*. Armed with such generalizations, we take up new cases and test them. That is to say, we ask, if I know this set of facts, what else do I know? And we answer that same question, the question of "what else," meaning at its foundation, "so what?"

For example, we may identify rituals important to Judaism and Islam and Buddhism. Can we then say what we mean by "ritual," defining the category out of data that we think belong in that category? Then we know something we may bring to new and unfamiliar data and try to make sense of them. Comparing religious traditions, then, opens the way to generalizing on some cases in quest of understanding about many more cases. Comparison and contrast open the way to answering the question, so what?

That quest for generalization about religion cannot be postponed, because religions—we cannot overstress—form a principal part of public life and culture in many, though not all, of the regions and nations of the world. And that also means, what people think about a given religion will shape the attitudes of nations toward one another. Even now, Western incomprehension of Islam spills over into fear of Muslims. And Islamic thinking about other religions also impedes Muslims' framing a comprehending attitude toward Christian minorities in Muslim countries and Christian, and secular, majorities in Western ones. Public policy in the coming century will encompass religions and our attitudes toward, our opinions of, various religious issues and entities. And because religion makes so vast a difference in so many parts of humanity, tolerance resting on indifference will not suffice. Conflicts loom. People make judgments. We can best confront difference in the benign setting of the academy, before we must face conflicts we cannot understand let alone avoid. To the work of sorting out difference, especially in religions, this labor of comparison and contrast therefore is essential. That means identifying what religions have in common, where they differ, and how to make sense of both. That is the work we undertake in this book and its companions. Where to begin?

We speak of practical things, urgent human questions to which all religions respond in one way or another. We have chosen three points to start with: religious traditions on family life, work, and personal virtue. We flatly claim that family, work, and virtue constitute categories of human existence that are close to universal. They constitute relationships and impose obligations to the others nearby, to the community at large, and to the self. "Family" pertains to relationships between me and those near at hand, "work" between me and those among whom I live, "virtue" between me and myself. Family, community, self—these take the measure of the lives we lead together, matters of public concern, not merely personal predeliction of no practical weight.

Accordingly, the scholars who join together in these pages concur that to study about religion, to seek generalizations that cases yield, one good starting point is to compare and contrast the views of the great religions on urgent and practical issues of everyday life. The reason is that, in our view, certain questions arise from experiences common to the bulk of humanity. That is why in this study religions meet on the neutral ground of what happens to every human being in the course of life.

Take death for example. If we ask Judaism, Islam, Buddhism, Christianity, and Hinduism to tell us what they have to say about what it means to live in the knowledge of the end to which life leads us all, the grave, we speak of what all must address. Not only so, but while diverse religions and cultures variously frame the issue of that shared experience, all take up precisely the same universal experience of humanity. Here our universal biology overrides our several, diverse cultures. When we speak of existential concerns common to the generality of humanity, that is what we mean. The case explains what we intend to do here. But here we choose practical issues of everyday life. That is because all religions take up the task of answering questions common to humanity in general. What are the universal human issues, the questions of shared and common existence, that we have chosen to take up in our exercise in comparing religious traditions?

1. Every person, whatever the particularities of circumstance, is born of a mother and father. The great world religions we examine here concur that special obligations link child to parent and parent to child. If, then, we wish to compare Judaism, Christianity, Islam, Hinduism, and Buddhism, we find a level plane in the common question: do I owe anything to my mother and father, and, if so, what do I owe my mother and my father, and what do they owe to me? In all five religions the family forms the building block of the social order. How does each define the family and the architecture of ethical obligations that family relationships entail?

2. Nearly every person lives in a community that accords to him or her its recognition and protection and assigns a position and a worthwhile task to participants in its shared life. So we reasonably set side by side the several world religions' answers to the question, what do I owe the community of which I am a part? For, once again, rising above the differences of context and circumstance, the human situation persists: we need guidance on the same matter, wherever we live. And that leads us to doctrines of work and rest, as religious theories of the social order.

3. Finally, and perhaps of greatest weight, everybody who lives at some point, in some way, must answer the question, who am I, and what is the meaning of my life? The language we have chosen is, what do I owe myself? The answers to these questions form a theory of personal virtue. And that makes us wonder how religions define the private person and transform him or her into the individual embodiment of public policy—as they surely do.

In framing these questions, then, we bring to the religious traditions an agenda of questions that pertain to the private lives of us all, wherever we are born and raised, whatever the religion we practice (if any). These questions of human existence, issues of private life, of home and family and the near-at-hand community—these prove relevant to all humanity, and, we claim, for all humanity in much the same way, in a shared and common context. For we think that birth to a mother and father, life in community, and the search for self-worth together form the great levelers of difference.

What does all this have to do with the comparison and contrast of religions in quest of generalization about religion? In learning from the five world religions described here, we address to them all one and the same question. That common question is uniformly divided up into the same parts, in the same language, for each of the religions examined in sequence. We see these questions as equally relevant, in proportion, in the same way, to all five religions. That is to say, Judaism, Christianity, Islam, Hinduism, and Buddhism all set forth doctrines of (1) family, (2) work, and (3) virtue. These doctrines provide clear and characteristic answers to the questions we have formulated. In other words, we have identified categories that, in our experience as scholars, fit well for the religions that we study, respectively.

Let us now turn to the categories we have chosen. How have we framed the questions? A few words of explanation are in order. In the several chapters, all of us follow a single outline. For the initial volumes of this exercise in comparing religious traditions, here are the outlines that dictate the presentation of each religion.

I. THE ETHICS OF FAMILY LIFE: WHAT DO WE OWE ONE ANOTHER?
    1. Conventional expectation versus this religious tradition: what do husbands and wives owe one another?
    2. What do parents owe their children?
    3. What do children owe their parents?
    4. When the family breaks down: what happens then?
    5. Unconventional families, supernatural families

II. MAKING AN HONEST LIVING: WHAT DO WE OWE THE COMMUNITY?
    1. Why must we work?
    2. How ought we to work? kinds of work to be preferred or avoided
    3. Why must we help others? private gain and public benefit
    4. When work does not work: unemployment, exploitation, and alternatives to proper work
    5. Unconventional work: working for God

III. THE LIFE OF VIRTUE: WHAT DO WE OWE OURSELVES?
    1. Conventional answers versus this religious tradition: who are we really? [conceptions of the person, or, in other words, theological anthropology]
    2. What are the social virtues? [for example, generosity, trust, gratitude]
    3. What is personal virtue? [for example, dignity, self-respect, hope]
    4. How does this religion define character, good and bad?
    5. Beyond the normal virtues: who is the extraordinary person? [for example, the saint]

So much for the common questions addressed to five religious traditions, questions that make possible the comparison and contrast of those traditions.

For all three topical expositions, a single pattern governs. We move from the conventional to the unconventional, and from the system when it works to the system when it breaks down. In each exposition we begin with the conventional issues of ordinary life. This means that through the first three sections we answer the question, what do people ordinarily mean by the matter under discussion, and what are the answers that this religion in everyday terms gives to the question? We then turn at the fourth section to how a given religion deals with failure. At the end, at the fifth section, we ask how a given religion altogether revises the conventional, this-worldly definition. Having laid out an account of matters that is uniform in structure for the religions portrayed here, we leave it to students to draw their own conclusions, frame their own judgments, in discussion beyond the pages of this book.

In the volume on family life, we begin with the family understood in a this-worldly framework, a conventional family, meaning husband, wife, and children, extending outward beyond the nuclear family to grandparents, uncles and aunts, dependents of various kinds, and castes. Then, second, we ask about how this religion deals with the breakdown of the norm, for example, with the family when it breaks down. Finally, we turn from the conventional to the unconventional definition of the same matter, for example, the supernatural family, the family defined in an other-than-this-worldly framework.

When it comes to work, we begin with the ordinary meaning of work, that is, what we do to support our families and ourselves, to earn our keep, and to contribute to the common good. Then we ask about doctrines that deal with the breakdown of the ordinary arrangements for everyday labor. Finally, we take up work in a different, unconventional context.

The same pattern governs the discussion of virtue, by which we mean, how we view ourselves. In this context we take for granted that people ordinarily aspire to think well of themselves, to live lives of virtue. That topic encompasses how this religious tradition defines a human being. Within that broad question are doctrines on public virtues, that is, admirable traits that make for a better society, as well as those on personal ones. The latter characterize individuals and point toward how a given religion defines a truly virtuous person. On the basis of doctrines of virtue we generalize in terms of character: what does this religion admire in the overall quality of a person; what marks a person as basically good or fundamentally evil? And, finally, we turn from the routine to the extraordinary: how does this religion identify the saint, the embodiment of virtue.

So we have undertaken an experiment in comparing religious traditions. Why have we done so? Once more: the payoff comes in the quest for generalizations, in the present instance, how religion shapes the traits of family, work, and virtue. We concentrate on practical questions of comparison, not only because we claim the issues addressed here face nearly all religions and the societies shaped by them, but also because these issues confront all of us as we make our way through life from birth to death. When we compare religions' patterns of belief and behavior, we may or may not cover topics of immediate relevance to our own circumstances. But when we ask about family, work, and virtue, we certainly inquire into what matters in the here and the now. That is the point at which generalization may take place.

For, as we shall see, religions really do concur on some practical matters, and they actually do make the same difference, each in its own context. That does not make them all alike, and it does not validate the ignorant dismissal of difference, "It doesn't matter what you believe as long as you're a good person." Nor does that concurrence permit us to reduce religions to religion, to define a generic religion. What we mean to show is the possibility of generalization, of moving from knowing this fact to explaining other facts, moving from the known to the unknown. That is how we meet our responsibility as academic scholars of religion and how we contribute to others outside of university life as well. All comes down to our sustained response to this simple question: if we know this, what else do we know?

Why the emphasis on practical matters? The academic study of religion maintains that we study about religions and religion and do not advocate the truth of one religion over another, and all of us in these pages affirm that conviction. But no one can imagine that the academic study of religion ought never present us with choices worthy of our consideration, ideas of other men and women that we may make our own. We represent the religions treated here as worthy of the close attention of inquiring minds, in quest, in the end, of insight into the human condition. No other single force in the social order, not politics, not economics, not psychology, not any of the other important elements in making the world what it is—none of them exceeds in power, or in pathos, the force of religion.

The partners in this project express thanks to Wadsworth Publishing Company for adopting the enterprise and guiding it from beginning to end. We benefited, especially, from the oversight and counsel of our editor, Peter Adams. We are also grateful for the helpful comments provided by the reviewers: Leslie Aldritt, Northland College; S. Daniel Breslauer, University of Kansas; Aminah Beverly McCloud, DePaul University; Preston McKever-Floyd, Coastal Carolina University.

The editor thanks the partners in this project for doing the work on time and with panache. He also expresses his personal gratitude to Bard College, for a research grant and for other support for his work as teacher and scholar.

Jacob Neusner
Editor
Bard College

Contributors

BRUCE CHILTON is Bernard Iddings Bell Professor of Religion at Bard
College.

CHARLES HALLISEY is John L. Loeb Associate Professor of the Humanities at
Harvard University, teaching on the Committee on the Study of Religion
and in the Department of Sanskrit and Indian Studies.

JACOB NEUSNER is Research Professor of Religion and Theology at Bard
College.

BRIAN K. SMITH is Professor of Religious Studies at the University of California at Riverside.

TAMARA SONN is Kenan Professor of Religious Studies at the College of
William and Mary.

1

Judaism

BY JACOB NEUSNER

CONVENTIONAL ANSWERS VERSUS THIS RELIGIOUS TRADITION: WHO ARE WE REALLY?

We human beings really are created in God's image, after God's likeness, and if we want to know God, we look into the face of the other. That is the message of the Torah, which the world calls "Judaism." We also, in our physical traits, form models of the natural world, corresponding to the glories of nature as much as to the sanctity of God. And it is in that context, within that vision of humanity, that we find out what we owe ourselves.

Let us start with an explicit statement that man—Adam and Eve—is in God's image, after God's likeness:[1]

> Said R. Hoshiah, "When the Holy One, blessed be he, came to create the first Man, the ministering angels mistook him [for God, since Man was in God's image,] and wanted to say before him, 'Holy, [holy, holy is the Lord of hosts].'
>
> "To what may the matter be compared? To the case of a king and a governor who were set in a chariot, and the provincials wanted to greet the king, 'Sovereign!' But they did not know which one of them was which. What did the king do? He turned the governor out and put him away from the chariot, so that people would know who was king.
>
> "So too when the Holy One, blessed be he, created the first Man, the angels mistook him [for God]. What did the Holy One, blessed be he, do? He put him to sleep, so everyone knew that he was a mere Man.
>
> "That is in line with the following verse of Scripture: 'Cease you from Man, in whose nostrils is a breath, for how little is he to be accounted' (Is. 2:22)."
>
> Genesis Rabbah VIII:X.1

Who we are, really, are creatures in God's image. Judaism over the ages has interpreted that teaching in diverse ways. Some maintain the literal sense of the passage just cited; others see the aspect of man that is in God's image in our free-

---

[1] All translations are by the author.

dom of will. We have the power to love or withhold love, to obey willingly or to rebel perversely. Who we are really is a mixture of traits, both virtuous and otherwise. God knew that at the outset.

> Said R. Simon, "When the Holy One, blessed be he, came to create the first Man, the ministering angels formed parties and sects.
>
> "Some of them said, 'Let him be created,' and some of them said, 'Let him not be created.'
>
> "That is in line with the following verse of Scripture: 'Mercy and truth fought together, righteousness and peace warred with each other' (Ps. 85:11).
>
> "Mercy said, 'Let him be created, for he will perform acts of mercy.'
>
> "Truth said, 'Let him not be created, for he is a complete fake.'
>
> "Righteousness said, 'Let him be created, for he will perform acts of righteousness.'
>
> "Peace said, 'Let him not be created, for he is one mass of contention.'
>
> "What then did the Holy One, blessed be he, do? He took truth and threw it to the ground. The ministering angels then said before the Holy One, blessed be he, 'Master of the ages, how can you disgrace your seal [which is truth]? Let truth be raised up from the ground!'
>
> "That is in line with the following verse of Scripture: 'Let truth spring up from the earth' (Ps. 85:2)."
>
> R. Huna the elder of Sepphoris said, "While the ministering angels were engaged in contentious arguments with one another, keeping one another preoccupied, the Holy One, blessed be he, created him.
>
> "He then said to them, 'What good are you doing [with your contentions]? Man has already been made!'"

God's creation of man represented an act of mercy and love that defied all rational considerations of truth, righteousness, and peace. The message is that in creating man, God expressed his special love for him. The stress is that the ministering angels opposed the creation of man; because of their divisive character, God was able to do it anyhow. The full character of the Aggadic revision of the story begins to emerge now. The debates over the creation of man on the part of the angels, their participation in God's deliberations, God's clear awareness of the possibilities of failure—these all recast Scripture's story.

But these readings of the biblical story that defines who we are, really, speak in their distinctive context, and before we can examine the Judaic virtues, we have to see them in their proper setting. Virtues out of context—whether humility or generosity or forbearance or temperance—bear no meaning particular to the faith at hand. Diverse religions may well concur on principal virtues such as these, yet mean by them very different things or assign to them different importance. But out of context those virtues are random, not part of a coherent system. Then we do not know how to decipher their message. For Judaism, which calls itself the Torah, the account of virtue begins in the Torah's picture of world order based on God's virtue, not the virtue of humanity. God's traits of justice and equity, love and compassion, form the model for those of God's creatures. Moreover, the Torah knows humanity as the children of Adam via Noah to Abraham. Accordingly, Judaism in its classical statement treats virtue as a component of a much larger doctrine that concerns the meaning of the life of humanity. The Torah tells the story of humanity's life from creation through Sinai to redemption at the end of time, and from birth to the grave and ultimate resurrection. Within that doctrine, what Judaism identifies as virtue in men and women finds its context.

Who we really are is simply said: we are "children of Adam and Eve, descendants of Noah," and, for the supernatural social entity Scripture knows as "Israel," "children of Abraham" and Sarah as well. Using the language, "children of . . . ," conveys the meaning "modeled after." As soon as we introduce the name of Adam and Eve—created by God "in our image . . . after our likeness" (Genesis 1:26), the matter of virtue finds its context in Adam's and Eve's relationship with God. That relationship was disrupted by Adam's and Eve's disobedience to God's commandment. So who are we really? On the one side, like Adam and Eve, we too are in God's image, after God's likeness. In their model, we by our nature both enjoy free will and disobey God's commandments.

Consequently, virtue stands for those traits that bring about reconciliation between Adam and Eve and God, and vice for those that disrupt the relationship. So the working system of the Torah finds its dynamic in the struggle between God's plan for creation—to create a perfect world of justice—and the free will of humanity. All virtuous traits, then, find their place within that encompassing vision that explains who we are by telling the story of creation culminating in Adam, Eve, and Eden. That is to say, in Judaism "we" are Adam and Eve, fallen from Eden, and, when possessed of the Torah, able to regain Eden. All virtue is defined in that context, and the story that Scripture tells sets forth that context.

When sages wish to investigate a question, they turn to Scripture, their principal source of facts concerning the record of humanity. There they meet God and in Scripture they amass those established data that supply the answer to any important question. In the Torah they find out that arrogance is a vice and causes sin, while humility is a virtue; and there they learn the reason why: virtue begins in our relationship to God, commencing with that of Adam and Eve—humility and obedience or arrogance and rebellion. Here is how the sages discover the governing principles of virtuous living:

Whence [in Scripture] do we derive an admonition against the arrogant?
    Said Raba said Zeiri, "'Listen and give ear, do not be proud' (Jer. 13:15)."
    R. Nahman bar Isaac said, "From the following: 'Your heart will be lifted up, and you will forget the Lord your God' (Dt. 8:14).
    "And it is written, 'Beware, lest you forget the Lord your God' (Dt. 8:11)."
    R. Avira expounded, sometimes in the name of R. Assi and sometimes in the name of R. Ammi, "Whoever is arrogant in the end will be diminished,
    "as it is said, 'They are exalted, there will be a diminution' (Job. 24:24).
    "And lest you maintain that they continue in the world [alive], Scripture states, 'And they are gone' (Job. 24:24).

"But if [the arrogant person] repents, he will be gathered up [in death] at the time allotted to him [and not before],

"as was the case with our father, Abraham,

"as it is said, 'But when they are lowly, they are gathered in like all' (Job 24:24)—like Abraham, Isaac, and Jacob, concerning whom 'all' is written [at Gen. 24:1, 27:33, 33:11].

"And if not: 'They are cut off as the tops of the ears of corn' (Job 24:24)."

"With him also who is of a contrite and humble spirit" (Is. 57:15).

R. Huna and R. Hisda:

One said, "I [God] am with the contrite."

The other said, "I [God] am the contrite."

Logic favors the view of him who has said, "I [God] am with the contrite," for lo, the Holy One, blessed be he, neglected all mountains and heights and brought his Presence to rest on Mount Sinai,

and he did not raise Mount Sinai upward [to himself].

R. Joseph said, "A person should always learn from the attitude of his Creator, for lo, the Holy One, blessed be he, neglected all mountains and heights and brought his Presence to rest on Mount Sinai,

"and he neglected all valuable trees and brought his Presence to rest in the bush."

Said R. Eleazar, "Whoever is arrogant is worthy of being cut down like an *asherah* [a tree that is worshipped].

"Here it is written, 'The high ones of stature shall be cut down' (Is. 10:33),

"and elsewhere it is written, 'And you shall hew down their Asherim' (Dt. 7:5)."

And R. Eleazar said, "Whoever is arrogant—his dust will not be stirred up [in the resurrection of the dead]. [Such a person will be judged for eternal death, when the dead are resurrected.]

"For it is said, 'Awake and sing, you that dwell in the dust' (Is. 26:19).

"It is stated not 'you who lie in the dust' but 'you who dwell in the dust,' meaning, one who has become a neighbor to the dust [by constant humility] even in his lifetime."

And R. Eleazar said, "For whoever is arrogant the Presence of God laments,

"as it is said, 'But the haughty he knows from afar' (Ps. 138:6)."

R. Avira expounded, and some say it was R. Eleazar, "Come and take note of the fact that not like the trait of the Holy One, blessed be he, is the trait of flesh and blood.

"The trait of flesh and blood is that those who are high take note of those who are high, but the one who is high does not take note of the one who is low.

"But the trait of the Holy One, blessed be he, is not that way. He is high, but he takes note of the low,

"as it is said, 'For though the Lord is high, yet he takes note of the low' (Ps. 138:6)."

Said R. Hisda, and some say it was Mar Uqba, "Concerning whoever is arrogant said the Holy One, blessed be he, he and I cannot live in the same world,

"as it is said, 'Whoever slanders his neighbor in secret—him will I destroy; him who has a haughty look and a proud heart I will not endure' (Ps. 101:5).

"Do not read, 'him [I cannot endure]' but 'with him [I cannot endure].'"

There are those who apply the foregoing teaching to those who slander, as it is said, "Whoever slanders his neighbor in secret—him will I destroy" (Ps. 101:5).

Said R. Ashi, "Whoever is arrogant in the end will be diminished,

"as it is said, 'For a rising and for a scab' (Lev. 14:56), and rising refers only to elevation, as it is said, 'Upon all the high mountains and upon all the hills that are lifted up' (Is. 2:14).

"Scab means only 'attachment,' as it is said, 'Attach me, I ask you, to one of the priests' offices, so that I may eat a piece of bread' (1 Sam. 2:36)."

Said R. Joshua b. Levi, "Come and take note of how great are the humble in the sight of the Holy One, blessed be he.

"For when the sanctuary stood, a person would bring a burnt-offering, gaining thereby the reward for bringing a burnt-offering, or a meal-offering, and gaining the reward for a meal offering.

"But a person who is genuinely humble does Scripture treat as if he had made offerings of all the sacrifices,

"as it is said, 'The sacrifices [plural] of God are a broken spirit' (Ps. 51:19).

"And not only so, but his prayer is not rejected, as it is said, 'A broken and contrite heart, O God, you will not despise' (Ps. 51:19)."

And R. Joshua b. Levi said, "Whoever properly sets his ways in this world will have the merit of witnessing the salvation of the Holy One, blessed be he,

"as it is said, 'To him who orders his way I will show the salvation of God' (Ps. 50:23).

"Do not read 'orders' but 'properly sets' [his] way."

Bavli Sotah 1:1–2 V.13ff./5A

Arrogance embodies the bad attitude, and reason leads to the expectation that the arrogant will be cut down to size. If the arrogant person repents, however, then he abandons the bad attitude and adopts the good one, of humility, which is the condition of repentance. God is the model of humility, so too Moses. The resurrection of the dead involves the exaltation of the humble—dust itself. Scripture and parable serve to convey these points, but the system at its core insists upon them.

Let me briefly spell out the theological framework of the Torah in which virtue—humility against arrogance—finds its place. There are three important doctrines that define the setting.

1. God formed creation in accord with a plan, which the Torah reveals. World order can be shown by the facts of nature and society set forth in the Torah's plan to conform to a pattern of reason based upon justice. Those who possess the Torah—Israel, defined as the people to whom God

is made manifest through the Torah—know God. Those who do not—
the gentiles, defined as idolaters—reject God in favor of idols. What happens to each of the two sectors of humanity, respectively, responds to their
relationship with God. Israel in the present age is subordinate to the nations, because God has designated the gentiles as the medium for penaliz-
ing Israel's rebellion, meaning through Israel's subordination and exile to
provoke Israel to repent. Private life as much as the public order conforms
to the principle that God rules justly in a creation of perfection and stasis.

2. What disrupts the perfection of creation is the sole power capable of standing on its own against God's power, and that is humanity's will. What humanity controls and God cannot coerce is humanity's capacity to form
intention and therefore choose either arrogantly to defy, or humbly to
love, God. This is where Judaism's definition of virtues makes its appearance. In the context established by the pattern of human creation and conduct, the principal virtue is humility, not arrogance. Because humanity
defies God, the sin that results from man's rebellion flaws creation and disrupts world order. The paradigm of the rebellion of Adam in Eden governs, the act of arrogant rebellion leading to exile from Eden and thus
accounting for the condition of humanity.

3. But, as in the original transaction of alienation and consequent exile, God
retains the power to encourage repentance through punishing man's arrogance. In mercy, moreover, God exercises the power to respond to repentance with forgiveness, that is, a change of attitude evoking a counterpart
change. Since, commanding his own will, humanity also has the power to
initiate the process of reconciliation with God, through repentance, an act
of humility, humanity may restore the perfection of that order that through
arrogance he has marred. Here we meet a divine virtue that humanity can
replicate: mercy, forgiveness, reconciliation. And yet a third class of virtues,
those involved in repentance and atonement, the confession of sin and the
determination to do good, will surely follow. But everything begins in the
virtue of humility.

But let us not neglect the end of the story. God ultimately will restore the
perfection that embodied his plan for creation. In the work of restoration, death
that comes about by reason of sin itself will die, the dead will be raised and
judged for their deeds in this life, and most of them, having been justified, will
go on to eternal life in the world to come. The paradigm of humanity restored
to Eden is realized in Israel's return to the Land of Israel. That is the view of the
Oral Torah. In that world or age to come, however, that sector of humanity that
through the Torah knows God will encompass all of humanity. Idolaters will
perish, and humanity that comprises Israel at the end will know the one, true
God and spend eternity in his light. The dead will rise out of their graves, and
the age to come will see humanity restored to Eden.

Now, recorded in this way, the story told by the Torah proves remarkably
familiar, with its stress on God's justice (to which his mercy is integral), man's
correspondence with God in his possession of the power of will, man's sin, and

God's response. It follows that Judaism forms its conception of who we are to begin with out of the story of the creation of man and woman in Eden, and it answers the question "who are we really?" by reflecting on the story of humanity's beginning, middle, and ending. All of us, Judaism maintains, are formed in the model of Adam and Eve.

If humble obedience to God's will defines virtue, and arrogant rebellion vice, then the question arises, on what account does humanity act with so much pride? For it is not as though humanity had much in which to take pride or foundation for its arrogant attitude. On the contrary, Aqabiah b. Mehalalel says, if we reflect on whence we come and whither we go, we shall attain humility:

> Aqabiah b. Mehalalel says, "Contemplate three things, and you will not come to commit a transgression. Know whence you have come, from a fetid drop; and where you are going, to worms and corruption; and before whom you are going to have to give a full accounting of yourself, before the King of kings of kings, the Holy One, blessed be he"
>
> M. Abot 3:1

> R. Abba b. R. Kahana in the name of R. Pappi and R. Joshua of Sikhnin in the name of R. Levi: "All three matters did Aqabiah derive by exegesis from a single word [that is, BWRK, 'your Creator']: Remember your well (beerka), your pit (BRK), and your Creator (BWRK). 'Remember your well'—this refers to the fetid drop. 'Remember your pit'—this refers to worms and corruption. 'Remember your Creator'—this refers to the King of kings of kings, the Holy One, before whom one is destined to render a full accounting."
>
> Leviticus Rabbah XVIII:I.1

The amplification of Aqabiah's saying by the later authority links the definition of humanity to the story of creation, birth, and death. Conscience—not sinning—comes about through consciousness of who we really are.

But the sages set forth a doctrine that compares in its grand vision to the one that finds humanity in God's image and likeness. They further maintain that the human being is formed in the model of nature, created as the counterpart to the natural world, so that whatever characterizes the creation of nature also marks the creation of man. The sage then treats the human being as a microcosm of nature, as much as "in our image, after our likeness," in God's image, after God's likeness. It would be difficult to state a more elevated conception of who we really are than this invocation of nature and God as embodied in humanity. Here is how, in concrete language, the sage makes the statement that we are the counterpart to the natural world:

> R. Yosé the Galilean says, "Whatever the Holy One, blessed be he, created on earth, he created also in man. To what may the matter be compared? To someone who took a piece of wood and wanted to make many forms on it but had no room to make them, so he was distressed. But someone who draws forms on the earth can go on drawing and can spread them out as far as he likes. But the Holy One, blessed be he, may his great name be blessed for ever and ever, in his wisdom and understanding created the whole of the

world, created the heaven and the earth, above and below, and created in man whatever he created in his world.

"In the world he created forests, and in man he created forests: the hairs on his head. In the world he created wild beasts and in man he created wild beasts: lice. In the world he created channels and in man he created channels: his ears. In the world he created wind and in man he created wind: his breath. In the world he created the sun and in man he created the sun: his forehead. Stagnant waters in the world, stagnant waters in man: his nose, [namely, rheum]. Salt water in the world, salt water in man: his urine. Streams in the world, streams in man: man's tears. Walls in the world, walls in man: his lips. Doors in the world, doors in man, his teeth. Firmaments in the world, firmaments in man, his tongue. Fresh water in the world, fresh water in man: his spit. Stars in the world, stars in the man: his cheeks. Towers in the world, towers in man: his neck. masts in the world, masts in man: his arms. Pins in the world, pins in man: his fingers. A King in the world, a king in man: his heart. Grape clusters in the world, grape clusters in man: his breasts. Counselors in the world, counselors in man: his kidneys. Millstones in the world, millstones in man: his intestines [which grind up food]. mashing mills in the world, and mashing mills in man: the spleen. Pits in the world, a pit in man: the belly button. Flowing streams in the world and a flowing stream in man: his blood. Trees in the world and trees in man: his bones. Hills in the world and hills in man: his buttocks. Pestle and mortar in the world and pestle and mortar in man: the joints. Horses in the world and horses in man: the legs. The angel of death in the world and the angel of death in man: his heels. Mountains and valleys in the world and mountains and valleys in man: when he is standing, he is like a mountain, when he is lying down, he is like a valley.

"Thus you have learned that whatever the Holy One, blessed be he, created on earth, he created also in man."

The Fathers according to Rabbi Nathan XXXI:III.1

Here is a vision of humanity that recalls the psalmist's cry, "What is man that you are mindful of him, and the son of man that you pay attention to him? Yet you have crowned him with glory and honor." So much for humanity in God's image, formed in the model of nature and its glories, a remarkable vision.

WHAT ARE THE SOCIAL VIRTUES?

The social virtues begin with righteousness, which bears the meaning in Hebrew of charity. To be righteous is to love God. That love is best expressed through acts of charity (philanthropy), which define righteousness better than any other. The mark of righteousness is to desire God, and the righteous always direct their hearts to God:

"But the Lord afflicted Pharaoh and his house with great plagues because of Sarai, Abram's wife" (Gen. 12:17):

"The righteous shall flourish like the palm tree, he shall grow like a cedar in Lebanon" (Ps. 92:13).

Just as a palm tree and a cedar produce neither crooked curves nor growths, so the righteous do not produce either crooked curves or growths. Just as the shade of the palm tree and cedar is distant from the base of the tree so the giving of the reward that is coming to the righteous seems distant. Just as, in the case of the palm tree and the cedar, the very core of the tree points upward, so in the case of the righteous, their heart is pointed toward the Holy One, blessed be he.

That is in line with the following verse of Scripture: "My eyes are ever toward the Lord, for he will bring forth my feet out of the net" (Ps. 25:15). Just as the palm tree and cedar are subject to desire, so the righteous are subject to desire. And what might it be? What they desire is the Holy One, blessed be he.

Leviticus Rabbah XLI:I.1

Charity and righteousness are called by one and the same word, *sedaqah,* because the act of philanthropy represents righteousness above all else. Charity and righteous deeds outweigh all other commandments in the Torah.[2] Acts of charity are to be conducted with dignity and respect for the poor. Anyone who gives a penny to the poor is blessed with six blessings, and anyone who speaks to him in a comforting manner is blessed with eleven. Anyone who gives a penny to the poor is blessed with six blessings: 'Is it not to deal your bread to the hungry and bring the poor to your house . . . when you see the naked' (Is. 58:7) 'then shall your light break forth. . . .' And anyone who speaks to him in a comforting manner is blessed with eleven: 'If you draw out your soul to the hungry and satisfy the afflicted soul, then shall your light rise in the darkness and your darkness be as noonday, and the Lord shall guide you continually and satisfy your soul in drought . . . and they shall build from you the old waste places and you shall raise up the foundations of many generations' (Is. 58:10–12)."[3] God responds to acts of charity: "Every act of charity and mercy that Israelites do in this world brings about peace and great reconciliation between Israel and their father in heaven: 'Thus says the Lord, do not enter into the house of mourning, nor go to lament, nor bemoan them, for I have taken away my peace from this people . . . even loving kindness and tender mercies'[4] (Jer. 16:4)— loving kindness refers to acts of mercy, and 'tender mercies' to charity."

But what God really admires is acts of selflessness, and the highest virtue of all, so far as the Torah is concerned, is the act that God cannot coerce but very much yearns for, that act of love that transcends the self. Virtue begins in obedience to the Torah, but reaches its pinnacle through deeds beyond the strict requirements of the Torah, and even the limits of the law altogether, that transform the hero into a holy man, whose holiness served just like that of a sage marked as such by knowledge of the Torah. To understand how sages make their statement,

---

[2]Tosefta Peah 4:19

[3]Bavli Baba Batra 1:5 IV.28–29/9b

[4]Bavli Baba Batra 1:5 IV.37–38/10a.

we have to keep in mind two facts. First, they believed that God hears and answers prayer, and that if God answers prayer, it is a mark of Heaven's favorable recognition of the one who says it. Therefore if someone has the reputation of saying prayers that are answered, sages want to know why. Second, sages believed that Torah-study defined the highest ideal that a man could attain, and they maintained that God wanted them to live a life of Torah-study. But in these stories, they discover people who could pray with effect in ways that they, the sages themselves, could not. And they further discovered that some people won Heaven's favor not by a lifelong devotion to the divine service but by doing a single remarkable action. So the sages themselves are going to tell us stories about how one enormous deed outweighed a life of Torah-study. The first story concerns a poor man who asked for charity:

> A certain man came before one of the relatives of R. Yannai. He said to him, "Rabbi, attain *zekhut* through me [by giving me charity]."
>
> He said to him, "And didn't your father leave you money?"
>
> He said to him, "No."
>
> He said to him, "Go and collect what your father left in deposit with others."
>
> He said to him, "I have heard concerning property my father deposited with others that it was gained by violence [so I don't want it]."
>
> He said to him, "You are worthy of praying and having your prayers answered."
>
> Yerushalmi Taanit 1:4.I

The word *zekhut* stands for "the merit, source of divine favor." It is the language that is used by the beggar to the donor: you will gain merit by an act of philanthropy to me. The point, of course, is self-evidently a reference to the possession of entitlement to supernatural favor, and it is gained, we see, through deeds that the law of the Torah cannot require but must favor: what one does on one's own volition, beyond the measure of the law. Here we see the opposite of sin. A sin is what one has done by one's own volition beyond all limits of the law. So an act that generates *zekhut* for the individual is the counterpart and opposite: what one does by one's own volition that also is beyond all requirements of the law.

A more complex body of meritorious actions is set forth in the following story, which captures the entire range of virtues that sages valued:

> A pious man from Kefar Imi appeared [in a dream] to the rabbis. He prayed for rain and it rained. The rabbis went up to him. His householders told them that he was sitting on a hill. They went out to him, saying to him, "Greetings," but he did not answer them.
>
> He was sitting and eating, and he did not say to them, "You break bread too."
>
> When he went back home, he made a bundle of faggots and put his cloak on top of the bundle [instead of on his shoulder].
>
> When he came home, he said to his household [wife], "These rabbis are here [because] they want me to pray for rain. If I pray and it rains, it is a dis-

grace for them, and if not, it is a profanation of the Name of Heaven. But come, you and I will go up [to the roof] and pray. If it rains, we shall tell them, 'We are not worthy to pray and have our prayers answered.'"

They went up and prayed and it rained.

They came down to them [and asked], "Why have the rabbis troubled themselves to come here today?"

They said to him, "We wanted you to pray so that it would rain."

He said to them, "Now do you really need my prayers? Heaven already has done its miracle."

They said to him, "Why, when you were on the hill, did we say hello to you, and you did not reply?"

He said to them, "I was then doing my job. Should I then interrupt my concentration [on my work]?"

They said to him, "And why, when you sat down to eat, did you not say to us 'You break bread too'?"

He said to them, "Because I had only my small ration of bread. Why would I have invited you to eat by way of mere flattery [when I knew I could not give you anything at all]?"

They said to him, "And why when you came to go down, did you put your cloak on top of the bundle?"

He said to them, "Because the cloak was not mine. It was borrowed for use at prayer. I did not want to tear it."

They said to him, "And why, when you were on the hill, did your wife wear dirty clothes, but when you came down from the mountain, did she put on clean clothes?"

He said to them, "When I was on the hill, she put on dirty clothes, so that no one would gaze at her. But when I came home from the hill, she put on clean clothes, so that I would not gaze on any other woman."

They said to him, "It is well that you pray and have your prayers answered."

Yerushalmi Taanit 1:4.I

The pious man, finally, enjoys the recognition of the sages by reason of his lien upon Heaven, able as he is to pray and bring rain. What has so endowed him with *zekhut*? Acts of punctiliousness of a moral order: concentrating on his work, avoiding an act of dissimulation, integrity in the disposition of a borrowed object, his wife's concern not to attract other men and her equal concern to make herself attractive to her husband. None of these stories refers explicitly to *zekhut*; all of them tell us about what it means to enjoy not an entitlement by inheritance but a lien accomplished by one's own supererogatory acts of restraint.

Zekhut forms a measure of one's own relationship with Heaven, as the power of one person, but not another, to pray and so bring rain attests. What sort of relationship does *zekhut*, as the opposite of sin, then posit? It is not one of coercion, for Heaven cannot force us to do those types of deeds that yield *zekhut*, and that, story after story suggests, is the definition of a deed that generates *zekhut*: doing what we ought to do but do not have to do. But then, we cannot coerce Heaven to do what we want done either, for example, by carrying out the commandments. These are obligatory, but do not obligate Heaven. *Zekhut* pertains to deeds of a supererogatory character—to which Heaven responds by deeds of a supererogatory character: supernatural favor to this one, who through deeds of ingratiation of the other or self-abnegation or restraint exhibits the attitude that in Heaven precipitates a counterpart attitude, hence generating *zekhut,* rather than to that one, who does not. The simple fact that rabbis cannot pray and bring rain, but a simple ass-driver can, tells the whole story. The relationship measured by *zekhut*—Heaven's response by an act of uncoerced favor to a person's uncoerced gift (e.g., act of gentility, restraint, or self-abnegation)—contains an element of unpredictability for which appeal to the *zekhut* inherited from ancestors accounts. So while I cannot coerce Heaven, I can through *zekhut* gain acts of favor from Heaven, and that is by doing what Heaven cannot require of me. Heaven then responds to my attitude in carrying out my duties—and more than my duties. That act of pure disinterest is the one that gains for me Heaven's deepest interest. The ultimate act of virtue turns out to be an act of pure grace, to which God responds with pure grace.

We turn to the opposite of restraint and self-abnegation, which is arrogance. If acts of humility, embodied in prayer, charity, and repentance, right the relationship with God, acts of arrogance upset it. The sages identify as an act of supreme arrogance losing one's temper.

God's presence is offended by displays of temper, and temper is a mark of arrogance, a source of sin, so M. Ned. 4:4 I.16–18/22b: Said Rabbah bar R. Huna, "Whoever loses his temper—even the Presence of God is not important to him: 'The wicked, through the pride of his countenance, will not seek God; God is not in all his thoughts' (Ps. 10:4)." R. Jeremiah of Difti said, "Whoever loses his temper—he forgets what he has learned and increases foolishness: 'For anger rests in the heart of fools' (Qoh. 7:9), and 'But the fool lays open his folly' (Prov. 13:16)." R. Nahman bar Isaac said, "One may be sure that his sins outnumber his merits: 'And a furious man abounds in transgressions' (Prov. 29:22)." Said R. Ada b. R. Hanina, "If the Israelites had not sinned, to them would have been given only the Five Books of the Torah and the book of Joshua alone, which involves the division of the Land of Israel. How come? 'For much wisdom proceeds from much anger' (Qoh. 1:18)." The anger of God caused him to send prophets with their wise teachings.

Sages admire restraint and temperance, marks of humility, so it stands to reason that loss of restraint and intemperance will signify arrogance. Sages do not treat respectfully the person who takes vows. Vow-takers yield to the undisciplined will, to emotion unguided by rational considerations. But intentionality must (ideally) take form out of both emotion and reflection. Vows explode, the fuel of emotion ignited by the heat of the occasion. "Qonam be any benefit I get from you" hardly forms a rational judgment of a stable relationship; it bespeaks a loss of temper, a response to provocation with provocation. Right at the outset the Halakhah gives a powerful signal of its opinion of the whole: suitable folk to begin with do not take vows, only wicked people do. That explains in so many words why, if one says something is subject to "the vows of suitable folk," he has said nothing. Suitable people—*kesheyrim*—make no vows at all, ever.

A distaste for vowing and disdain for people who make vows, then, characterize the law. People who take vows are deemed irresponsible; they are adults who
have classified themselves as children. They possess the power of intentionality but
not the responsibility for its wise use. That is why they are given openings toward
the unbinding of their vows; they are forced at the same time to take seriously what
they have said. Vows are treated as a testing of Heaven, a trial of Heavenly patience
and grace. Sanctification can affect a person or a mess of porridge, and there is a
difference. Expletives make that difference; these are not admired. To sages language is holy; it is how God forms a relationship with humanity, the medium of
divine communication. Vows constitute a disreputable use of the powerful and the
holy. And language is holy because language gives form and effect to intentionality. That is why we do admit intentionality—not foresight but intentionality as to
honor—into the repertoire of reasons for nullifying vows, as we note in the law
of vows that is set forth at Mishnah-tractate Nedarim:

> They unloose a vow for a man by reference to his own honor and by refer-
> ence to the honor of his children.
>
> They say to him, "Had you known that the next day they would say about
> you, 'That's the way of So-and-so, going around divorcing his wives,'
>
> "and that about your daughters they'd be saying, 'They're daughters of a
> divorcée! What did their mother do to get herself divorced' [would you have
> taken a vow]?"
>
> And [if] he then said, "Had I known that things would be that way, I
> should never have taken such a vow,"
>
> lo, this [vow] is not binding.
>
> Mishnah-tractate Nedarim 9:9

> [If one said,] "Qonam if I marry that ugly Miss So-and-so," and lo, she is
> beautiful,
>
> ". . . dark . . . ," and lo, she is light,
>
> ". . . short . . . ," and lo, she is tall,
>
> he is permitted [to marry] her,
>
> not because she was ugly and turned beautiful, dark and turned light, short
> and turned tall, but because the vow [to begin with] was based on erroneous
> facts.
>
> M'SH B: A certain man prohibited by vow that from the daughter of his
> sister he should derive benefit.
>
> And they brought her into the house of R. Ishmael and made her
> beautiful.
>
> Said to him R. Ishmael, "My son, did you ever take a vow about this
> lass?"
>
> He said to him, "Never!"
>
> And R. Ishmael declared his [vow] not binding.
>
> That moment R. Ishmael wept and said, "Israelite girls really are beautiful,
> but poverty makes them ugly."
>
> And when R. Ishmael died, Israelite girls took up a lamentation, saying,
> "Israelite girls, weep over R. Ishmael."

And that is what [Scripture] says for Saul, "Israelite girls, weep for Saul who clothed you in scarlet delicately, who put ornaments of gold upon your apparel" (2 Sam. 1:24).

Mishnah-tractate Nedarim 9:10

The normative law rejects unforeseen events as a routine excuse for nullifying a vow; foresight on its own ("had you known . . . would you have vowed?") plays a dubious role. But when it comes to the intentionality involving honor of parents or children, that forms a consideration of such overriding power as to nullify the vow.

Our final encounter with the social virtues carries us to the notion that the higher virtue is the one that encompasses lesser ones. And the highest virtue is good will, which encompasses every other social virtue of generosity, foresight, neighborliness, and the rest. The worst vice is not envy, bad neighborliness, defaulting on a loan, but ill will:

Rabbah Yohanan ben Zakkai said to the disciples, "Go and see what is the straight path to which someone should stick."

R. Eliezer says, "A generous spirit."

R. Joshua says, "A good friend."

R. Yosé says, "A good neighbor."

R. Simeon says, "Foresight."

R. Eleazar says, "Good will."

He said to them, "I prefer the opinion of R. Eleazar b. Arakh, because in what he says is included everything you say."

He said to them, "Go out and see what is the bad road, which someone should avoid."

R. Eliezer says, "Envy."

R. Joshua says, "A bad friend."

R. Yosé says, "A bad neighbor."

R. Simeon says, "Defaulting on a loan."

(All the same is a loan owed to a human being and a loan owed to the Omnipresent, blessed be he, as it is said, "The wicked borrows and does not pay back, but the righteous person deals graciously and hands over [what he owes]" [Psalm 37:21].)

R. Eleazar says, "Bad will."

He said to them, "I prefer the opinion of R. Eleazar b. Arakh, because in what he says is included everything you say."

Mishnah-tractate Abot 2:8–9

The reason behind the position is explicit: the comprehensive definition is preferred over the episodic one. Yohanan finds in the attitude of good will the source of all specific virtues, because in his view attitude and intention in the end define the human being: we are what we want to be, the world is what we want to make of it. The entire message of the Torah for the virtuous man and woman is summed up in that conviction, which, furthermore, is embodied in the law of Judaism governing the social order.

WHAT IS PERSONAL VIRTUE?

The system of Judaism set forth by the sages forms a tight fabric, so that what sages say in a theological setting comes to expression also in the norms of behavior—guided by law, not only by will—that they set forth. We see that fact when we take up the matter of hope. That defines one of the highest personal virtues—not to despair—and one of the personal virtues that Israel, a defeated and broken-hearted people, most required for itself. To make that statement, sages resorted to a legal point. The message is, when hope is abandoned, then, but only then, all is lost. This point is made in connection with the law of ownership of property. Ownership of property depends upon one's attitude toward the property. This comes to expression in several ways. If one consecrates the property, God through the Temple becomes the owner. An act of will alienates the rights of ownership. If squatters have taken one's field or house, when does the original owner lose title? It is when one relinquishes ownership by reason of despairing of recovering possession of the property, that he also loses the rights of ownership. So one may give up property either as a gift to Heaven or as a surrender to bad fortune. Ownership by itself therefore makes little difference; one's attitude toward one's property, on the one side, and one's disposition of possessions, on the other, govern. One does well, therefore, to hold with open arms; one does better to give up ownership of property to Heaven as an act of donation than to relinquish ownership to violence as an act of despair.

In addition to hope, sages identified personal virtues as cleanliness, cultic cleanness, leading to spiritual achievements, holiness, humility, fear of sin, true piety, and onward. These are set forth in a hierarchy, leading from one upward to the next, finally to the day of judgment and eternal life. They did not differentiate the carnal from the spiritual but saw all personal virtue as forming a single coherent whole, from the humble quality of promptness onward, up to the resurrection of the dead:

> In this connection R. Phineas b. Yair would say, "Promptness leads to [hygienic] cleanliness, cleanliness to [cultic] cleanness, cleanness to holiness, holiness to humility, humility to fear of sin, fear of sin to true piety, true piety to the Holy Spirit, the Holy Spirit to the resurrection of the dead, the resurrection of the dead to Elijah the prophet [bringing the Day of Judgment]" [Mishnah-tractate Sotah 9:15].
>
> "Promptness leads to [hygienic] cleanliness": "And when he made an end of atoning for the holy place" (Lev. 16:20).
>
> ". . . cleanliness to [cultic] cleanness": "And the priest shall make atonement for her, and she shall be clean" (Lev. 12:8).
>
> ". . . cleanness to holiness": "And he shall purify it and make it holy" (Lev. 16:9).
>
> ". . . holiness to humility": "For thus says the High and Lofty One, who inhabits eternity, whose name is holy, 'I dwell in the high and holy place, with the one who is of a contrite and humble spirit" (Is. 57:15).

". . . humility to fear of sin": "The reward of humility is the fear of the Lord" (Prov. 22:4).

". . . fear of sin to true piety": "Then you spoke in a vision to your saints" (Ps. 89:20).

". . . true piety to the Holy Spirit": "Then you spoke in a vision to your saints" (Ps. 89:20).

". . . the Holy Spirit to the resurrection of the dead": "And I will put my spirit in you and you shall live" (Ez. 37:14).

". . . the resurrection of the dead to Elijah the prophet of blessed memory": "Behold I will send you Elijah the prophet" (Mal. 3:23).

Song Rabbah I:V.3

What we see once more is how the system supplies context to all the details. The virtue of personal cleanliness so far as Judaism teaches it finds its meaning in the ladder that leads to holiness, encounter with the Holy Spirit, and ultimately the resurrection of the dead.

But, as we saw earlier, the right attitude, the appropriate intention—these matter most of all. How does individual virtue encompass matters of attitude and emotion? The Written Torah answers the question decisively. Certainly the right attitude that the individual should cultivate begins in the commandment, "You will love your neighbor as yourself" (Leviticus 19:18). Here is how sages amplify that matter:

> "You shall not hate your brother in your heart, [but reasoning, you shall reason with your neighbor, lest you bear sin because of him. You shall not take vengeance or bear any grudge against the sons of your own people, but you shall love your neighbor as yourself: I am the Lord]" (Lev. 19:17–18).
>
> Might one suppose that one should not curse him, set him straight, or contradict him?
>
> Scripture says, "in your heart."
>
> I spoke only concerning hatred that is in the heart.

Sages' first point is to define loving one's neighbor as oneself as loving the neighbor in the heart—not harboring a secret enmity, but expressing openly and honestly one's own grievance. So we bear responsibility for those actions that shape our intentionality and attitude; there are things we can do to improve our attitude toward the other and so to foster a proper intentionality toward him or her, and not bearing a grudge is critical. But that involves expressing what troubles us, not holding things in and secretly conspiring, in our own heart, to get even. So we are required to speak forthrightly to the person against whom we have a grievance:

> And how do we know that if one has rebuked him four or five times, he should still go and rebuke him again?
>
> Scripture says, "reasoning, you shall reason with your neighbor."
>
> Might one suppose that that is the case even if one rebukes him and his countenance blanches?
>
> Scripture says, "lest you bear sin."

That means not taking vengeance or bearing a grudge. As is their way, sages translate their teachings into narratives, which exemplify the point in a clear way:

> "You shall not take vengeance [or bear any grudge]":
>   To what extent is the force of vengeance?
>   If one says to him, "Lend me your sickle," and the other did not do so.
>   On the next day, the other says to him, "Lend me your spade."
>   The one then replies, "I am not going to lend it to, because you didn't lend me your sickle."
>   In that context, it is said, "You shall not take vengeance."
>   ". . . or bear any grudge":
>   To what extent is the force of a grudge?
>   If one says to him, "Lend me your spade," but he did not do so.
>   The next day the other one says to him, "Lend me your sickle,"
>   and the other replies, "I am not like you, for you didn't lend me your spade [but here, take the sickle]!"
>   In that context, it is said, "or bear any grudge."
>   "You shall not take vengeance or bear any grudge against the sons of your own people":
>   "You may take vengeance and bear a grudge against others."
>   ". . . but you shall love your neighbor as yourself: [I am the Lord]":
>   R. Aqiba says, "This is the encompassing principle of the Torah."
>   Ben Azzai says, "'This is the book of the generations of Adam' (Gen. 5:1) is a still more encompassing principle."
>
> Sifra CC:III

And we note, at the end, that the first-century authority, Rabbi Aqiba, deems love of neighbor to form the most important principle of the entire Torah.

In addition to love of neighbor, one other personal virtue takes priority, and that is, love of God. But sages also value fear of God, that is to say, reverence. Then they ask, which is the better motive for serving God, fear or love? The one coerces, like it or not; the other appeals to our own will, making God's will into our will, rather than our will into God's will. So sages admire those who serve God out of love, but they identify with those who serve God out of reverence. Here is how they state the matter:

> On that day did R. Joshua b. Hurqanos expound as follows: "Job served the Holy One, blessed be He, only out of love,
>   "since it is said, 'Though he slay me, yet will I wait for him' (Job. 13:15).
>   "But still the matter is in doubt [as to whether it means], 'I will wait for him,' or, 'I will not wait for him.'
>   "Scripture states, 'Until I die I will not put away mine integrity from me' (Job. 27:5).
>   "This teaches that he did what he did out of love."
>   Said R. Joshua, "Who will remove the dirt from your eyes, Rabban Yohanan b. Zakkai. For you used to expound for your entire life that Job served the Omnipresent only out of awe,

"since it is said, 'The man was perfect and upright and one who feared God and avoided evil' (Job. 1:8).

"And now has not Joshua, the disciple of your disciple, taught that he did what he did out of love."

Mishnah-tractate Sotah 5:5

Joshua takes the view that Job served God out of love, and Joshua does not share that view, valuing service out of reverence more. He refers to his master, Yohanan b. Zakkai, now deceased, who has not lived to hear the exegesis of which he would have disapproved.

In the name of R. Nathan they said, "'This will be my salvation, that a godless man shall not come before him' (Job 13: 16).

"One verse of Scripture says, 'And you shall love the Lord your God [with all your heart, and with all your soul, and with all your might]' (Dt. 6:5).

"And another verse of Scripture says, 'You shall fear the Lord your God; you shall serve him, [and swear by his name]' (Dt. 6:13).

"Do [his will] out of love, do his will out of fear.

"'Do [his will] out of love,' so that if you should come to hate, you will know that you love him, and one who loves cannot hate.

"'Do his will out of fear,' so that if you come to rebel against him, [you will know that] one who fears does not rebel."

Why is fear or reverence the greater personal virtue? Because—by now we can have predicted it—the one who fears will not rebel; that is, such a one is not going to be arrogant. If we serve God out of love, then our own feelings enter into the transaction; we can deny love. But if we serve God out of fear, then obligation takes over, and humility sets in. But that is not the whole story, as we shall see in a moment, for while Job served out of love, Abraham did so out of fear, and of them all, he was the only truly beloved one. In this same context, sages castigate a variety of Pharisees, who serve God in a show-offy way, displaying their piety in public.

There are seven types of [improper, wrong-headed] Pharisees: the shoulder-Pharisee; the wait-a-while Pharisee; the bookkeeping Pharisee; the niggardly Pharisee; the show-me-what-I-did-wrong Pharisee; the Pharisee-out-of-fear; and the Pharisee-out-of-love.

"The shoulder-Pharisee" carries the religious deeds he has done on his shoulder [for all to see].

"The wait-a-while Pharisee"—"Wait a minute, so I can go off and do a religious deed."

"The bookkeeping Pharisee"—He does one deed for which he is liable and one deed which is a religious duty, and then he balances one off against the other.

"The niggardly Pharisee"—"Who will show me how I can save so that I can do a religious deed."

"The show-me-what-I-did-wrong Pharisee"—"Show me what sin I have done, and I will do an equivalent religious duty."

"A Pharisee-out-of-fear," like Job.

"A Pharisee-out-of-love," like Abraham.

And the only one of them all who is truly beloved is the Pharisee-out-of-love, like Abraham.

Yerushalmi Sotah 5:5, I:2–3

The upshot is quickly stated: sages found both motives—love and fear—admirable, assigning the one to Job, the other to Abraham. But then, in their context, it is Abraham who forms the ideal.

HOW DOES THIS RELIGION DEFINE CHARACTER, GOOD AND BAD?

Good character is defined in various ways, all of them deriving from the Torah. The basic question of good character is answered by appeal to the commandments that, if one does them, mark a person as godly. But the Torah contains many commandments. Here is how sages define the truly good character. They affirm that all of the commandments serve to form good character, and disobedience to any of them marks bad character. But they recognize a hierarchy of character-forming obligations, a hierarchy that they find in the Written Torah.

> R. Simelai expounded, "Six hundred and thirteen commandments were given to Moses, three hundred and sixty-five negative ones, corresponding to the number of the days of the solar year, and two hundred forty-eight positive commandments, corresponding to the parts of man's body."
>
> "David came and reduced them to eleven: 'A Psalm of David: Lord, who shall sojourn in thy tabernacle, and who shall dwell in thy holy mountain? (i) He who walks uprightly and (ii) works righteousness and (iii) speaks truth in his heart and (iv) has no slander on his tongue and (v) does no evil to his fellow and (vi) does not take up a reproach against his neighbor, (vii) in whose eyes a vile person is despised but (viii) honors those who fear the Lord. (ix) He swears to his own hurt and changes not. (x) He does not lend on interest. (xi) He does not take a bribe against the innocent' (Psalm 15)."
>
> "Isaiah came and reduced them to six: '(i) He who walks righteously and (ii) speaks uprightly, (iii) he who despises the gain of oppressions, (iv) shakes his hand from holding bribes, (v) stops his ear from hearing of blood (vi) and shuts his eyes from looking upon evil, he shall dwell on high' (Isaiah 33:25–26)."
>
> "Micah came and reduced them to three: 'It has been told you, man, what is good, and what the Lord demands from you, (i) only to do justly and (ii) to love mercy, and (iii) to walk humbly before God' (Micah 6:8)."
>
> "Isaiah again came and reduced them to two: 'Thus says the Lord, (i) Keep justice and (ii) do righteousness' (Isaiah 56:1)."
>
> "Amos came and reduced them to a single one, as it is said, 'For thus says the Lord to the house of Israel. Seek Me and live.'
>
> "Habakkuk further came and based them on one, as it is said, 'But the righteous shall live by his faith' (Habakkuk 2:4)."

Bavli Makkot 23b–24a

Living by one's faith should not be misunderstood. Simelai does not mean by "faith" one's personal opinions or beliefs, and he is not commending the individual who stands against the world by reason of personal conviction. By "faith" Simelai understands Habakkuk to mean, "faithfulness," that is, trust in God, and "the righteous shall live by his faith" means "by confidence in God's providence." That accords with Amos's "Seek Me and live," and Micah's recommendation to walk humbly with God. Naturally, faithfulness to God yields, also, adherence to justice and mercy, as we have seen earlier, and the actions of those recommended as embodiments of self-abnegation—the ones whose prayers are answered—fit well into the picture before us.

What defines bad character? Once more, we are used to sages' preference for definition through deed. But all together, sages find bad character to embody traits of selfishness and pride and arrogance. These are the attitudes that yield idolatry, fornication, love for gossip, and other forms of self-aggrandizement. Above all else, idolatry, fornication, and murder represent the cardinal sins—the actions by which one manipulates the world round about, trying to govern God, exploit and even eliminate the other:

> Another matter: "For the earth is filled with violence" (Gen. 6:13).
> Said R. Levi, "The word for violence refers to idolatry, fornication, and murder.
> "Idolatry: 'For the earth is filled with violence' (Gen. 6:13).
> "Fornication: 'The violence done to me and to my flesh be upon Babylonia' (Jer. 51:35). [And the word for 'flesh' refers to incest, as at Lev. 18:6].
> "Murder: 'For the violence against the children of Judah, because they have shed innocent blood' (Joel 4:19).
> "Further, the word for 'violence' stands for its ordinary meaning as well."
>
> Genesis Rabbah XXXI:VI.1

And yet, there is a social vice that matters even more, being commonplace and easy to carry out. When it comes to assessing a person's character, gossip outweighs even idolatry, fornication, and murder:

> These are four things for the performance of which one is punished in this world, while the principal [i.e., eternal punishment] remains for the world to come, and these are they:
> (1) idolatrous worship, (2) sexual misbehavior, (3) murder, and (4) gossip, which is worse than all of them [together].
>
> Tosefta-tractate Peah 1:2

The three cardinal sins are forgivable, but rejection of the Torah is not:

> R. Huna, R. Jeremiah in the name of R. Samuel bar R. Isaac: "We find that the Holy One, blessed be he, forgave Israel for idolatry, fornication, and murder. [But] for their rejection of the Torah he never forgave them."
> What is the scriptural basis for that view?
> It is not written, "Because they practiced idolatry, fornication, and murder," but rather, "And the Lord said, 'Because they have forsaken my Torah.'"

Said R. Hiyya bar Ba, "'If they were to forsake me, I should forgive them, for they may yet keep my Torah. For if they should forsake me but keep my Torah, the leaven that is in [the Torah] will bring them closer to me.'"

R. Huna said, "Study Torah [even if it is] not for its own sake, for, out of [doing so] not for its own sake, you will come [to study it] for its own sake."

Yerushalmi-tractate Hagigah 1:7/I:3

Why is rejection of the Torah not forgivable? Because the Torah affords knowledge of God and God's will, and rejecting the Torah then brings about all other vices and sins, constituting the ultimate act of arrogance.

Why, then, do people sin, and what is the key to bad character? Sages see two conflicting impulses in the human being, the impulse to do good and the impulse to do evil. That impulse is identified in many passages of the Oral Torah with sexual sins (not sexuality per se). Sages identify the mark of bad character as the dominant trait not only of the gossip but also of the fornicator:

R. Hunia in the name of R. Dosa b. R. Tebet: "Two impulses to do evil did the Holy One, blessed be He, create in his world, the impulse to worship idols, and the impulse to fornicate. The impulse to worship idols has already been eliminated, but the impulse to fornicate still endures.

"Said the Holy One, blessed be He, 'Whoever can withstand the impulse to fornicate do I credit as though he had withstood them both.'"

Said R. Judah, "The matter may be compared to the case of a snake-charmer who had [two] snakes. He charmed the larger and left the smaller, saying, 'Whoever can withstand this one is certainly credited as though he had withstood them both.'

"So the Holy One, blessed be He, eliminated the impulse to worship idols but left the impulse to fornicate. He said, 'Whoever can withstand the impulse to fornicate do I credit as though he had withstood them both.'"

Song of Songs Rabbah XCVI:i.1

The impulse to do evil also bears a good side, so Gen. R. IX:VII.1: Nahman in the name of R. Samuel: "'Behold, it was very good' refers to the impulse to do good. '*And* behold, it was very good' encompasses also the impulse to do evil. And is the impulse to do evil '*very* good'? Indeed so, for if it were not for the impulse to do evil, a man would not build a house, marry a wife, and produce children. So does Solomon say, 'Again I considered all labor and all excelling in work, that is rivalry with his neighbor' (Qoh. 4:4)."

The person of poor character pays a heavy price: that person will never see God. Who are such types? They are scoffers, flatterers, liars, and slanderers:

And said R. Hisda said R. Jeremiah bar Abba, "There are four categories who will not receive the face of the Presence of God:

"The categories of scoffers, flatterers, liars, and slanderers.

"The category of scoffers, as it is written, 'He has stretched out his hand against scorners' (Hos. 7:5).

"The category of flatterers, as it is written, 'He who speaks lies shall not be established in my sight' (Job. 13:16).

"The category of liars, as it is written, 'He who speaks lies shall not be established in my sight' (Ps. 101:7).

"The category of slanderers, as it is written, 'For you are not a God who has pleasure in wickedness; evil will not dwell with you' (Ps. 5:5). 'You are righteous, O Lord, and evil will not dwell in your house' [Ps. 5 addresses slander.]"

Bavli-tractate Sanhedrin 11:2 X.4/103a

What these have in common is the use of the power of language for wicked purposes. These are not people who murder, fornicate, or worship idols. These persons will not see God because of things that they say, not do. Once more, we return to sages' basic conviction that attitude and intentionality, reaching expression in language as much as in deed, make all the difference. What is the antidote? It is the shaping of one's attitude and intentionality in the proper way. And how is this done? It is through close study of the Torah, both the written and the oral parts thereof. Everything is captured in a single statement, "God wants the heart," which is amplified by another, "The commandments were given only to purify the heart of humanity." Then who is the person who ought to embody and represent that pure heart that the Torah so highly appreciates? It must be the master of Torah, the sage.

BEYOND THE NORMAL VIRTUES:
WHO IS THE EXTRAORDINARY PERSON?

The type of person who transcends the normal virtues and serves as the model for the rest of humanity is the sage. He[5] is valued in heaven by reason of his learning on earth. Sages on earth may not occupy positions of power and influence, but in heaven they do. The arrogant on earth are humbled in heaven, the humble on earth are exalted in heaven:

Joseph b. R. Joshua fell sick and went into a coma. Afterward his father said to him, "So what did you see?"

"I saw an upside down world, what is on high is down below, and what is below is on high."

He said to him, "You saw a world of clarity."

"And as to us, how are we perceived?"

He said to him, "As we are valued here, so we are valued there. I heard them saying, 'Happy is he who comes here with his learning fully in hand.' And I heard them saying, 'As to those put to death [as martyrs] by the government, no creature can stand within their precincts.'"

Bavli Pesahim 50A 3:7–8 II:4

---

[5]In the formative age, the first seven centuries of the common era, sages were men; the modes of acquiring knowledge of the Torah, involving study in a relationship of discipleship to a master, were not open to women. Hence here we shall speak of "him," not "him or her." In our own times the doors of the schools where the Torah is taught have opened to women as well. Women become rabbis in Reform, Reconstructionist, Conservative, and other Judaisms, and some Orthodox Judaisms make provision for women to study and teach the Torah as well.

The sage enjoyed Heaven's high esteem because he spent his life trying to know God through mastery of God's self manifestation in the Torah. He was, therefore, a man sanctified through study of the Torah in discipleship, a link in the chain of Oral Torah from Sinai. Because they embody the law of the Torah, the actions of the sage define norms and supply exemplary models; the sage then constitutes a native category, holding together a vast corpus of exemplary statements, for example, of what this or that named master did or refrained from doing. Because of his mastery of the Torah, a disciple of a sage is equivalent to an actual Torah-scroll, the physical object, and is treated with the same respect that is paid to the Torah. He who sees a disciple of a sage who has died is as if he sees a scroll of the Torah that has been burned.[6]

The sage is treated like a scroll of the Torah. With special reference to the death of a sage, we have the following:

> R. Sheshet, and some say, R. Yohanan, said, "Removing the Torah contained in the sage must be like the giving of the Torah; just as the giving of the Torah involved six hundred thousand, so taking away the Torah involves six hundred thousand. But this is with regard to one who has recited Scripture and repeated Mishnah traditions. But in the case of one who repeated Tannaite statements to others, there is no upper limit at all."
>
> Bavli-tractate Ketubot 23:1–2 I.19/17a

Why should the sage make such a difference? Because through what he masters in the Torah, he meets God; he brings God's presence to rest upon Israel. This is expressed in the following way:

> "And it came to pass in the days of Ahaz" (Is. 7:1).
> What was the misfortune that took place at that time?
> "The Syrians on the east and the Philistines on the west [devour Israel with open mouth]" (Is. 9:12).
> The matter [the position of Israel] may be compared to a king who handed over his son to a tutor, who hated [the son]. The tutor thought, "If I kill him now, I shall turn out to be liable to the death penalty before the king. So what I'll do is take away his wet nurse, and he will die on his own."
> So thought Ahaz, "If there are no kids, there will be no he-goats. If there are no he-goats, there will be no flock. If there is no flock, there will be no shepherd. If there is no shepherd, there will be no world.
> So did Ahaz plan, "If there are no children, there will be no disciples; if there are no disciples, there will be no sages; if there are no sages, there will be no Torah; if there is no Torah, there will be no synagogues and schools; if there are no synagogues and schools, then the Holy One, blessed be he, will not allow his Presence to come to rest in the world."
> What did he do? He went and locked the synagogues and schools.
>
> Leviticus Rabbah XI:VII 3

---

[6]Tosefta-tractate Taanit 3:7 I.10.

Through the Torah God comes into the world, and the sages, who master the Torah and teach it, therefore bring God into the world. That is why to deny the teachings of the sages is to deny God. That proposition is elaborately spelled out.

"But if you will not hearken to me [and will not do all these commandments, if you spurn my statutes and if your soul abhors my ordinances, so that you will not do all my commandments but break my covenant, I will do this to you]":

"But if you will not hearken to me" means, if you will not listen to the exposition of sages.

Might one suppose that reference is made to Scripture [rather than sages' teachings]?

When Scripture says, "and will not do all these commandments," lo, reference clearly is made to what is written in the Torah.

Then how shall I interpret, "But if you will not hearken to me"?

It means, if you will not listen to the exposition of sages.

"But if you will not hearken":

What is the point of Scripture here?

This refers to one who knows God's lordship and intentionally rebels against it.

And so Scripture says, "Like Nimrod, a mighty hunter [before the Lord]" (Gen. 10:9).

Now what is the point of saying "before the Lord"?

[It really means, rebellion, for the letters of the name for Nimrod can spell out "rebel," so that] this refers to one who knows God's lordship and intentionally rebels against it.

"But if you will not hearken to me [and will not do all these commandments]":

What is the point of Scripture in saying, "will not do"?

You have someone who does not learn but who carries out [the teachings of the Torah].

In that connection, Scripture says, "But if you will not hearken to me and will not do."

Lo, whoever does not learn [the Torah] also does not carry it out.

And you have someone who does not learn [the Torah] and also does not carry it out, but he does not despise others [who do so].

In that connection, Scripture says, "if you spurn my statutes."

Lo, whoever does not learn the Torah and does not carry it out in the end will despise others who do so.

And you furthermore have someone who does not learn [the Torah], and also does not carry it out, and he does despise others [who do so], but he does not hate the sages.

In that connection, Scripture says, "and if your soul abhors my ordinances"—

Lo, whoever does not learn [the Torah], also does not carry it out, and does despise others [who do so], in the end will hate the sages.

And you furthermore have someone who does not learn [the Torah], does not carry it out, despises others [who do so], and hates the sages, but who lets others carry out [the Torah].

Scripture says, "so that you will not do [all my commandments but break my covenant]"—

lo, whoever does not learn [the Torah], does not carry it out, despises others [who do so], and hates the sages, in the end will not let others carry out [the Torah].

Or you may have someone who does not learn [the Torah], does not carry it out, despises others [who do so], hates the sages, does not let others carry out [the Torah], but he confesses that the religious duties were spoken from Sinai.

Scripture says, "all my commandments"—

lo, whoever does not learn [the Torah], does not carry it out, despises others [who do so], hates the sages, does not let others carry out [the Torah], in the end will deny that the religious duties were spoken from Sinai.

Or you may have someone who exhibits all these traits but does not deny the very Principle [of God's existence and rule].

Scripture says, "but break my covenant"—

lo, whoever exhibits all these traits in the end will deny the very Principle [of God's existence and rule].

                                                        Sifra CCLXIV:I.1, 2, 4

Why such a heavy emphasis on the sainthood of the sage and on his Torah? The reason is that the study of the Torah changed the one who studied because through it he entered into the mind of God, learning how God's mind worked when God formed the Torah, written and oral alike, and (in the explicit view of Genesis Rabbah 1:1) consulted the Torah and created the world. And there, in the intellect of God, in their judgment humanity gained access to the only means of uniting intellect with existential condition as to salvation. The Mishnah had set forth the rules that governed the natural world in relationship to heaven. But knowledge of the Torah now joined the one world, known through nature, with the other world, the world of supernature, where, in the end, intellect merely served in the quest for salvation. Through Torah-study sages claimed for themselves a place in that very process of thought that had given birth to nature; but it was a supernatural process, and knowledge of that process on its own terms would transform and, in the nature of things, save. That explains the integrative power of imputing supernatural power to learning.

One becomes a disciple of a sage by hearing and repeating and memorizing the words of the sage set forth as Torah. Reciting words of Torah is obligatory for the disciple, and doing so in constant interchange with colleagues is the sole valid way. Thus, "If two disciples of sages go along without words of Torah between them, they are worthy of being burned in fire, as it is said, 'And it came to pass, as they still went on, that, behold, a chariot of fire' (2 Kgs. 2:11). The reason that the chariot of fire appeared is that they were talking. Lo, if there had not been talk of Torah, they would have been worthy of being burned."[7] What is the mark of a sage? A sage exhibits traits of intelligence and

---

[7]Bavli-tractate Sotah 9:12 V.3.

civility: there are seven traits to an unformed clod, and seven to a sage. (1) A sage does not speak before someone greater than he in wisdom. (2) And he does not interrupt his fellow. (3) And he is not at a loss for an answer. (4) He asks a relevant question and answers properly. (5) And he addresses each matter in its proper sequence, first, then second. (6) And concerning something he has not heard, he says, "I have not heard the answer." (7) And he concedes the truth when the other party demonstrates it. And the opposite of these traits apply to a clod.[8]

So much for the sage, whose intellectual capacities—ability to learn what the Torah says and to reason in a rational way about it—are supposed to—and in some cases do—impart those qualities of character and conscience that realize what it means to be "in our image, after our likeness." But sages themselves paint yet another, and conflicting, picture of the extraordinarily virtuous person. They have the notion that the most ignorant of ignorant persons, who devote their lives to sin, can through a single action accomplish what a life devoted to Torah-study cannot achieve. And that brings us back to our starting point, the merit of the act of selfless love, the act God cannot compel or coerce but craves of humanity. The commandment to love God—"you shall love the Lord your God with all your heart, your soul, and your might" (Deuteronomy 4:9)—and the commandment to love the other—"you shall love your neighbor as yourself" (Leviticus 19:18)—meet and form a single statement. It is that to which God aspires for us, but what God cannot impose upon us. God can command love, but not coerce it, favor but not force it. But then God responds to the act of selfless generosity with an act of grace—precisely that act that humanity for its part cannot compel or coerce out of God, cannot cajole from God, but can only beseech.

And no wonder, in sages' account of matters, such a remarkable action done once not only makes up for a dissolute life but in that single moment wins Heaven's perpetual favor:

> In a dream of R. Abbahu, Mr. Pentakaka ["Five sins"] appeared, who prayed that rain would come, and it rained. R. Abbahu sent and summoned him. He said to him, "What is your trade?"
>
> He said to him, "Five sins does that man [I] do every day, [for I am a pimp:] [1] hiring whores, [2] cleaning up the theater, [3] bringing home their garments for washing, [4] dancing, and [4] 'performing' before them."
>
> He said to him, "And what sort of decent thing have you ever done?"
>
> He said to him, "One day that man [I] was cleaning the theater, and a woman came and stood behind a pillar and cried. I said to her, 'What's with you?' And she said to me, 'That woman's [my] husband is in prison, and I wanted to see what I can do to free him,' so I sold my bed and cover, and I gave the proceeds to her. I said to her, 'Here is your money, free your husband, but do not sin.'"
>
> He said to him, "You are worthy of praying and having your prayers answered."
>
> Yerushalmi Taanit 1:4.I

---

[8]Mishnah–tractate Abot 5:7.

Mr. Five-Sins has done everything sinful that (within sages' imagination) one can do, and, more to the point, he does it every day. What he should do is carry out the commandments, and he should study the Torah every day. So what he has done is what he should not have done, and what he has not done is what he should have done—every day. And yet in a single action, in a moment, everything changes. So the singularity of the act of *zekhut,* which suffices if done only one time, encompasses its power to outweigh a life of sin—again, an act of *zekhut* as the mirror image and opposite of sin. Here again, the single act of saving a woman from a "fate worse than death" has sufficed. Mr. Five Sins has carried out an act of grace, to which Heaven, uncoerced and uncompelled, responds with that love in which God so richly abounds for humanity. The extraordinary person is the one who sacrifices for the other in an act of selfless love—and that can be anybody, at any time, anywhere. That is why, for Judaism, the great commandment is one of love: "You shall love the Lord your God with all your heart, with all your soul, and with all your might," as the creed of Judaism maintains. The one thing one person cannot command of another person is love. That, by definition, is freely given, or not given at all. It cannot be coerced or commanded. Then virtue consists in doing on one's own what God yearns for but cannot impose, which is, to love God.

COMMENTARIES

Christianity on Judaism

by Bruce Chilton

Christianity can only endorse the insight that humanity is created in the image and likeness of God (Genesis 1:26). The affinity between divine and human identity is pursued in the ethical realm, when Jesus links two quite disparate commands in the Torah, to love God (Deuteronomy 6:4) and to love one's neighbor (Leviticus 19:18), by his careful insistence that they are like one another (Matthew 22:34–30; Mark 12:28–34). The Scriptures of Israel had discovered within the vision of the divine Throne that an image of humanity was present with God (see Ezekiel 1:26; Daniel 7:13), and Jesus joined himself to that vision (Luke 12:8–9). In the Revelation of John, the crucified Jesus is himself part of the Throne (chapters 4–5), and that signals an essential aspect of the teaching of his resurrection: even put to death, and particularly experienced alive after his death, Jesus was the inherent image of divine humanity.

The defection of the primordial man and woman as the emblem of who we are does not seal our fate, but is part of the master plan of the restoration of humanity to God's image and likeness. That is a hope Christianity also shares with Judaism, but Israel's return to the Land of Israel is no longer seen as a necessary part of that hope. As Paul expresses the matter, "just as through one person's obedience many were caused to be sinners, so also through one's obedience many shall be caused to be righteous" (Romans 5:19). Human salvation is no longer here a matter of place, but of the medium of life itself; the first Adam was a living being, the last Adam a life-giving spirit (1 Corinthians 15:45). Christianity's anthropology is of a new, restored humanity in Christ, attested both by Jesus' resurrection and by the promptings of the Holy Spirit within us.

Spelling out how the case of Jesus can resonate with humanity as such involves a detailed analysis of how humans are connected to one another, as well as to God. Philo of Alexandria, an older contemporary of Jesus, developed just such a theology in his treatise "On the Creation of the World." In his exposition, the pattern of divine creation (the "Word," Logos) corresponds to the model of humanity, so that we all share a correspondence with the creative ideal in God's mind, with the natural world around us, and with one another. The Fathers according to Rabbi Nathan XXXI:III.1 represents a Rabbinic exposition of that analysis, just as the Gospel according to John 1:1–18 does so from the point of view of Christianity. What is immediately striking, when one sets these texts side by side, is that the terms of reference of the correspondences detailed are as categorically cosmographic in the Rabbinic application as they are soteriological in the Christian application. Both aspects are present in Philo (and neither is excluded in Judaism or Christianity), but the difference of emphasis is notable.

John's Gospel itself adumbrates this distinction at the close of its famous prologue regarding the word of God (1:17):

> Because from his fullness we all received, even grace in place of grace, because the law was given through Moses; grace and truth occurred through Christ Jesus.

The principle of *zekhut* or grace undergirds our lives, because only divine generosity gave us being, and the uncoerced mirroring of that by humanity is among Heaven's greatest joys. As in every case of divine pleasure, this embrace of grace results in a new creation: the restored humanity promised in Christ and first effected in his resurrection. His spirit becomes accessible to all, which is why, in Christianity, the single unforgivable sin is not against the Torah or the Christ, but against the Spirit of God (Matthew 12:31–32; Mark 3:28–30).

Islam on Judaism

by TAMARA SONN

Islam differs markedly from Judaism in its vision of human nature. In Islam, God is considered incomparable, infinitely beyond any comparison we can make about him. We speak of God's will and God's mind, for example, but this type of language is considered to be metaphorical. To accept the language literally is to commit the offense of anthropomorphism: making God like human beings. In our encounters with God, we experience qualities or characteristics such as mind and will (to use the same examples) that seem to us like our own. Therefore we describe them as such. But we must always understand that, in God, such qualities exist in ways we cannot understand fully. We simply accept what God has revealed to us. And what God has revealed to us overall is that he is creator and judge, benevolent and compassionate, and that we were created in order to "establish justice," as the Qur'an puts it (Qur'an 4:135), not to try to be like God. Our job is to contribute to the creation of a society that reflects the equality all people share in the eyes of their creator. That is God's will. True recognition of divinity is evidenced in our submission to that will. We are therefore cherished servants of God in the Islamic view. The creation story explains that we were entrusted by God with the task of doing his will, despite the challenges created by our ignorance and natural weaknesses. To the extent that we overcome those faults and choose God's will over our own, we will be rewarded. The law has been given by God to help us do that. Therefore, Islam agrees with Judaism that the law mediates the struggle between God's will for a just world and human selfishness. Islam agrees with Judaism as well that the divine law, God's will, is both reasonable and just. But Islam rejects the Judaic notion that God is powerless against human will. In Islamic belief, God is omnipotent; nothing limits divine power. Human beings are responsible for their own decisions, but the Qur'an confirms that nothing happens without God's will. God created us with the ability to reject the good guidance provided by the Qur'an and Sunna (the Prophet Muhammad's example). We will therefore be rewarded or punished according to our choices. Therefore, Islam agrees with Judaism about the importance of hope. The Qur'an condemns despair and constantly reminds believers that they were created with divine purpose by God who is all-merciful and forgiving. Loss of hope is therefore tantamount to disbelief. The greatest virtue, by contrast, is *taqwa,* taking refuge in God through righteousness. Things may not always turn out as we intended, but provided our intentions were honorable, our failings will be forgiven. And provided we trust in God, guidance will be forthcoming.

Hinduism on Judaism

by BRIAN K. SMITH

The notion that God's traits "form the model for those of God's creatures" finds a parallel in some of the theistic traditions of Hinduism. As it says in the Bhagavad Gita, for example, God is active in the world, and thus so should be human beings. But God also acts in a virtuous manner, in this case meaning disinterestedly, without desire and without all motivations that stem from desire. And so, says the Gita, should humans act. They should imitate God by fulfilling their duty, to the very best of their ability, but without an eye to the "fruits" of action. Here, as in Judaism, human virtue is conceived as imitative of God's virtue and as the means for human beings to dedicate their activity to God.

But in most forms of Hindu theology we are not so much "modeled after" God as we are, originally, emanations of him. The driving force of much of Judaism's teachings on virtue—obedience to God and what he expects of us, our role in his divine plan—finds no real parallel in Hinduism. Virtues such as humility and vices such as arrogance, which do exist in Hinduism as well as in Judaism, are set within very different theological contexts. So too are what would seem to be comparable social virtues revolving around "selflessness."

Professor Neusner writes that in Judaism, "Conscience—not sinning—comes about through consciousness of who we really are." Self-knowledge appears to be pivotal to virtuous behavior in Judaism, and the same can certainly be said of Hinduism. The differences—and they are big ones—derive from very different ideas about self-identity. The two traditions may ask the same question

("Who are we really?"), but the answers they offer are indicative of the large divide between them. For Judaism, we are (and are *to be*) the humble servants of God, our creator and king. In traditional Hinduism, the first answer to the question of self-identity (and thus to how to behave virtuously) is that we are human beings born (due to our past karma) into a particular caste with particular duties to perform in order to fulfill our innate destiny. We must, in a certain sense, perform these duties "selflessly," that is, without the overweening drives of selfish desire. But also in most forms of Hinduism we are, in the deepest sense, no different from God (or the *brahman* or however the Cosmic One is conceived), and union with that One—a more radical vision of "selflessness"—is the ultimate goal.

Buddhism on Judaism

by CHARLES HALLISEY

There might appear to be a profound difference in orientation to the life of virtue in the Buddhist and Jewish traditions. The latter defines its whole vision of what it means to be human, including the life of virtue, within the context of the image of God that is inherent in each human being. In some cases, it is God's traits that serve as models for particular human virtues, while in others, it is qualities that are generated by human relations with God that serve as yardsticks for other human virtues. The Buddhist traditions are well known for their disinterest in a creator, and in this sense, the Buddhist traditions have sometimes been called atheistic.

This might just be a surface difference, however. We can in fact see similar patterns in Buddhist interactions with Buddhas, as supreme and accessible Lords, to what can be observed in Jewish approaches to God, and these patterns echo throughout Buddhist accounts of the life of virtue. Thus, a Buddha's compassion and tolerance serve as models for our own self-transformation, just as God's traits of justice and equity form a model for those of God's creatures. And, if the social virtues begin, in Judaism, with righteousness that is best experienced in a loving relationship to God, similarly, the social virtues in Buddhism can be said to begin in gratitude, an attitude that is best known in a mindful relationship with a Buddha.

The insistence on locating the life of human virtue within a divine framework comes at a cost that Buddhists would find very high. Most notably, Buddhists would look for more attention to how we relate directly to our neighbor. That is, when we look into the face of our neighbor in order to see God's likeness, how do we still see our neighbor and his very particular and unique needs for our compassion and aid?

SUMMARY

We are really in God's image, after God's likeness, but, in the narrative of mythic monotheism, we are children of Adam and Eve and, as survivors of the world flood, children of Noah as well. Just as God acts in full freedom will, so too do we. Sin results from the arrogance of exercising free will in contradiction to God's will. Virtue is attained through humility, expressed by freely loving God and obeying the Torah in which God makes himself manifest. The social virtues begin with righteousness, meaning, love for God. God responds to voluntary acts of self-sacrifice by uncoerced love. Good character involves seeking God and living faithfully. The extraordinary person is the one who devotes his or her life to meeting God in the Torah.

GLOSSARY

Abodah labor; also, Temple service, performing the sacrificial cult in the Temple of Jerusalem; also prayer

Abot "the Fathers," the sayings of the principal authorities of the Oral Torah of Judaism; a tractate attached to the Mishnah, ca. 200 C.E., at about 250 C.E.

Aggadah lore, narrative, exegesis of Scripture, theology

B.C.E. before the Common Era = B.C.

Baba Mesia The Middle Gate, a tractate of the Mishnah that deals with aspects of civil law, subject to commentary in the Bavli and the Yerushalmi

Bavli the Talmud of Babylonia, ca. 600 C.E., a systematic commentary to thirty-seven of the sixty-three tractates of the Mishnah

C.E. Common Era = A.D.

Elijah the prophet the harbinger of the coming of the Messiah

Erubin a tractate of the Mishnah that deals with transporting objects on the Sabbath from public to private domain and vice versa; and the provision of a Sabbath boundary, mingling ownership of property within the boundary into a single domain for purpose of Sabbath observance

Fathers According to Rabbi Nathan A talmud to Abot; provides biographies to the sages whose sayings are mentioned in Abot

Fathers see Abot

Genesis Rabbah Rabbinic commentary to the book of Genesis, produced at ca. 450 C.E. Emphasizes the connection between Israel's life as portrayed in Scripture with its situation in real time.

Hagigah tractate of the Halakhah of the Mishnah-Tosefta-Yerushalmi-Bavli that deals with the festal offering presented by pilgrims to the Jerusalem Temple during the festival celebrations of Passover, Pentecost, and Tabernacles

Halakhah law, norms of behavior

Hillel and Shammai Two principal authorities of the Mishnah, flourished around the beginning of the first century C.E.

Kesherim people who are honorable and virtue, literally, "kosher-people"

Ketubot a tractate of the Mishnah that deals with marriage-agreements, guaranteeing support for a wife in the event of death or divorce

Leviticus Rabbah Commentary to the book of Leviticus, ca. 450 C.E.

Makkot tractate of the Halakhah of the Mishnah-Tosefta-Yerushalmi-Bavli that deals with sins punished by flogging, with the punishment for manslaughter, and with administering the flogging

Megillah a tractate of the Mishnah that deals with the festival of Purim, described in the biblical book of Esther; and with the life of synagogues, with special attention to the public declamation of the Torah

Mekhilta attributed to R. Ishmael Commentary to the book of Exodus, probably of ca. 250 C.E.

Mishnah a six-part exposition of the law, divided into sixty-three tractates, or subject-areas, of the Oral Torah revealed by God to Moses at Mount Sinai and formulated and transmitted wholly in memory until formalized in ca. 200 C.E. under the auspices of Judah the Patriarch, the ruler of the Jewish population of Roman Palestine of that period

Nedarim tractate of the Halakhah of the Mishnah-Tosefta-Yerushalmi-Bavli that deals with taking vows and releasing them

Pesahim a tractate of the Mishnah that deals with the festival of Passover, with special attention to the prohibition of leaven on that holy day and the sacrifice of the Pascal lamb; and the Passover meal in the home

Pesiqta deRab Kahana Rabbinic commentary on passages of Scripture highlighted on various Sabbaths and festivals

Qiddushin a tractate of the Mishnah that deals with betrothals

Qonam a euphemism for "qorban," meaning, "offering," thus a declaration that something is holy as is an offering in the Temple and therefore not available for secular, everyday use

Sanhedrin tractate of the Halakhah of the Mishnah-Tosefta-Yerushalmi-Bavli that deals with the operation of the courts of justice, both civil and criminal; and with the crimes or sins that are punished by the four media for inflicting the death penalty, respectively

Shabbat Hebrew word for the Sabbath; the seventh day, a day of rest, commemorating the creation of the world in six days and God's repose on the Seventh

Sifra Rabbinic commentary to the book of Leviticus, emphasizes that Scripture forms the valid source for the laws of the Mishnah

Song Rabbah Song of Songs Rabbah, the rabbinic commentary to the book of the Song of Songs; underscores that the love poem embodies God's love for Israel and Israel's love for God

Sotah tractate of the Mishnah-Tosefta-Yerushalmi-Bavli that deals with the wife accused of adultery, as portrayed at Numbers 5

Taanit a tractate of the Mishnah-Tosefta-Yerushalmi-Bavli that deals with fasting in times of crisis, and also the delegation of priests of a given village and its activities when it goes up to Jerusalem to conduct the Temple rites

Talmud a systematic commentary to a tractate of the Mishnah, clarifying the source in Scripture of a law in the Mishnah, the meanings of words and phrases, and the broader implications of a rule; also augmenting the presentation of the law by the Mishnah through a systematic exposition of correlative topics, whether of law or of theology; the whole characterized by contentious analytical argument

Torah the Five books of Moses, Genesis, Exodus, Leviticus Numbers, Deuteronomy; more generally, God's teaching to Moses at Mount Sinai, written and oral

Tosefta A compilation of legal rulings that complement those in the Mishnah and are attributed to the same authorities as are cited in the Mishnah, reached closure at ca. 300 C.E.

Tractate a topical exposition of a category of law (halakhah) in Judaism, with special reference to the Mishnah's, Tosefta's, Yerushalmi's, and Bavli's topical divisions

Yerushalmi The Talmud of the Land of Israel ("Jerusalem"), produced in ca. 400 C.E. in Galilee by the sages of the Torah, commenting on thirty-nine of the sixty-three tractates of the Mishnah

Yohanan ben Zakkai The Rabbinic leader who escaped from Jerusalem before it fell to the Romans in the summer of 68 C.E. and who founded the study-circle that preserved knowledge of the Torah after the calamity and that produced the Mishnah and related traditions

Zekhut unearned, uncoerced grace, bestowed by God in response to unearned acts of self-sacrifice or of other unusual merit that God craves but cannot coerce

DISCUSSION QUESTIONS

1. How does Judaism link virtue to its fundamental theological convictions, and what is the role of narrative in its picture of human and divine virtue? What links right attitude and intentionality to the theological narrative of the creation of humanity and the fall from Eden?

2. Why does Judaism lay such stress on the virtue of humility and the vice of arrogance? Why should these represent the most important traits of personality, positive, and negative, that Judaism identifies? Do you see a connection between Judaism's fundamental theological convictions, expressed through narrative, and its definition of the principal virtues?

3. Why does God most admire selflessness? What does self-abnegation signal about a personality?

4. What are the hallmarks of humility? How does that theological virtue get amplified into a series of social virtues?

5. Why does "good will" (literally, "a good heart") embody all the other virtues in the opinion of Yohanan ben Zakkai?

6. What makes service of God out of fear more virtuous than service of God out of love, and vice versa? Why should that issue preoccupy the sages of Judaism?

☞ INFOTRAC

If you would like additional information related to the material discussed here, you can visit our Web site: http://www.wadsworth.com

2

Christianity

BY BRUCE CHILTON

CONVENTIONAL ANSWERS VERSUS
THIS RELIGIOUS TRADITION:
WHO ARE WE REALLY?

hristianity conceives of people as having a deep affinity with God, and at the same time it acknowledges that between God and humanity an unbridgable chasm sometimes seems to intrude. Paul is the preeminent Christian theologian of the ambivalence of this relationship. Paul wrote very extensively to a Christian community in Rome around 57 C.E. (four years after he wrote to the Galatians in Asia Minor). His letter to the Romans is the result, the fullest explanation of Paul's theology. In an opening section, Paul concerns himself with the issue of how God may be conceived of as judging people, when they do not even know him. His response is that God's power and divinity is primordially evident to people from the world around them (Romans 1:19–20):

> What is known of God is evident to them, because he has manifested it to them. His invisible qualities, his eternal power and divinity, have been demonstrated perceptibly from the creation of the world by the things that have been made.

The topic of judgment illuminates how Paul understands God to be known to humanity at large. To Paul the particular qualities of God, because they are behind the world rather than in it, are invisible. The fact of God's being God means that he is transcendent in his divinity, beyond the terms of reference of time and space. But his power is also evident, demonstrated by our perception of things made in the world around us. The world is not just an accident of our environment, but that which is created by God. Paul's conviction is consonant with the story of the creation in Genesis 1, and with much else in the Scriptures of Israel.

When Paul refers to God separating him from his mother's womb in Galatians 1:15, there is nothing abstract or theoretical about the imagery of creation. The emphasis, rather, falls on the immediate and personal link between God and Paul's own being. The imagery is not original with Paul: he is picking up the language of the Old Testament, for example in the book of Psalms. Psalm 22:9 and Psalm 71:6 offer praise to God for taking the speaker from the womb and keeping him safe from childhood. The image is also used in the prophetic literature, when the prophet is said to have been taken from the womb for the purpose of giving his prophecy (Isaiah 49:1; Jeremiah 1:5). In all these cases, as in Paul's usage, the imagery expresses not only a sense of being in an ordered creation, but of experiencing God's care within that creation. The prophetic usage enhances the emphasis on one's personal sense of purpose by applying the image to a specified mission one is to accomplish. Paul shares that emphasis, as well.

The prophetic dimension of Paul's reference to God comes out again in his description of God "calling" him. The motif that God "calls" is so widespread in the biblical tradition, its significance might be overlooked. The basic meaning of the motif is expressed in the story of the prophet Samuel's call (1 Samuel 3:1–14). The boy Samuel is staying with the priest Eli, attending the ark and its sacrificial worship. It was a time when "the word of the Lord" and vision were rare. But when Samuel slept at night near the ark, the Lord called to him to so clearly, Samuel thought it was Eli calling him. Three times he went to Eli, to ask what he wanted, and Eli finally instructed him to answer, "Speak, Lord, for thy servant hears." The result is that God begins to tell Samuel what he is about to do. Samuel commences his prophetic ministry, which leads to the anointing of David as king of Israel.

"Calling," then, is understood to establish a link between God and the person he calls, so that God's word may be delivered. Who is called? It might be a prophet, or all Israel, or Jesus himself. Matthew 2:15 presents the infant Jesus as called from Egypt for his vocation in Israel, in citing the prophetic book of Hosea (11:1). Hosea applies "Out of Egypt I called my Son" to the people Israel, liberated at the time of the Exodus. That wording is then interpreted afresh in Matthew to refer to Jesus. That is possible because much of the language of the Old Testament, including reference to God's calling and God's separating a person from the womb, is deliberately developed in the New Testament. The usage of the Old Testament is the point of departure for new applications and unusual developments, designed to convey a sense of intimacy with God.

God initiates the biblical call, but the call must be answered for it to be productive of the communication that is the purpose of the calling. Indeed, the fact of God's call can be the basis upon which people take it upon themselves to call upon God. "Answer me when I call, O God of my righteousness" (Psalm 4:1) is an appeal that is predicated on the previous response to God's call on the part of the psalmist and the psalmist's community.

Paul particularly develops the reciprocity of call and response in his teaching in regard to the Spirit of God. 1 Corinthians 2 shows how, in a letter written a year or two before Romans, Paul sees Spirit at work. If one asks how we can know what God has prepared for us, the answer is that Spirit alone is able to communicate divine purposes.

Paul develops his position by quoting a passage from Isaiah 64:4 (in 2:9), which speaks of things beyond human understanding that God has readied for those who love him, and then goes on to say (2:10–11):

> God has revealed them to us through the Spirit; for the Spirit searches all things, even the depths of God. For who among men knows the things of man except the spirit of man which is in him? So also no one has known the things of God except the Spirit of God.

As Paul sees human relations, one person can only know what another thinks and feels on the basis of their shared "spirit." "Spirit" is the name for what links one person with another, and by means of that link we can also know what God thinks and feels. The Spirit at issue in knowing God, Paul goes on to say, is not "the spirit of the world," but "the Spirit which is of God" (1 Corinthians 2:12). The human spirit that is the medium of ordinary, human exchange becomes as the result of God's effective calling the vehicle of divine revelation.

Paul's remark in 1 Corinthians 2 is part of a complete anthropology, which is spelled out further in 1 Corinthians 15, his classic explanation of what resurrection involves. When Paul thinks of a person, he conceives of a body as composed of flesh. Flesh in his definition is physical substance that varies from one created thing to another (for example, people, animals, birds, and fish; 1 Corinthians 15:39). But in addition to being physical bodies, people are also what Paul calls a "psychic body," by which he means bodies with souls (1 Corinthians 15:44). (Unfortunately, the phrase is wrongly translated in many modern versions, but its dependence on the noun for "soul" [*psukhe*] shows what the real sense is.) In other words, people as bodies are not just lumps of flesh, but they are self-aware. That self-awareness is precisely what makes them "psychic body."

Now in addition to being physical body and psychic body, Paul says we are or can become "spiritual body" (1 Corinthians 15:44). That is, we can relate thoughts and feelings to one another and to God, as 1 Corinthians 2 has already shown us. Jesus is therefore the last Adam, a "life-giving spirit" (1 Corinthians 15:45) just as the first Adam was a "living being" or "soul" (the two words are the same in Greek, *psukhe*). Jesus is the basis on which we can realize our identities as God's children, the brothers and sisters of Christ, and know the power of the resurrection. In presenting Jesus in this way, Paul defines a distinctive Christology as well as a characteristic spirituality.

The initial terms of Paul's knowledge of God, therefore, are his awareness of God's power and care, and his access to the Spirit of God. But that is by no means the whole of Paul's knowledge of God. Its distinctive feature is that God was pleased "to reveal his Son in me" (Galatians 1:15): that is how Paul knows in the first place that he has been separated from the womb and called by God. The revelation of God's Son in the midst of one's being is the distinctive basis of Christian knowledge of God. In fact, Paul conceives of the moment of receiving God's Spirit in a highly specific manner, linked inextricably to Jesus (Galatians 4:6): "Because you are sons, God sent the Spirit of his Son into our heart, crying, Abba—Father." Baptism is the moment at which, by accepting the revelation of the Son, one can accept that Spirit which is truly divine. Only what has come from God can acknowledge and respond to God: that is the revelation of God's Son within.

Paul brings us, then, to the most characteristic aspect of the Christian understanding of the knowledge of God—its emphasis upon Jesus, the Son of God, as the central mediator of that knowledge. One's own acknowledgement of and response to God remain vital, but they are understood to be possible only because God has already been at work within, shaping a spiritual eye to see him at work and a spiritual ear to hear his call. As Paul conceives of Jesus, he is first of all the Son of God revealed within us. Of course, Paul is aware of the primitive teaching concerning Jesus' deeds and teaching, including a graphic account of his crucifixion (see Galatians 3:1). But his interest in Jesus is not historical. Rather, his attention is taken up by how the revelation of the Son of God might shape our minds and hearts to know God.

The most famous expression of this theme occurs in the letter to the Philippians, which was probably composed after Paul's death, by his follower Timothy (ca. 90 C.E.). It represents a mature Pauline theology, much of it on the basis of what Paul personally had thought. It was composed at a time at which Christians in the Graeco-Roman world were largely of the servant class, so that its appeal to the form of Jesus as a servant is especially poignant (Philippians 2:5–8):

> Let this thought prevail among you, which was also in Jesus Christ: Who, being in God's form, did not consider the presumption of equality with God, but emptied himself, taking a servant's form; existing in men's likeness, and found as a man in shape, he humbled himself, becoming obedient unto death, death on a cross.

The point of Paul and Timothy together (Philippians 1:1) is that it is possible, on the basis of the revelation of the Son of God within one, to think as Jesus did, although in one's own circumstances. This is a prime example of the imperative to imitate Christ within the New Testament. Its object is not a slavish mimicry of the historical person, but an embrace of that humble disposition of Christ that makes the knowledge of God possible, proceeding as it does from God's own loving nature.

Knowledge of God, then, involves the capacity to acknowledge God as the source of one's being, the ability to respond to God's call and to hear him, and an acceptance within oneself of Christ's own loving disposition, his humility unto death. How, then, do we know ourselves? By discovering and reshaping who we truly are in the image of God's Son. Christianity's anthropology directly reflects its call to humanity to enter into the vision of God and to be transformed by the divine Spirit.

WHAT ARE THE SOCIAL VIRTUES?

A single, determinative choice, made during the second century C.E. and confirmed in countless ways ever since, made engagement with the world around us the primary medium of virtue within Christianity. That engagement typically includes the imperative of overcoming evil. The creed (called the Apostles' Creed) that emerged during the second century to articulate the rule of faith began with an embrace of the God of Israel as creator and with an equally emphatic (if indirect) rejection of any dualism that would remove God from the realities of our world. Expressed in that way, the emphasis falls on the reality of Christ's appearance in human flesh, and on Christ's capacity to transform human life in the flesh into the image of God. And that is indeed the incarnational emphasis that governs the creed. But the statement of belief in "God the Father Almighty, maker of heaven and earth" obviously also involves a commitment to the experience of this world as actually attesting the presence of God.

No one needs someone else's list to think of many different ways in which our experience of the world does just the opposite of attesting the presence of God. What are we to make of the suffering of the innocent? Or of the prosperity of the wicked? Of disease and disaster, famine and war and crime and accident? All those and more are part of the experience of which we hear every day, and which we all come to know directly, at least in part. The fact of our human mortality carries innumerable forms of suffering and pain with it, and that would seem to make it extremely difficult to understand how God, as a loving and merciful father, can have created a world so riven with evil. The problem is not just the imperfection of what we see around us, but the seemingly unanswerable claim that this world attests evil at least as much as it witnesses to good as its source.

There were many different options during the second century for viewing the world and the evil within it. What brought the Church to the creed, and then what made for the appeal of the creed within the Church, was not any naive embrace of this world as being inherently good or pleasant through and through. The second century in fact brought with it powerful incentives, both intellectual and practical, to deny that God was directly responsible for this world.

The broad appeal of Gnosticism during the second century (discussed in the chapter on Christianity in the second volume of this series) shows how appealing it could be to abstract God from the world around us. Instead, it could be argued that some other force was in command of the events we all confront, and most fear to confront. Gnostics portrayed the physical circumstances of existence as a sham, a fake creation developed by a false god, far removed from the actual Father who provides us with our spiritual being. Although Gnosticism was a remarkably diverse phenomenon, that was an underlying feature that united its adherents. This feature is worth stressing, because it is frequently not emphasized, or even ignored, in modern accounts of Gnosticism. There is a tendency to treat Gnostics as if they were simply some sort of liberal thinkers in antiquity, when in fact they insisted that only they had the knowledge (the *gnosis*) to discover and maintain spiritual existence in the face of the claims of a false world.

Yet the same Paul who would die in Rome during Nero's pogrom against Christians could insist as late as 57 C.E. in his letter to the Romans (13:1–2):

> Let every person be subject to the governing authorities. For there is no authority except from God, and those that exist have been instated by God.
> Therefore one who resists the authorities resists what God has appointed, and those who resist will incur judgment.

Peter is said to have died in the same pogrom (crucified, rather than beheaded, as it is said Paul was),[1] and yet the letter called 1 Peter (composed around 90 C.E., during another period of persecution) attributes the following advice to

---

[1]See Eusebius, *The History of the Church from Christ to Constantine*, (translated by G. A. Williamson (Baltimore: Penguin Books, 1967), 2.25.

him (4:19): "Therefore let those who suffer according to God's will do right and entrust their souls to a faithful Creator." There was every intellectual and practical reason to deny that current experience comes from God. Gnosticism (including Gnostic Christianity) offered the possibility of refusing the intellectual legitimacy of the ruling powers, and therefore of accommodating practically any form of words they might demand. Yet that is exactly what early Christianity did *not* do.

There is a particularly poignant passage in an account of martyrs during the second century called "The Acts of the Scillitan Martyrs," in which a Roman judge attempts to reason with some people who have been denounced for their Christianity, but are not guilty of any other crime. He explains to them, very patiently, that they can easily walk away from the court, simply by burning some incense before an image of the emperor, and swearing an oath of allegiance to him as God's son. His patience extends to a conscientious recognition that the act does not actually require belief: only conformity to the due form is required. Many Gnostic Christians would have had no difficulty complying with the judge's request, and no doubt there were other Early Christians, loyal to the creed, who nonetheless went along with such friendly advice. But, to the judge's exasperation, the Scillitan martyrs oblige the judge to condemn them to death, which he eventually does. To his mind (as to that of Marcus Aurelius; *Meditations* 11:3), they were obstinate. Christians were proud of such behavior in their ranks, and produced an entire literature of martyrdom.

The insistence in 1 Peter 4:19 provides the key to this Christian persistence (or obstinacy, depending upon one's point of view). The fact of God's creation of this world seals it as ultimately good, no matter what our immediate experience of it might make it seem. The beginning of the passage makes its perspective clear (1 Peter 4:12–13):

> Beloved, do not be surprised at the fiery ordeal that is taking place among you to test you, as though something strange were happening to you. But rejoice insofar as you are sharing Christ's sufferings, so that you may also be glad and shout for joy when his glory is revealed.

God's creation of this world in 1 Peter, in the New Testament as a whole, and in the rule of faith as articulated in the creed, is not to be understood simply as a theoretical expression of where things originally came from. Of course, Christians do and always have understood that God is good and that what he made (and makes) is very good, in the unmistakable assertion of Genesis 1:31. But they do not say on that basis that what seems bad is really good, or that evil is merely illusory or the work of some other power. Instead, they see present experience as in the process of a transformation, sometimes a painful transformation, in which all goodness (including God's) will be vindicated. Christian faith in creation is more eschatological than anything else: it is concerned with what will happen at the end (the *eskhaton* in Greek) of all things.

Because Christianity is committed to eschatology as the single perspective that makes sense of human experience, it has been obliged to spell out for itself what its eschatology means, how the anticipated transformation of the world is to be worked out. Three types of eschatological thinking have characterized Christianity over time, and they are closely related to one another. All three of them, at any one time, have been represented, although given periods usually represent a commitment to one of the types more than the others. Which of the three is emphasized has a profound impact on how a person and a community deal with suffering, and with how they actually perceive pain. For that reason, the distinctions among the three—and their relationship to one another—are quite important to understand. They represent the strategies Christianity has crafted for engagement with the world on the basis of the virtue of the society of God.

Temporal Eschatology

By its very nature, eschatology must involve the end of time as we know and conceive of time. But there is no actual necessity that eschatological expectation should develop into what is defined as an apocalyptic expectation. After all, Jesus instructed his disciples to pray, "Your kingdom will come,"[2] without giving a precise indication of when that moment was to come. Apocalyptic thought involves the claim to understand the sequence and timing of the ultimate events in human affairs, up until and including the end.

Jesus does not appear to have taught any single apocalyptic scheme, and it is even said that, after his resurrection, he explicitly told his followers that "It is not yours to know the times and periods which the Father has set by his own authority" (Acts 1:7). But the fact is that, even without Jesus' encouragement, apocalyptic calendars thrived in primitive Christianity, as evidenced in books in the New Testament such as the Revelation of John, 2 Thessalonians, 2 Peter, and Jude, all of which were produced near the end of the first century. There is no one such calendar, so it seems obvious that Jesus did not endorse any single apocalyptic scheme. But then, the variety of the calendars shows how vibrant and diverse apocalyptic expectation was.

Although other forms of eschatology have tended to dominate over temporal eschatology in the subsequent history of the Church, there have been notable examples of renewed apocalyptic fervor, especially during times of extreme social change. Examples include the Anabaptists during the Reformation in Europe, and groups such as the Shakers in the United States during the nineteenth century. Today, denominations such as the Jehovah's Witnesses represent the tradition of apocalyptic eschatology.

Transcendent Eschatology

Because thought in the modern (and the so-called postmodern) world is, on the whole, not eschatological, it is easy to dismiss eschatology as a primitive and outdated view of the world. The scientific thought of ancient Greece, which has deeply influenced our own view of science, often conceived of physical reality as static and unchanging, and that has inclined us to prefer views of the world that are also static. Now, however, science itself shows us just how conditional human existence is. Physically, not even the universe appears permanent; solid

---

[2]For the emphatic wording of the prayer of Jesus, and its Aramaic original, see Bruce Chilton, *Jesus' Prayer and Jesus' Eucharist. His Personal Practice of Spirituality* (Valley Forge, PA: Trinity Press International, 1997).

matter seems to be a myth; the very survival of human beings is called into question by the rapid extinction of many other animal and plant species.

Just as our own world has started to seem less stable and unchanging to us, the world of ancient eschatology has proven to be much less simplistic and "primitive" than was once thought to be the case. It was fashionable a century ago to depict eschatology as a strictly temporal teaching, as if time was its only concern. We have just seen that some eschatology is indeed temporal in its emphasis. But to see God as final in human affairs also involves seeing God's kingdom as working now, transforming the very environment in which we live. As Jesus put it, the kingdom of God "is like yeast, which a woman takes, hides in three measures of dough, until the whole is yeasted" (Luke 13:21; Matthew 13:33). Because space, as well as time, is a dimension of God's activity, eschatology also involves seeing God at work now in his final revelation, and it involves the possibility of joining God in his kingdom.

The point of the revelation of the kingdom within our world is that it points beyond our world. The kingdom is transcendent: it comes from outside us, transforms us, and directs us outside our selves. No theologian more forcefully or influentially emphasized this aspect of eschatology than Origen, who taught and wrote (first in Egypt, then in Palestine) during the third century. He died as a consequence of wounds he received during torture under the emperor Decius (who authorized persecution during 249–250 C.E.). In order to explain the value of the promises that are ours in Christ, Origen cites John 17:14, when Jesus asserts that neither he nor his disciples are of the world, and Origen then goes on to explain (*On First Principles* 2.3.6):

> But there is no doubt that the Savior refers to something more glorious and splendid than this present world, and invites and incites all who believe in him to direct their course towards it. But whether that world, which he wishes us to know of, is one that stands apart and separate from this world in space and quality and glory, or whether, as seems more likely to me, it excels in quality and glory but is nevertheless contained within the limits of this world, is uncertain, and in my opinion an unsuitable subject for the mind and thoughts of human beings.

Origen here expresses a characteristic feature of Christian teaching concerning transcendence. The point is not to speak of something so different that we have no inkling of what God would do with us. Rather, God may be perceived to be immanent in the world, and in his immanence to direct our course toward that which he would have us be. ("Immanence" is the usual category used to refer to the divine as existing within the universe as people may perceive it.) Because Christian teaching of divine transcendence is eschatological, it links this world with the world to come in the expectation and the experience of the believer.

Juridical Eschatology

Jesus' well-known parable of a feast to which the host makes surprising, insistent invitations—and equally categorical exclusions—voices another emphatic dimension of his own eschatology (Matthew 22:1–14; Luke 14:16–24). God is portrayed as celebrating in his kingdom with those who would join him, and as refusing to include those who have rejected the appointed way of entering his kingdom. Because Jesus was and is rightly known as the supreme teacher of divine love, this aspect of his teaching is frequently (and all too conveniently) ignored. But there is finally no compromise in love: it supersedes what would resist it. As the book of Psalms puts it, God's being king puts an end to everything wicked and those who represent wickedness, whether individuals or nations (Psalm 10:15–16).

The lively expectation of the judgment that is involved in God's final disclosure is a typical, sometimes a dominant, feature of Christianity. In this, Augustine of Hippo delineates the sort of practice that would emerge during the Middle Ages. Speaking during the season of Lent, when the congregation prepared for the celebration of Easter and Christ's temptation in the wilderness is recalled, Augustine preached as follows (*Sermon* 206.1):

> Life in this world is certainly the time of our humiliation. These days show—
> by the recurrence of this holy season—how the sufferings of the Lord Christ,
> who once suffered for us by death, are renewed each year. For what was done
> once and for all time so that our life might be renewed is solemnized each
> year so that the memory may be kept fresh. If, therefore, we ought to be
> humble of heart with sentiments of most sincere reverence throughout the
> entire period of our earthly sojourn when we live in the midst of temptations,
> how much more necessary is humility during these days, when we not only
> pass the time of our humiliation by living, but call attention to it by special
> devotion! The humility of Christ has taught us to be humble because he
> yielded to the wicked in his death; the exaltation of Christ lifts us up because
> by rising again he cleared the way for his devoted followers. Because, "if we
> have died with him, we shall also live with him; if we endure, we shall also
> reign with him" (2 Timothy 2:11–12). One of these conditions we now cele-
> brate with due observance in view of his approaching passion; the other we
> shall celebrate after Easter when his resurrection is, in like manner, accom-
> plished again.

What Augustine is here signaling to us, in the clearest of terms, is the link between devotion to Christ and eschatology. Devotion to him, the imitation of Christ, is not merely encouraged because of Jesus' goodness, but because his life, death, and resurrection maps the path into God's kingdom. Jesus' example charts the single course for passing through the divine judgment that is necessarily a part of the coming of the kingdom.

The three types of eschatology mentioned here are particularly mentioned because they correspond to major movements during the formative centuries of Christianity. Temporal eschatology typified the first two centuries; transcendent eschatology characterized the emergence of Christianity's philosophical dominance between the third century and the seventh century; juridical eschatology, of which Augustine is an early example, became the hallmark of Christianity from the Middle Ages onward. Although it may seem confusing to think of eschatology in these different ways, they are all a part of conceiving God as truly final. His finality is such that he will definitively change time, but also space and the nature of justice in human relations. Time and space and ethics are not totally different categories, but are essential dimensions of human experience, so that eschatology rightly involves them all.[3]

Eschatology in all of its rich nuance constitutes the fundamental perspective from which Christianity addresses the problem of suffering and urges a positive engagement with the world. The God who makes the world also redeems the world, and he redeems the world we know, as it is. That may involve waiting over time (temporal eschatology), transforming the place where we stand (transcendent eschatology), and/or entering into a judgment that will change us (juridical eschatology), but in any and all cases, suffering is not the last word, but the transitional word before glory, and occasions eschatological transformation when the faithful respond according to the pattern of Christ.

WHAT IS PERSONAL VIRTUE?

Considerable space has been devoted to the issues involved in understanding eschatology, because the type of eschatology Christianity embraces has determined its portrayal of how we encounter our world. That portrayal, in turn, relates to the anticipation of how God in Christ is to transform the world. The virtue that arises from each eschatology is understood as "power": *virtus* in the Latin sense of the word. That transforming virtue is what is activated by the conduct of every Christian, who becomes a mirror of Christ's transformation of the world.

Once time is perceived as the principal dimension within which God acts definitively, the obvious question becomes: just when will that be? We have already seen above that 1 Peter urges its readers to treat their current persecution as a "fiery ordeal," a test whose end would be glory for those who were proven (1 Peter 4:12–13). But how long was the ordeal to last? Does faith involve the simple assurance that in the end God will triumph, without knowledge of his plan for his people? Or does faith appropriately include a more precise insight into one's own redemption and the redemption of one's fellows? It is no coincidence that the letter called 2 Peter addresses just these questions.

2 Peter is a work of the second century that is attributed to Peter, who (as we have seen) probably died under Nero in Rome in 64 C.E. It takes up the trait of apocalyptic literature of being attributed to a great visionary from the past. (That trait is also represented in the book of Daniel in the Old Testament and 2 Esdras in the Apocrypha.) Here, 2 Peter beautifully and classically sets out an

---

[3]In fact, Jesus' own eschatology included two further dimensions. His definition of the kingdom provided for a distinctive view of what made for the purity acceptable to God and for an emphasis on the outward, inclusive range of the kingdom. See Bruce Chilton, *Pure Kingdom: Jesus' Vision of God: Studying the Historical Jesus*, vol. 1 (Grand Rapids, MI: Eerdmans, 1996). Those dimensions are not included here because they did not amount to distinctive types of eschatology within the formative periods of Christianity. Still, emphasis upon the purity and upon the outward extension of God's kingdom are characteristic of Christianity in most periods.

account of how the pain of eschatological delay is experienced within apocalyptic Christianity, and how it might be addressed (2 Peter 3:1–9):

> This is already, beloved, a second letter I write to you; in them I arouse by reminder your sincere intent, to remember the sayings told in advance by the holy prophets and the commandment of your apostles of the Lord and Savior. First, know this: There will come at the last days scoffers with scoffing, going according to their own desires, and saying,
>
> Where is the promise of his coming? Because although the patriarchs perished, everything remains the same from the beginning of creation!
>
> This escapes those who like to think this way: Heavens existed from of old and earth from water and through water subsisted by the word of God. Through them the world then was destroyed, deluged with water. But the present heavens and the earth by the same word are stored for fire, kept for the day of judgment and the destruction of the godless. Do not let this one thing escape you, beloved: one day with the Lord is as a thousand years, and a thousand years as one day (Psalm 90:4). The Lord does not delay his promise, as some people suppose delay, but he is generous to you, not wishing you to be destroyed, but that all might attain to repentance.

The pain of time, that it remains unfulfilled by the presence of God, is dealt with by the understanding that it provides an interim for the purpose of repentance. That pain becomes an opportunity, to the extent that it is used as a preparation. Patient penitence is part of the power that transforms the world.

Just as Origen believed that God through Christ had prepared "something more glorious and splendid than this present world," as we have seen, so he pondered what it means to conceive of God and of divine reward as beyond our ordinary terms of reference. His discussion appears within his use of the imagery of light to understand God (*On First Principles* 1.1.5):[4]

> Having then refuted, to the best of our ability, every interpretation which suggests that we should attribute to God any material characteristics, we assert that he is in truth incomprehensible and immeasurable. For whatever may be the knowledge which we have been able to obtain about God, whether by perception or reflection, we must of necessity believe that he is far and away better than our thoughts about him. For if we see a man who can scarcely look at a glimmer of the light of the smallest lamp, and if we wish to teach such a one, whose eyesight is not strong enough to receive more light than we have said, about the brightness and splendor of the sun, shall we not have to tell him that the splendor of the sun is unspeakably and immeasurably better and more glorious than all this light he can see?

Here the imagery of pain is more than a matter of the discomfort one might feel in the ordinary course of living. The point is rather that our lives at their

---

[4]For the examples and their elucidation, we are indebted to John Dillon, "Looking on the Light: Some Remarks on the Imagery of Light in the first chapter of the *Peri Archon*," in *The Golden Chain: Studies in the Development of Platonism and Christianity* (Aldershot, England: Variorum, 1990), 215–230 (essay XXII).

best do not prepare us to come in contact with God, and the little we know already is itself not something we can sustain. As in the myth of the cave in Plato's *Republic,* a person living in the dark will not readily be accustomed to light.

The difference between Origen and Plato is that, while in the myth of the cave, the person can come into the sun's light, for Origen we cannot know God as God truly is in this life.[5] For that reason, pain is experienced in two directions at once. First, we are not naturally prepared to discover as much of God's light as we do, and that is a painful condition, as in Plato's myth. But second, we are also intrinsically unable to proceed from the intimations of God to the reality they point to, so that we cannot be completely fulfilled even after we have prepared ourselves for the light. So the pain of this life is that it offers both too much of the reality of God and too little of it. The dilemma can only be resolved when we are in a different place, when the transcendence of God, which presently impinges on our lives, becomes the whole of life as we know it. And because that can only occur beyond our world, present experience is not merely painful, but is itself a kind of pain. That is the reason for which Origen emphasizes the irreducible importance for every Christian of the vision of God. Only that vision enables us to both understand and endure our present predicament, because it anticipates the full reality that is to come.

In *Sermon* 205.1, preceding the sermon in which he explains the eschatological link between humility and exaltation, Augustine portrays the Christian life as inherently painful, and yet as inherently hopeful for that reason. What he says at the start of the season of Lent is a classic exposition, which charts a course for the development of spirituality during the Middle Ages:

> Today we commence the observance of Lent, the season now encountering us in the course of the liturgical year. You are owed an appropriately solemn sermon, so that the word of God, brought to you through my ministry, may sustain you in spirit while you fast in body, and so that the inner man, thus refreshed by suitable food, may be able to accomplish and to persevere bravely in the disciplining of the outer man. For to my spirit of devotion it seems right that we, who are going to revere the Passion of our crucified Lord in the very near future, should construct for ourselves a cross of the bodily pleasures in need of restraint, as the Apostle says, "And they who belong to Christ have crucified their flesh with its passions and desires." (Galatians 5:24)

Pain here is actually a gate to the promise of transformation. The fact of our selfish desires, which we experience in our flesh, is what keeps us from appreciating and joining ourselves to the love of God in Augustine's thought (see especially his magisterial work, *The City of God*).[6] So the willing experience of pain actually permits us to know our true selves, to form a cross of what alienates us from

---

[5]This is Dillon's main point (see p. 225), and his citation of *On First Principles* 1.1.6 demonstrates it admirably.

[6]See Bruce D. Chilton and Jacob Neusner, editors, *Trading Places Sourcebook: Readings in the Intersecting Histories of Judaism and Christianity* (Cleveland: Pilgrim Press, 1996), 203–209.

God, and so through the death of selfishness to understand who we truly are before God.

Juridical eschatology is the source of Christianity's profound skepticism about the value of human life in the flesh. The problem is not so much the material of which we are made, as what has become of it by means of human selfishness. Flesh is where we try to make gods of ourselves, and in so doing dishonor each other in our abuse of passion as much as we dishonor God. For Augustine, war, crime, exploitation, and the violent results of all three are not happenstances. When he learns of such things, the news does not come to him as a sudden realization that life as he knows it (in the flesh) is beset by evil. Rather, he recognizes that these evils must be overcome by a recognition of our truer selves, selves not subservient to that selfishness. That became the most predominant virtue in Christianity from the time of the Middle Ages.

HOW DOES THIS RELIGION DEFINE CHARACTER, GOOD AND BAD?

Gregory of Nyssa inhabited a very different world from Paul's. By his time, Christianity was in fashion within the Roman Empire. He was the brother of Basil of Caesarea in the Cappodocian region of Asia Minor, and Gregory himself was bishop of Nyssa (between 371 and 394). Together with their friend Gregory, son of the bishop of Nazianzus, they are known as the "Cappodocian Fathers." Champions of the emerging Trinitarian doctrine of their day, Gregory especially represents the interpenetration of the Hellenistic literary tradition with the orientation of Christianity. Deeply influenced by Origen, he also remained married long into his episcopate, and only took monastic vows after his wife's death. More eloquently than any other Christian teacher, he identified the problem of the sincerity of believers, which obviously needed to be questioned as soon as the Christian faith became fashionable. Insincerity, the appearance of Christianity on the grounds of convenience, has since his time been recognized as the chief weakness within Christian character.

Gregory devoted a considerable letter and a notable rhetorical image to this issue in "On What Is Meant by the Profession 'Christian'":

> In now sending this letter to your Reverence, I am behaving like those
> debtors who happen upon some good fortune and pay the entire amount
> owed at one fell swoop. For after being constantly in your debt (because
> among Christians a promise is a debt), I now wish to fill in the past lapse of
> letters, which I contracted unwillingly, by extending this letter to such a
> length that it will count as many when it is judged by the customary length of
> letters. But, in order that I may not go on idly writing at length, I think that
> it will be good for me to imitate in my epistolary style the conversations we
> used to have when we were face to face. Indeed, I remember very well that
> the occasion of our discussions every time was a concern for virtue and exercise related to the service of God. You always reacted attentively to what was

said, although you did not accept it without examining it, and we, advancing in time, solved everything we sought by following our discussion. If it were possible, even now, for the impetus of discussion to be derived from your presence, it would be better in every way. There would be a mutual benefit from our seeing each other (what is sweeter to me in life than this?) and, under the plectrum of your intelligence, our old lyre would reawaken. But, since the necessity of life causes us to be separated in body, even if our souls are always united, it is necessary to assume your role also, if some logical conclusion is to develop for us. First of all, however, it would be best to propose a hypothesis profitable to the soul for the scope of our letter, and, then, to direct our argument to what lies before us. Therefore, let us ask as in a logical problem: What is meant by the profession "Christian"?

For surely, a consideration of this issue will not be without profit, since, if what is indicated by this name is determined accurately, we shall have much assistance for a life in accordance with virtue, provided, as our name implies, that we are eager for a lofty discipline. A person who wants to be called a doctor or an orator or a geometrician is not worthy of the title until he has some training in the subject and until he discovers from experience what he is being called, and the person wishing to be thus addressed in accordance with truth, so that the form of address will not be a misnomer, will want the use of the title to depend on the practice itself. In the same way, if we seek the true meaning of the word "Christian" and find it, we will not choose not to conform to what the name implies when it is used of us, in order that the popular story about the monkey may not also be applicable to us.

They say that a certain showman in the city of Alexandria trained a monkey to dance with some grace, and dressed him in a dancer's mask and a suitable costume. He put him in a chorus and gained fame by the monkey's twisting himself in time with the music and concealing his nature in every way by what he was doing and what he appeared to be. While the audience was enthralled by the novelty of the spectacle, one of the clever persons present, by means of a trick, showed those watching the performance that the dancer was a monkey. When everyone was crying out and applauding the gesticulations of the monkey, who was moving rhythmically with the music, they say that he threw onto the dancing place some of the sweets which arouse the greediness of such animals. The monkey, without a moment's delay, when he saw the almonds scattered in front of the chorus, forgetting the dancing and the applause and the elaborate costume, ran after them and grabbed what he found in the palms of his hands. And in order that the mask would not get in the way of his mouth, he energetically thrust aside the disguise with his nails and shredded the clever workmanship; he immediately evoked a laugh from the spectators in place of the praise and admiration, as he emerged ugly and ridiculous from the mask. Therefore, just as the clever device was not sufficient for that creature to be considered a man, once his nature was disclosed in greediness for the sweets, so those individuals not truly shaping their own natures by faith will easily be disclosed in the kinds of greediness which come from the devil as being something other than what they are called. For, instead of a fig or an almond or some such thing, conceit and love of honor and love of gain and love of pleasure, and whatever else the evil assembly of the devil places before greedy men instead of sweets, easily bring to light the ape-like souls who, through pretense of imitation play the role of the Christian and then remove the mask of moderation or meekness or some other virtue in a moment of personal crisis. It is necessary, therefore, for us to understand what the profession of Christianity means, for then, perhaps, we will become what the term means to say and not be seen through by the One who perceives what is hidden. It must not be found that we have disguised ourselves by a bare confession and by the pretense of the name alone, when we are actually something contrary to what we appear to be.

Let us, then, consider, first of all, from the term itself what Christianity means. From those who are wiser it is, of course, possible for us to discover a significance more profound and more noble in every way, more in keeping with the dignity of the word. However, what we begin with is this: the word "Christ," exchanged for a clearer and more familiar word, means "the king," and Holy Scripture, in accordance with proper usage, indicates royal dignity with such a word. But since, as Scripture says, the divine is inexpressible, incomprehensible, exceeding all comprehensible thought, the Holy Spirit must inspire prophets and apostles, and they contribute with many words and insights to our understanding of the incorruptible nature, one setting us right about one divine idea and another about another. His dominion over all is suggested by the name of Kingdom, and his purity and freedom from every passion and every evil is indicated by the names of the virtues, each being understood as referring to higher signification. Such expressions are used as "justice itself" and "wisdom and power" and "truth" and "goodness" and "life" and "salvation" and "incorruptibility" and "permanence" and "lack of change" and whatever elevated concept there is, and Christ is and is said to be all of them. If, therefore, the comprehension of every lofty idea is conceived of in the name of Christ (for the other qualities mentioned are included under the higher designation, each of them being implied in the notion of Kingdom), perhaps some understanding of the interpretation of Christianity will follow. If we, who are joined to him by faith in him, are called by his name whose incorruptible nature is beyond verbal interpretation, it is altogether necessary for us to become what is contemplated in connection with that incorruptible nature and to achieve an identity which follows along with it. For just as by participating in Christ we are given the title "Christian," so also are we drawn into a share in the lofty ideas which it implies. Just as in a chain, what draws the loop at the top also draws the next loops, in like manner, since the rest of the words interpreting his ineffable and multiform blessedness are joined to the word "Christ," it is necessary for the person drawn along with him to share these qualities with him.

If, therefore, someone puts on the name of Christ, but does not exhibit in his life what is indicated by the term, such a person belies the name and puts on a lifeless mask in accordance with the model proposed to us (of humanly formed features put on a monkey). For it is not possible for Christ not to be justice and purity and truth and estrangement from all evil, nor is it possible to be a Christian (that is, truly a Christian) without displaying in oneself a participation in these qualities. If one can give a definition of the meaning of Christianity, we shall define it as follows: Christianity is an imitation of the divine nature. Now, let no one object to the definition as being immoderate and exceeding the lowliness of our nature; it does not go beyond our nature. Indeed, if anyone considers the first condition of man, he will find through the Scriptural teachings that the definition does not exceed the measure of our nature. The first constitution of man was as an imitation of the likeness of God. So Moses, in philosophizing about man, where he says that God made man, states that: "He created him in the image of God," and the profession "Christianity," therefore, brings man back to his original good fortune.

But, if man was originally a likeness of God, perhaps we have not gone beyond the limit in declaring that Christianity is an imitation of the divine nature. Great, indeed, is the promise of this title. Perhaps it would be fitting to investigate also whether not conforming to the definition in one's life is without danger for one who makes use of the word. What is meant here might become clear from examples. Let it be supposed that a professional painter is given a commission to paint a picture of the king for those living far away. If he draws an ugly and ill-formed shape on the wood and calls this unseemly figure an image of the king, would it not be likely that authority as such should be annoyed, on the grounds that the handsome original had been insulted among those who had never seen the king through this bad painting? For people will necessarily think that the original is what the form on the icon shows him to be. If, then, the definition says that Christianity is an imitation of God, the person who has never been given an explanation of this mystery will think that the divine is such as he sees life among us to be, accepting it as a valid imitation of God. So that, if he sees models of complete good, he will believe that the divine revered by us is good. But, if someone is emotional and brutal, changing from one passion to another, and reflecting forms of beasts in his character (for it is easily possible to see how the changes in our nature correspond to beasts) when such a one calls himself a Christian and it is clear to all that the promise of the name professes an imitation of God, then, that person makes the divine, which is believed to be reflected in our private life, an object of censure among unbelievers. Scripture, therefore, utters a kind of fearful threat to such persons, crying: "Woe to those on account of whom my name is blasphemed among the nations." And our Lord seems to me to be guiding our thoughts in this direction when he says to those able to hear: "You are to be perfect, even as your heavenly Father is perfect." For, in naming the true Father as Father of the faithful, he wishes those born through him to have the same perfection of the good things seen in the Father.

Then you will ask me: "How could it come about that human lowliness could be extended to the blessedness seen in God, since the implausibility in the command is immediately evident? How could it be possible for the earthly to be like the One in heaven, the very difference in nature proving that the imitation is out of reach? For it is as hopeless to make oneself equal in appearance to the heavenly greatness and the beauties in it as it is for man on earth to make himself like the God of heaven." But the explanation of this is clear. The Gospel does not order human nature to be compounded with divine nature, but it does order good actions to be imitated in life as much as possible. But what actions of ours are like the actions of God? Those that are alien from all evil, purifying themselves as far as possible in deed and word and thought from all vileness. This is truly the imitation of the divine and the perfection connected with the God of heaven.

It does not seem to me that the Gospel is speaking of the firmament of heaven as some remote habitation of God when it advises us to be perfect as our heavenly Father is perfect. The divine is equally present in all things, and, in like manner, it pervades all creation and it does not exist separated from being, but the divine nature touches each element of being with equal honor, encompassing all things within its own comprehensive power. And the prophet instructs with this saying, "even if I am in heaven in my thought, even if I examine what is below the earth in my calculation, even if I extend the intellectual part of my soul to the boundaries of being, I see all things in the power of your right hand," for the text is as follows: "If I go up to the heavens, you are there; if I sink to the nether world, you are present there. If I take the wings of the dawn, or settle at the farthest limits of the sea, even there your hand shall guide me, and your right hand hold me fast." It is taught from these words that not being separated by choice from God is the heavenly habitation. Since the world above is known to be pure of evil (Holy Scripture often mentions this to us symbolically), and since experiences connected with evil take place in this more material life below, here the inventor of evil, the serpent, crawls and creeps through life on earth, as is said of it in the symbolic statement: "On your belly shall you crawl and dust shall you eat, all the days of your life."

This kind of movement and this type of food explain to us that this refers to the life on earth which accepts the serpent of manifold evil and nurtures this creature that creeps upon it. Therefore, the one who orders us to imitate our heavenly Father orders us to purify ourselves from earthly passions. This is a separation which does not come about through a change of place, but is achieved only through the operation of choice. If, then, alienation from evil is accomplished only by the impetus of thought, the evangelical word enjoins nothing impossible upon us. There is no trouble connected with the impetus of thought, since it is possible for us without exertion to be present through thought wherever we wish to be, so that a heavenly sojourn is easy for anyone who wants it, even on earth. As the Gospel suggests, by our thinking heavenly thoughts and depositing in the treasury, there is a wealth of virtue: "Do not lay up for yourselves treasures on earth," it says, "but lay up for yourselves treasures in heaven, where neither moth nor rust consumes nor thieves break in and steal." By these words, he indicates the incorruptible power that governs blessedness above. For in the midst of the ruin of life here, one produces many different kinds of evil for oneself in the course of human encounters. Either one begets through thought a moth, which, because of its corroding and destroying power, renders useless anything it grows upon unless it is shaken off, and creeps towards whatever is lying about, suggesting through its movement a path of destruction for those it comes near; or, if all is secure within, there is a conspiracy of external circumstances. Either the treasure of the heart is shut off through pleasure or the receptacle of the soul is rendered empty of virtue through some other experience, being distracted by desire or grief or some such emotion. But since the Lord says that in the treasures above neither moth nor rust is present, nor evil from theft which teaches us to be suspicious, we must transfer our activities to a region where what is stored is not only safe and undiminished forever, but where it also produces many kinds of interest. Because of the nature of the one receiving the deposit, it is altogether necessary that the return be amplified. For just as we, in accordance with our nature, accomplish little in making our deposit because we are what we are, so, also, it follows that the One who is rich in every way will give to the depositor a return which reflects his nature. So let no one be discouraged when he brings into the divine treasury what is in keeping with his own power, assuming that he will go off with what corresponds to the amount he has given, but let him anticipate, according to the Gospel which says he will receive in exchange large for small, the heavenly for the earthly, the eternal for the temporal, such things as are not able to be grasped by thought or explained by word, concerning which the inspired Scripture teaches: "Eye has not seen, ear has not heard, nor has it entered into the heart of man, what things God has prepared for those who love him."

So, esteemed head, we have given you payment in full, not only for the letters not sent before, but also in advance for the ones which may not be written hereafter. May you fare well in the Lord and may what is pleasing to God be always in your mind and heart and in ours.

The power of Gregory's analysis is that he identifies precisely the primary engine of Christian ethics: the imitation of Christ. The prosperity of a Christianized Roman Empire put followers of Jesus in the odd position of being prominent and acceptable. It became conceivable and practicable to become a Christian out of convenience. Gregory reflects the response of exchanging the inquisition that once came from outside, from Roman magistrates, for a searching inquiry within, to test one's own motivations and sincerity.

BEYOND THE NORMAL VIRTUES:
WHO IS THE EXTRAORDINARY PERSON?

Engagement with the world, always a duty within Christianity, brings suffering with it in distinct ways. There is the suffering of time, the suffering of place, the suffering of self. Temporal eschatology longs for a different time, transcendent eschatology for a different place, juridical eschatology for a different self. (What is striking is that these anxieties—of time, place, and self—are precisely the most

persistent troubles of modernity. But where eschatology offers a prospect of resolution, secular therapies can provide only assuagement.) Yet just where one
might expect that these distinct kinds of suffering would develop into distinct re-
sponses, Christianity in fact teaches a single, unambiguous strategy, grounded in
the teaching of Jesus.

In his "Letter from Birmingham Jail," Martin Luther King Jr. set out the fundamental position behind his teaching of nonviolence: "One has not only a legal
but a moral responsibility to obey just laws. Conversely, one has a moral responsibility to disobey unjust laws. I would agree with St. Augustine that 'an unjust law is no law at all.'" Brave and lucid though that policy is, it is grounded
in the more radical teaching of Jesus, perhaps best expressed in the following advice (Matthew 5:38–42):

> You have heard that it was said, An eye for an eye and a tooth for a tooth.
> But I say to you not to resist the evil one. But to someone who strikes you
> on the right cheek, turn also the other. And to one who wants to enter judg-
> ment with you to take your shirt, give your cloak, too! And with someone
> who compels a mile's journey from you, travel with him two. Give to the
> one who asks of you, and do not turn away from one who wants to borrow
> from you.

Of all the teachings of Jesus, none is more straightforward, and none more chal-
lenging. Evil is to be overcome by means of what is usually called nonresistance.

What follows in Matthew states the principle of Jesus' teaching, that we are
to love in the way that God does (Matthew 5:43–48; Luke 6:36). The fundamental quality of that teaching within Christianity is unquestionable (Matthew
22:34–40; Mark 12:28–34; Luke 10:25–28; Romans 13:8–10). But in the
teaching about turning the other cheek, giving the cloak, going the extra mile,
offering the money, everything comes down to particular conditions that pre-
vailed during the Roman occupation of the Near East. The fact that this formulation only appears in Matthew (written around 80 C.E.) has given rise to the
legitimate question whether it should be attributed to Jesus in its present form.
The imagery corresponds to the circumstances of the Roman occupation in an
urban area, where a soldier of the empire might well demand provisions and service and money, and all with the threat of force. But even if we acknowledge (as
seems only reasonable) that Matthew's Gospel has pitched Jesus' policy in the
idiom of its own experience, the policy itself should still be attributed to Jesus.

Why should what is usually called nonresistance to evil be recommended? It
needs to be stressed that nonresistance is not the same as acquiescence. The injustice that is done is never accepted as if it were just. The acts of turning the
other cheek, giving the cloak, going the additional mile, offering the money, all
are designed to be excessive, so that the fact of the injustice of what is demanded
is underlined. Indeed, it is not really accurate to call the behavior "nonresistance." The point is for the person who makes demands that are unjust to realize they are unjust. Just that policy served Christians and their faith well during
the centuries of persecution under the Roman Empire. It was effective because
it brought about an awareness within the empire, even among the enemies of

Christianity, that the policy of violent persecution was unjust (and, for that matter, ineffective). Rather than a teaching of nonresistance, this is a version of the advice of how to retaliate. Instead of an eye for an eye, it suggests a cheek after a cheek. This is not nonresistance; it is exemplary response. That is, it is a form of retaliation: not to harm, but to show another way.

The hope that the other way—God's way—will be seen by means of exemplary response, and that once it has been seen it will be followed, is basic to Jesus' policy of retaliatory love. That hope is articulated by the three types of eschatology we have seen, in each of which God's ultimate vindication is what awaits the believer at the end. But in every case (as we will go on now to see), the same basic policy of exemplary response is urged as the only authentically Christian response to suffering in the present.

Just after 1 Peter 4:12–13 (cited above) refers to the promise involved in sharing Christ's sufferings, it spells out its own advice of exemplary response (1 Peter 4:14–19):

> If you are reviled for the name of Christ, you are blessed, because the Spirit of glory—even God's own Spirit—rests upon you. Because none of you is to suffer as a murderer or thief or doer of bad or meddler: but if as a Christian, let him not be ashamed, but give glory to God by this name. Because now is time for judgment to begin with the house of God; and if first with us, what will the end be of those who disobey the gospel of God? And if the just person is barely saved, where shall the irreverent and the sinful appear? So let those who suffer according to the will of God commend their lives to a faithful creator in doing good.

The reality of suffering is not only acknowledged, but celebrated, because the pain of the present time, a function of the injustice of the world, is transitional to the glory that is to come. The only real danger, within this temporal eschatology, is that Christians might begin to commit injustice, since they are treated as criminals in any case. The letter addresses just that worry, while it firmly articulates a classic response to the reality of unjustly suffering pain.

So classic is this expression of the Christian response to suffering and pain, we find it incorporated within the distinct eschatologies already described. Origen, in *On First Principles,* provides insight into how a transcendent eschatology may take up the imperative of exemplary response. For Origen, the source of suffering is not physical pain as such. That may seem ironic, since he without question experienced more torture than all the other theologians mentioned here. But Origen's was not merely a personal theology. To his mind, our actual source of pain is what occurs within our own passions and desires when they are disordered so as not to prepare themselves for the knowledge of God. Yet Origen is also categorical in insisting that Christianity is not about the denial of passion or desire as such (*On First Principles* 3.2.2):

> Are we to think that the devil is the cause of our being hungry or thirsty? I guess there is no one who would venture to maintain such a thing. If then he is not the cause of our being hungry or thirsty, what of that time when an

individual has reached the age of puberty and this involves the arousal of natural desire? It follows without a doubt that, as the devil is not the cause of our
being hungry or thirsty, so neither is he the cause of that impulse which is
naturally present at maturity, the desire for sexual intercourse. It is certain that
this impulse is by no means always incited by the devil, so as to lead us to
think that if there were no devil our bodies would not have the wish for such
intercourse.

This unusually blunt statement makes it clear that, for Origen, the problem of
the evil people cannot be pawned off on the flesh or the devil. The source of
evil is rather what we do with our natural (and naturally good) desires.

That is what leads Origen to the conclusion that we must treat our own desires as Matthew's Jesus would have us treat Roman soldiers: with an exemplary
response (*On First Principles* 3.2.4):

> We must bear in mind, all the while, that nothing more happens to us as a re-
> sult of good or evil thoughts which are suggested to our heart, but a simple
> agitation and excitement which urges us on to deed of good or evil. It is pos-
> sible for us, when an evil power has begun to urge us on to a deed of evil, to
> dismiss the evil suggestion and to resist the mean enticement, and to do noth-
> ing at all worthy of blame. And it is possible on the other hand when a divine
> power has urged us on to better things, not to follow its guidance, since our
> capacity of free will is maintained for us in either case.

Even a suggestion to do injustice need not be enacted along the lines of its evil
intent, and may be followed and pursued to the extent that it includes what is
good in itself. Origen, one of the greatest teachers of spirituality, shows us how
the rule of exemplary response may be followed within our hearts, to nurture
our passions toward the transcendent vision of God.

Now as it happens, Augustine—in quite a different analysis of hunger and
thirst—offers an alternative for understanding pain (*Sermon* 240.3):

> Now if I said that the body would rise again to be hungry and thirsty, to be
> sick and suffer, to be subject to decay, you would rightly refuse to believe me.
> True, the flesh now suffers these needs and afflictions. Why? Sin is the cause.
> We have all sinned in one man [Augustine refers here to Adam], and we have
> all been born into corruption. Sin is the cause of all our evils. In fact, it is not
> without reason that people suffer all these evils. God is just; God is omnipo-
> tent. We would not suffer these evils in any way if we did not deserve them.
> But since we were subjected to these punishments to which we are obliged
> because of our sins, our Lord Jesus Christ wished to partake of our punish-
> ments without any guilt on his part. By enduring the penalty without any
> guilt, he canceled both the guilt and the penalty. He canceled the guilt by
> forgiving sins, the penalty, by rising from the dead. He promised this and he
> wished us to walk in hope. Let us persevere, and we will come to the reward.

With extraordinary clarity, Augustine sets out the juridical eschatology that would
be a controlling influence in the West during the Middle Ages and the Refor-

mation. Pain is now what we accept with an exemplary response that itself takes up the model of Jesus Christ. Suffering patiently brings the reward that has been possible because of the single one who suffered innocently. The humanity that was lost in the case of Adam is more than recovered in the case of Christ.

Christianity is committed irrevocably to the goodness of what God created. It is realistic about acknowledging—and even emphasizing—the pain and the suffering involved in being human. The resolution between divine goodness and our suffering is found in the teaching of eschatology: God is transforming our world to make us participants in God's glory. Whether that transformation is conceived as happening more over time (temporal eschatology), through the space that God creates anew (transcendent eschatology), or by the purification of our moral natures (juridical eschatology), Christians are in agreement that it is our exemplary response to evil, after the pattern of Jesus, which permits us access to God's living transformation. That emphasis is so all-consuming that the imitation of Christ (often called the *imitatio Christi,* from the Latin phrasing) has come to be the focus of Christian ethics.

COMMENTARIES

Judaism on Christianity

by JACOB NEUSNER

Because Judaism and Christianity accept as authoritative the same Scriptures, called by Christianity "the Old Testament," and by Judaism "the Written Torah," or simply "the Hebrew Scriptures," they concur on many fundamental questions. Chief among these is the conception that man is like God, but man is fundamentally separate from God. God is always God, known to man only as he makes himself manifest. That is, for Judaism, in the Torah, the written part as well as the oral part ultimately set down in the Rabbinic writings of ancient times. For Christianity, it is in Christ, God incarnate. But if the ancient Rabbis were to read Paul's account of his being called, as Professor Chilton lays matters out, they would have found that picture surprising. For to them Scripture—the Torah properly understood—contained the record of God's picture of man, his quest for man. While some few of the Rabbinic sages told of supernatural encounters, none would claim personally to have been called by God. All of them underwent a long experience of discipleship to a master, and that is how they entered into the world of the Torah, written and oral. They formed a link in the chain of tradition to Sinai, a tradition received and handed on in a long process of discipleship to a master, beginning with Moses' study of Torah with God himself.

When it comes to attesting to the presence of God, with special reference to the suffering of the righteous and the prosperity of the wicked, Judaism in its classical statement found a solution to the anomalies of injustice. It was in the doctrine of the return to Eden after a last judgment, at which all who had ever lived would pass under God's judgment. Those that were found justified would enter into Eden for eternity. Those that did not, and they would not be many, would return to the grave for eternal death. Restorationist eschatology flows from the same cogent logic that has dictated theological doctrine from the beginning of this systematic account. The last things are to be known from the first. In the just plan of creation, man was meant to live in Eden, and Israel in the Land of Israel in time without end. The restoration will bring about that long and tragically postponed perfection of the world order, sealing the demonstration of the justice of God's plan for creation. Risen from the dead, having atoned through death, man will be judged in accord with his deeds. So the consequences of Adam's and Eve's rebellion and sin having been overcome, the struggle of man's will and God's word having been resolved, God's original plan will be realized at the last. The simple, global logic of the system, with its focus on the world order of justice established by God but disrupted by man, leads inexorably to this eschatology of restoration, the restoration of balance, order, proportion—eternity.

What does Judaism offer in response to the imitation of Christ? It is the imitation of God. That doctrine is explicitly stated in the following way:

> "And the Lord said to Moses, Say to all the congregation of the people of Israel, You shall be holy, [for I the Lord your God am holy. Every one of you shall revere his mother and his father, and you shall keep my Sabbaths; I am the Lord your God. Do not turn to idols or make for yourselves molten gods; I am the Lord your God]" (Lev. 19:1–4):
> "You shall be holy":
> "You shall be separate."
> "You shall be holy, for I the Lord your God am holy":
> That is to say, "if you sanctify yourselves, I shall credit it to you as though you had sanctified me, and if you do not sanctify yourselves, I shall hold that it is as if you have not sanctified me."
> Or perhaps the sense is this: "If you sanctify me, then lo, I shall be sanctified, and if not, I shall not be sanctified"?
> Scripture says, "For I . . . am holy," meaning, I remain in my state of sanctification, whether or not you sanctify me.
> Abba Saul says, "The king has a retinue, and what is the task thereof? It is to imitate the king."
>
> Sifra CXCV:I.2–3

Here is Judaism's explicit statement of what it means to be like God. In the comparison and contrast, we see how the two great religions both compare and contrast. In their basic structures, they compare. In their articulation of those structures, they contrast.

Islam on Christianity

by TAMARA SONN

Islam agrees with Christianity that God is utterly transcendent, beyond our limited power to know directly. Islam also agrees with Christianity that God is manifest in the world to all human beings, and not only to those who have received a particular scripture. And Islam accepts that Jesus, the Messiah, brought revelation that was unique at the time. However, Jesus did so not as a divine being, but as a prophet sent by the one God. His message, and that of all prophets, has been recapitulated and completed in the Qur'an. Still, as in Christianity, Islam holds the example of Jesus' humility and compassion to be eminently worthy of emulation. But Islam rejects the ethic of submitting peacefully to any authorities, even to the point of martyrdom. Rather, the Qur'an commands that believers "do good and prevent evil" (Qur'an 3:111), that they fight the oppressors wherever they find them, transforming the world from corruption to goodness and justice. Martyrdom in Islam consists not in submission to injustice but in struggling against it. Humility is indeed a major virtue in Islam, but acquiescence in the face of evil is not considered humility. Rather, one is commanded to expend every effort in the struggle against evil. Humility consists in attributing any success therein to the God who inspires the effort. In order to encourage our efforts, Islam, like Christianity, calls for restraint in the form of an annual month-long fast during Ramadan. But the fast has less to do with world transformation and eschatology than with self-transformation: recognizing one's utter dependence on God and, at the same time, one's equality with all other human beings in that dependency. For contrary to the Augustinian view, Islam does not view the physical world as one to be transcended or overcome in favor of the spiritual during our lifetimes. Rather, the physical world is the arena in which we demonstrate our commitment to God's will by working against oppression, injustice, and deprivation of all kinds. All human beings, in the Islamic ideal, are entitled to the necessities required for a comfortable life.

Hinduism on Christianity

by Brian K. Smith

Many of the distinctive differences between Hinduism and Judaism on the question of virtue hold also for a comparison between Hinduism and Christianity. The "self-knowledge" that guides virtue in Christianity—we are all God's children and "the brothers and sisters of Christ"—may here too be contrasted to the very different understanding of the "self" and thus virtuous action in Hindusm. And while there are certainly moral exemplars in Hinduism (holy men and women, gurus, and also incarnations of the divine called avatars), none of these plays the specific mediating role Christians assign to Christ in the cosmic and historical unfolding of things.

The so-called "problem of evil" in Christianity ("how God, as a loving and merciful father, can have created a world so riven with evil") is more or less obviated in Hinduism by the law of karma and rebirth. There is evil in the world because we, in our past lives, have created the karmic seeds and conditions for it. Karma is an automatically working operation that ensures justice (albeit over lifetimes), and does so usually apart from the divine will. In some theistic sects of Hinduism, there is the notion that faith and devotion to God can "override" one's karmic record, but in any case God is never held to be in any way responsible for evil.

Nor is the world as a whole regarded as in the process of any kind of redemption or transformation. The world will go on until it ends, and then will be reborn again—just like the individual lives of human beings. The critical importance in Christianity of eschatological thinking (in its three main varieties discussed above) is thus absent in Hinduism. There are, to be sure, theories in Hinduism regarding the end-times, and also theories about new beginnings that emerge out of the apocalypse. Such is, however, the nature of all things in the world: birth, life, death, and rebirth. In the Hindu view, the end of the world is only a stage in the eternal cycle of samsara. It has no particular meaning, it is not a part of any deity's "plan," and has no redemptive potential. Whereas in Christian thinking, eschatological visions have served important roles in shaping ideas regarding virtue, in Hinduism they are relegated to a relatively minor place in religious thought.

Buddhism on Christianity

by CHARLES HALLISEY

As with Judaism, Buddhism departs from Christianity in its disinterest in God, as creator and as a defining condition for all of human life. Buddhism also has no sense of an absolute end of time, an eschatology.

A more significant contrast may lie in Buddhist surprise in the awareness of judgment in the life of virtue as conceived by Christians. For Buddhists, compassion, which is expressed without judgment, is at the heart of the life of virtue. A story of one of the Buddha's previous lives portrays the process of his deciding to sacrifice his own body for a starving tigress in the following way:

> There can only be two reasons for taking no notice when someone else is in difficulties: selfish concern for one's own well-being, or sheer helplessness. But I cannot be happy as long as there is someone who is unhappy. And anyway, how can I take no notice when it is in my power to help? Suppose there were some criminal in abject misery and I took no notice of him even though I could be of help. It would be the same as committing a crime: I would burn with remorse, like deadwood in a forest fire.[1]

We can see that compassion for others is an absolute in the life of virtue and it knows no real constraints. Moreover, compassion for others is something that one owes to oneself because it is the only way that one can be happy.

SUMMARY

"Virtue" in Christianity lives up to its meaning in Latin (*virtus*): it refers to power. Indeed, Christians have conceived that power in ultimate terms, because

---

[1]Peter Khoroche, translator. *Once the Buddha Was a Monkey: Arya Sura's Jatakamala* (Chicago: University of Chicago Press, 1989), 25.

it derives from the might of God in Creation. The affinity between human spirit and divine Spirit opens the wellspring of virtue to those who heed God's calling.

That prophetic vocation, of responding to God's Spirit, results in a transformation of any human being that believes in God, and also of the world as a whole. Christianity remained committed to its Judaic heritage in its attachment to the world as reflecting divine glory, but those who remained loyal to Christ in the midst of persecution were only too aware of the experience of unjust suffering in Creation. Still, in its extended argument with Gnosticism, Christianity endorsed both the goodness of the natural order and the legitimate authority of the Roman Empire (despite the suffering endured at the hands of Roman magistrates). That was because the world in the full sense, natural and social, was being transformed to the eye of faith. In the end, Christians believed, God would triumph over evil and transform the world. The ultimate transformation was conceived of as occurring in differing ways: as intervening at the end of all time, as transcending any space we can know, and as culminating in the moral judgment of all peoples. Each of these conceptions represents the cumulative character of Christian eschatology, the finale of the world as we know if it.

Depending on the sort of eschatology Christians have embraced, they have stressed the importance of patient waiting (for the end of time), of discerning divine transcendence (within one's present experience), and/or of moral regeneration (in daily life and conduct). Yet in the adjustment to those differing conceptions, theologians of varying times and places have stressed the crucial importance of a single ethical norm. Jesus' teaching that love is the only appropriate retaliation to evil has endured as the keystone of Christian moral theology.

GLOSSARY

Apocalyptic an uncovering or disclosure (from the Greek *apokalupsis*). The term might refer to any revelation of heavenly mysteries, but it is often used in a more specific sense, of an insight such as is conveyed in the last book of the New Testament, the Revelation of John (also known as the Apocalypse). There, persistent attention is paid to the calendar of events, linked to present circumstances, that will lead up to and include the destruction and transformation of the world as we know it.

Eschatology (from the Greek *eskhata*, "last things") might refer to any teaching in regard to the end and purpose of human existence and the world. Typically, it is applied to prophetic promises such as Isaiah's prediction of "new heavens and a new earth" (Isaiah 65:17). The term is used to refer to the hope and expectation of how the transformed world will one day be. In contrast, the term apocalyptic refers more to the visionary means of disclosing that just what that new world will really be and the sequence of events leading up to the eschatological transformation.

Immanence the complement of transcendence. Removed though God is from the ordinary circumstances of our world, and however distant he might seem from the world he made, God's power and will is nonetheless discernible in all that he made, as well as in the human beings whom he created in his image and likeness, no matter what their subsequent transgressions.

Imitation   (from the Latin *imitatio* and the Greek *mimesis*) can easily be mistaken in English for mere mimicry. Its deeper sense was captured by Aristotle, who said, "The objects of imitation are actions, with agents who are necessarily either good men or bad—the diversity of human character being nearly always derivative from this . . ." (*Poetics* 2 [1448ª 1–5]). In other words, by the things people do, learned by observing others, they frame the identity and character of who they are in the social world.

Transcendence   refers literally (from its Latin origin in *transcendere*) to the movement from one place to another, surpassing a boundary. When the divine capacity to proceed across boundaries is at issue, the point is to speak of God as being removed from all the terms and conditions in space, which constrain human beings.

DISCUSSION QUESTIONS

1. How does Paul conceive of the relationship between human beings and God? How did his conception relate to the biblical pattern of prophetic vocation?

2. Explain why the motif of the imitation of Christ (*imitatio Christi*) has been perennially discussed in Christian theology.

3. What is the foundation of the teaching that Christians should be obedient to the duly constituted authorities of this world?

4. How might the varying eschatologies of the early Church be described as both distinctive and yet coherent with one another?

5. In what way is the transformation of the world linked to the moral imperative to live in a manner true to the vocation of Christ?

6. How did Jesus teach evil should be dealt with, and why is that teaching at the heart of Christianity?

 **INFOTRAC**

If you would like additional information related to the material discussed here, you can visit our Web site: http://www.wadsworth.com

3

Islam

BY TAMARA SONN

CONVENTIONAL ANSWERS VERSUS THIS RELIGIOUS TRADITION: WHO ARE WE REALLY?

Human beings are clearly described in the Qur'an as God's deputies or stewards, created by God with a task to fulfill. As discussed in the second volume of this series, the creation story in Islamic scripture describes God informing the angels that he intends to "place on earth my *khalifah*" (2:30), often translated as "vicegerent" by people who seem unaware that no one uses that term in English. *Khalifah* means successor, deputy, or vicar, in the sense of someone who is assigned by the one in charge to maintain the owner's property, and is responsible for making sure the owner's interests are protected and well cared for. In that sense, the term carries the meaning of steward, as in the biblical story of the person assigned to make sure the owner's orchards receive whatever attention they need in order to flourish. Human beings were created by God with this "trust" (*amanah*): "Indeed, we offered the trust to the heavens and the earth and the mountains but they refused to accept it and were afraid of it. But the human being carried it" (33:73). It is human beings' job, therefore, to "establish justice," for a just society, healthy and balanced, is what God wants us to establish and maintain.

The Qur'an reveals that a just society is one whose overall well-being is measured by that of its weakest members—orphans, widows, the elderly, the marginalized—not by that of its powerful elites. "Do you not see that God knows everything in the heavens and the earth? There is no secret meeting of three but that God is their fourth, nor of five but that he is their sixth, nor of less than these or more but that he is with them wherever they are," says the Qur'an (58:8). All creatures are of equal concern to their creator. The success or failure of God's deputies will be judged on the extent to which they exert themselves in the effort to re-create in society the equality all human beings share in the eyes of God.

As such, human beings are all God's servants. Our reason for existing is to do the divine will. As we have noted, the meaning of the term *islam* is "submission;" a *muslim* is one who submits to the will of God. The purpose of revelation is to make that will clear; the Qur'an therefore calls itself "guidance for people" (*hudan li'l-nas*). It establishes the basic rules and moral guidelines for a just society, and instructs human beings to use their intelligence to understand how best to put God's will into practice on a daily basis. Therefore, we are not servants in the sense of helpless or abject slaves. Instead, we have been endowed with intelligence and are instructed to use it, to seek knowledge, to understand our surroundings so that we may better fulfill our purpose for existing.

We are also given moral freedom. We may choose the right path or we may allow ourselves to be misled by greed and other self-destructive concerns. The Qur'an asserts repeatedly that God leads some people to goodness while he "seals the hearts" of others. It also states that some people will inevitably go to hell:

> We have created many of the jinn [creatures similar to humans but with greater physical powers and without the basic moral character of humans] and humans for hell; they have hearts but do not understand with them, and they have eyes but do not see with them, and they have ears but do not hear with them. They are like cows, but more misguided; they are heedless. (7:180)

Claims like this have led some to believe that Islam does not teach that human beings have free will. Instead, they believe, Islam teaches predestination—the idea that our fates are already established by God and there is nothing we can do to change them. The majority of scholars, however, believe this is a misinterpretation of Islamic teaching. It is true, of course, that Islam teaches that God is omniscient; like all monotheistic religions, Islam teaches that God knows everything. It is unthinkable, therefore, that God will be surprised to find out how we decide to lead our lives. But the idea of divine omniscience does not interfere with the notion of human ignorance. Regardless of who else knows what decisions we will make, the fact that we must struggle with the choices means that we are free moral agents. We must choose between right and wrong, and to the extent that we are aware of the difference, we are responsible for the consequences.

Accordingly, the verses in the Qur'an that seem to indicate that God is solely responsible for human misdeeds are more accurately understood as supporting the notion of human moral agency. In general, they refer to God's allowing people to be misled only after they have rejected goodness. For example:

> And they swear vehemently by God that if a sign came to them they would believe in it. Say, "Indeed God has signs but what will make you understand that when it comes, they will not believe. And we will confuse their hearts and their eyes, as they did not believe in them the first time and we will leave them in their sin to wander without direction." (6:110–11)

Similarly, "And punishment comes to those who reject our signs because they disobeyed" (6:50). Elsewhere, "They said, 'Our hearts are encased,' but God has cursed them for their disbelief" (2:89). In this way, the Qur'an clearly stresses that people are led astray through their own choices: "Evil is the situation of the example of those who treated our signs as lies, wronging themselves" (7:178). Secondarily, the Qur'an's claim that God leads some on the right path and al-

lows some to go astray makes the point that human beings need not take upon
themselves the responsibility of judging others; God is the sole judge. Human
beings' responsibility is to carry out God's will. For this they will be rewarded;
failure to do so will unquestionably result in punishment. This promise of reward and threat of punishment again emphasizes our moral responsibility, since
reward and punishment would be utterly unjust if people are not free to choose
their actions.

God has provided guidance for human beings throughout history to aid in
the effort to do the work we were created for. "And there is no community to
which a warner has not come" (35:25). "And those who disbelieve say, 'Why
was not a sign sent from his lord?' But you are a warner and there is a guide for
every people" (13:8). All communities, therefore, have been given sufficient
guidance to fulfill the divine will. If we fail, it is because we have made wrong
choices, and we are the ones who will bear the consequences.

The Qur'an acknowledges human weaknesses, our pride and selfishness:
"People are prone to selfishness" (4:129), "The human being is created impatient and greedy. When evil touches him he goes to pieces, and when good
comes to him, he hoards it" (70:20–22). Elsewhere: "The human being never
tires of praying for good but if evil touches him, he panics and gives up hope.
And if we make him taste our mercy after evil has come to him, indeed he says,
'I deserved this and I do not think the [final] hour will come'" (41:50–51). But
the Qur'an also assures us that we are created with sufficient moral power to
withstand temptation and make correct choices: "God burdens no one beyond
[her] his power" (2:287). And people are also assured that God is a merciful
judge: "Indeed your lord has forgiveness for people, despite their wrongdoings"
(13:7). In fact, every verse of the Qur'an opens with affirmation of God's mercy
and compassion: "In the name of God, the merciful, the benevolent."

Overall, the Qur'an's view of human beings is holistic. We are integrated
beings with physical and mental or spiritual aspects. The Qur'an does not draw
a radical distinction between those aspects. It often uses the term *nafs* when referring to individuals. Although it is usually translated "soul," this term actually
means "self" or "person" rather than some immaterial substance surviving
death in order to be reunited with a revived body at the end of time. In contrast to this perception, the Qur'an speaks of reviving the entire person from
death at the last judgement. Although this dualistic approach came to dominate
in Islam just as it had in Christianity, the significance of the Qur'an's attitude is
that there is no radical distinction between physical and spiritual well-being;
both are important for our happiness and for the well-being of others that we
are supposed to establish.[1] While it praises steadfastness in the face of troubles,
it does not valorize physical suffering for its own sake. Such valorization implies
that one can be physically miserable yet emotionally or spiritually healthy. By

---

[1]Later Islamic thinkers, such as eleventh- and twelfth-century jurist al-Ghazali, accepted
the mind-body distinction characteristic of Christian thinking, as discussed by Fazlur
Rahman, *Major Themes of the Qur'an* (Minneapolis: Bibliotheca Islamica, 1980), 17. See
also Fazlur Rahman, *Health and Medicine in the Islamic Tradition* (New York: Crossroad,
1989), 21ff.

contrast, the Qur'an assumes that the overall well-being of the human being depends upon its ability to meet its basic material needs while, at the same time, not being preoccupied with them. Sufficiency of material and physical comfort are essential for continued efforts to fulfill the will of God. And that is the ultimate purpose of human existence: *islam,* submission to God, or *'ibadah,* service to God.

WHAT ARE THE SOCIAL VIRTUES?

It is difficult to distinguish social from personal virtue in Islam because the two are so integrally related. As noted above, the human being is conceived holistically: a single being with physical and mental or spiritual characteristics. As such, we are social creatures; very little of what we do can be considered to affect society more than it affects ourselves, and vice versa. (One who does something that is good for other people has done something that is good for herself or himself, and vice versa.) Further, we have noted that the very purpose of human existence in Islamic teaching is to serve God, to do the will of God, and that will has been revealed as the mandate to re-create in society the equality all human beings share in the eyes of their creator. In this sense, all virtue in Islam is social virtue.

The interrelatedness of virtues in Islam is perhaps most eloquently expressed in the famous Qur'anic passage:

> It is not goodness that you turn your faces to the East or the West; but good is the one who believes in God and the last day and the angels and the book and the prophets and who spends money for love of Him on relatives and orphans and the needy and travelers and beggars and captives and who observes prayer and gives charity [zakat] and [those] who fulfill their promises when they make them and those who are patient in poverty and affliction and war. These are the ones who demonstrate righteousness and who are devout. (2:178)

The Qur'an therefore calls for belief in God and revelation. This, as we will discuss in the next section, can be considered a personal virtue. But just as soon as it calls for belief, the Qur'an moves on to social virtues. Indeed, the Qur'an gives the impression that the two cannot be separated. Claiming to believe and offering prayers are described as hypocrisy if they are not accompanied by charity and efforts to help the less fortunate:

> Have you seen the one who makes a mockery of religion? It is the one who mistreats orphans and works little for the feeding of the poor. Woe, then, to those who pray, yet are neglectful of their prayers—those who pray for show and withhold charity. (107:2–8)

In the Qur'an all virtue is tied to the overall goal of human life, to please God by working for social justice. That is the paradigmatic value; it establishes the context in which to judge all other actions as virtuous or not. Most characteristically, the Qur'an calls for charity and helping the poor as the way to achieve the goal. For example:

> Spending wealth for God's cause is like a grain of corn that grows seven ears, in each ear a hundred kernels. And God multiplies further for whomever he pleases. God is bountiful and all-knowing.
>
> Those who spend their wealth for God's cause and do not then criticize or insult will be rewarded by their lord and they [need] have no fear or grief.
>
> Judicious speech and forgiveness are better than charity followed by insult. And God is all-sufficient and merciful.
>
> Believers, do not nullify your charity through criticism and insult, like the one who spends his wealth to be seen by people and does not believe in God and the last day. He is like a smooth rock with soil on it that is laid bare in a downpour, leaving it smooth and hard. They will get nothing of what they earn. God does not guide the disbelieving people.
>
> And those who spend their wealth to please God and to strengthen themselves are like a garden on high ground. The rains fall on it and it produces double fruit, and if rain does not fall, then dew. God sees what you do. (2:262–266)

Charity is actually required by Islam of all adult Muslims, in the form of *zakat*. A portion of whatever wealth they have over and above that required to maintain their homes and meet their responsibilities is to be given to a local authority for the needs of the community: "for the poor and the needy and those who work for them and for those whose hearts are to be reconciled and for captives and debtors and for God's cause, and travelers—a ruling from God" (9:60). In other words, Muslims are required to support local social services, efforts to propagate the faith, diplomacy, hospitality, and whatever expenditures are necessary to further the overall cause of social justice.

In addition to required charity, other charity (*sadaqah*) is also recommended. Actually, the Qur'an says that charity that other people do not know about is best: "If you give charity openly, that is good, but if you hide it and give it to the poor, it is better for you and He will remove your offenses. And God is aware of what you do" (2:272). In fact, then, the Qur'an encourages people to give continually: "Those who spend their wealth by night and day, secretly and openly, will have their reward with their lord; they [need] have no fear or grief" (2:273).

The rationale for both required and recommended charity is that wealth is not given to people for their pleasure alone, but to further the will of God that all human beings be adequately cared for. Even the Prophet is advised that the victories he has been granted have a purpose and that distribution of the wealth acquired through conquest is a part of that plan: "Whatever God has given to his Messenger as spoils from the towns is for God and the Messenger and for relatives and orphans and the needy and travelers, so that it may not circulate [only] among the wealthy" (59:8). Again, all things are related to God's ultimate purpose for human existence.

The Qur'an always relates such efforts toward social well-being to correct belief: "Indeed, those who believe and do good deeds and establish prayer and give charity will have their reward with their lord, and [need] have no fear or grief" (2:278). The implication is that charity and good deeds are the natural manifestation of correct belief and prayer. In the Qur'an's worldview, the one is unthinkable without the other.

Similarly, Muslims are enjoined to treat one another as they would their own family members: "Indeed, believers are brothers [and sisters] so make peace among brothers and respect God and the mercy [will come] to you" (49:11). People must treat each other with respect, avoiding gossip and ridicule, the sources of mistrust among people (49:12; cf. 58:9–11). Trust among believers is essential, and differences of opinion should not distract people from the solidarity necessary to achieve a just society. The Qur'an says that differences among people are part of God's plan: "People, we have created you from a male and a female and made you into tribes and clans that you may come to know one another. Indeed, the noblest among you with God is the most righteous" (49:14). The bond among people should be their commitment to doing the will of God, and that should allow them to transcend their petty squabbles.

Nowhere does the Qur'an call for uniformity of belief, but only "competition in goodness," judged in terms of deeds done in "God's cause" (al-sabil Allah). That cause takes precedence even over family bonds. The Qur'an requires respect of children for parents and sound nurturing by parents of children. But the overall well-being of the community must take precedence over narrow family concerns: "Believers, be steadfast in justice, witnessing for God, even though it is against yourselves or parents or relatives, rich or poor; God is closer than either" (4:136). The Qur'an warns that if "fathers, sons, brothers, spouses, clans, wealth, trade, your houses" take precedence over struggling in God's cause, God will judge accordingly (9:25). The cause of God must also take precedence over sectarian bonds. The Qur'an clearly calls for cooperation even among religious groups in doing the will of God: "People of the Book [i.e., Jews, Christians, and Muslims], join together on a formula common among us that we serve only God" (3:64).

Indeed, the Qur'an explains that it was not incorrect teaching of the earlier prophets that led astray their communities—such as the Jews and Christians, whom the Qur'an discusses at length. Instead, it was those communities' failure to properly put their teachings into practice:

> If the People of the Book had believed and acted righteously we would have removed their evils and admitted them to Paradise. If they established the Torah, the Gospel, and what has been sent down to them from their lord, they would have eaten in abundance. Among them are moderate people but many of them do evil. (5:66–67)

It was not the messengers, therefore, but the followers who failed to grasp the essence of revelation. And the evidence is that their belief did not lead to pious behavior expressed in social responsibility.

> You who believe, indeed many rabbis and monks consume people's property by falsehood and turn from the way of God, and to those who store up gold

and silver and do not spend them in the way of God, give them news of severe punishment. (9:34)

It is in this very context that the Qur'an explains the mission of Prophet
Muhammad. He has been sent to establish a just community, a median community, *ummat al-wasit,* in the sense that it steers clear of the extremes of other
communities; it is a community bound by commitment to God's will. The
Qur'an says, "Thus we have made you a median community so that you may
be witnesses to people and the Messenger may be a witness for you" (2:144).
Elsewhere:

> You are the best community produced for humanity, commanding good and
> forbidding evil and believing in God. And if the People of the Book [those
> who received previous revelations, i.e., Jews and Christians] had believed, it
> would have been better for them. Among them are believers but most of
> them have strayed. (3:111)

WHAT IS PERSONAL VIRTUE?

Although personal and social virtues are part of an integrated human personality in Islam, it is possible to identify virtues specific to the individual. Typically,
however, the Qur'an identifies them in connection with doing good works, a
social virtue. For example:

> Indeed, those who believe and those Jews, and Christians, and Sabians who
> believe in God and the last day and do good works, for them is their reward
> with their lord and no fear nor grief. (2:63)

> Indeed, those who believe and those Jews and Sabians and Christians who be-
> lieve in God and the last day and do good works, no fear for them nor grief.
> (5:70)

Belief in God, therefore, is considered in the Qur'anic view to be the basis of all
virtues, that which motivates the good deeds necessary to accomplish the trust,
the *amanah,* for which we were created. The term for belief or faith is *iman,* and
in its centrality to the overall mission of Islam, it has been called Islam's most important ethical term. In fact, that term and others based on the same linguistic
root appear far more frequently in the Qur'an than does the term *islam.*

The term *iman* comes from an Arabic root that conveys the meaning of being
safe or secure and, closely related, trustworthy. The Qur'an uses the term and its
variants in a number of ways associated with the notion of security. For example: "And God set forth the parable of a village that was secure (*aminah*) and at
peace, its provisions coming to it plentifully from everywhere, but then it was
ungrateful for the favors of God so God made it taste the garment of hunger and
fear for what they did" (16:113). But its paradigm usage is the verse related above
describing the responsibility human beings took upon themselves at creation, the
amanah: "Indeed, we offered the trust to the heavens and the earth and the

mountains but they refused to accept it and were afraid, but the human beings accepted it" (33:73).

Again, we see the integrated approach to faith in Islam. The implication is that acceptance of one's purpose on earth and one's utter dependence on God are not only correct belief but the route to security and ultimate well-being. Human happiness and well-being in this view can only come from this recognition. Efforts to find security and fulfillment elsewhere are inevitably futile since God is the sole source of both. Yet the recognition is not mere intellectual assent. Simple acceptance of a creed, a formula describing specific aspects of a belief system, is an entirely different concept represented by another term. In Arabic that term is *'aqidah,* which is important but different from *iman* as such. Iman, properly conceived, is both intellectual acceptance of propositions concerning the unseen, and commitment to manifestation of that acceptance in the realm of the seen.

It is here that in Islam the eternal (the timeless world, from the Latin *aeterna*) and the earthly (the world bounded by time, the secular, from the Latin *saecula*) meet. For there is no way to judge true belief except through proper behavior in the social order. That is why the first "pillar" of Islam—the first requirement of all Muslims—is *shahadah,* or bearing witness. The Qur'an did not command mere intellectual belief, but rather, a certain kind of behavior or activity in accordance with beliefs. Beliefs are not, in general, to be held for their own sake, but for their role in influencing behavior in accordance with the will of God. Where there appears to be a discrepancy between expressed belief and behavior, behavior is clearly the more important factor. Revelation is the source of true belief, but revelation unheard—whether literally or figuratively—ceases to function as revelation. The circuit must be complete for the energy to function. Indeed, in Islam revelation is similar to energy: it motivates, it is effective. Why some people hear but do not hear, the Qur'an tells us, is known only by God. But how can we tell if someone has heard? Not by words claiming belief, but by activity reflecting belief. Thus, the first pillar of Islam is not simply saying or believing that "there is no god but the one God, Allah, and Muhammad is the messenger of God." The sense of the term *shahadah* is "bearing witness," that is, vowing to demonstrate in one's behavior the recognition that "there is no god but Allah and Muhammad is God's messenger."

Accordingly, the term *islam* itself represents a major virtue. Like the term *iman, islam* has a number of interrelated meanings. It comes from an Arabic root that can mean in various contexts to be safe, secure, intact, integrated, or whole. In one of its most common noun usages, it means peace; the Islamic greeting is *as-salam 'alaikum,* "Peace be with you." In another of its forms the verb means "to surrender" or "submit"—the root from which we get the term *islam,* naming the religion itself. Even though this term is used less frequently in the Qur'an than the term *iman,* its significance is no less profound. Again, it carries with it the existential nature of faith in Islam, the idea that true faith is inevitably demonstrated in action. As in Christianity, God in Islam is ultimately beyond the power of human beings to perceive. God is infinite and cannot be comprehended by our distinctly finite minds. But God has chosen to reveal himself to humanity in specific ways; what we know about God, therefore, is what God has revealed to us. And what God has revealed to us in Islam is what God wants us to do. This is often called "the prophetic imperative": the urgency of the desire to do what God wants us to do, to reflect the equality of all human beings in the social order, as a response to authentic recognition of divinity—in other words, the submission of our own wills to the divine will, *islam*.

For creatures other than human beings, submission to the will of God is simple. In fact, the Qur'an says that the whole universe is prostrate before God in complete submission: "And whoever is in the heavens and earth willingly or unwillingly prostrates before God along with their shadows, morning and evening" (13:16). Similarly, "And whatever is in the heavens and whatever creatures on earth and the angels prostrate before God and they are not proud" (16:50). The nature of all creation is to behave in the way and for the purpose for which it was created. Only human beings, having taken upon themselves "the trust," have the capacity to go against our very nature, attempting to thwart the will of God. Because God is the ultimate power, such efforts are doomed to failure, along with those who make them. Therefore, the Qur'an specifies certain actions for believers, designed to remind them of their creator and their commitment to do his will. Those acts are generally classified as kinds of worship: prayer, fasting, and pilgrimage. But each of these must be done mindfully; simple repetition of ritual is not meritorious in Islam. For that reason, performance of the deeds must be preceded by declaration of proper intention. One must consciously dedicate one's actions to God, expressing the desire to submit to God's will or, as it is often put, to please God. Only in that way can performance of ritual be considered virtuous. As the Qur'an reminds people, the benefit resulting from such deeds is not for God but for people (22:38). Reminding themselves of the reason for their existence, renewing their commitment to doing the will of God, and reestablishing their shared humanity through group worship all help strengthen human beings' faith as well as their commitment to put it into action.

Perhaps the most generalized of Islamic virtues is the state or condition of having achieved mindfulness of God, such that our actions automatically reflect true belief. That condition is called *taqwa* by the Qur'an. Coming from a root meaning similar to *iman* and *islam* in Arabic, the term is difficult to translate. Its core meaning is to guard, shelter, protect, or preserve. In one form it means "to be on guard," which may be why *taqwa* is so often translated into English as "fear of God," although this phrase makes as little sense in Arabic as it does in English. The Qur'an uses the term most often to indicate a "safe course" in the sense that the kind of behavior discussed is most likely to lead to the well-being of those who engage in it. For example, in verses quoted in the previous section, the term translated as "pious" or "acting righteously" is actually the noun form indicating "those who have *taqwa*." Thus:

> It is not goodness that you turn your faces to the East or the West; but good
> is the one who believes in God and the last day and the angels and the book
> and the prophets and who spends money for love of Him on relatives and or-
> phans and the needy and travelers and beggars and captives and who observes

prayer and gives charity and who fulfill their promises when they make them
and those who are patient in poverty and affliction and war. These are the
ones who demonstrate righteousness and who have *taqwa*. (2:178)

We referred above to the verse in which the Qur'an says that sacrifices are
not for God but for the well-being of the people who make them. Speaking of
the benefit of animal sacrifice, the Qur'an says, "Their flesh does not reach God
nor does their blood, but *taqwa* among you reaches him" (22:38). When the
Qur'an talks about proper motivation for performing religious rituals, it says it
must be *taqwa* (22:33). When it speaks of being fair in dealings with people, even
those considered to be enemies, it says that is a manifestation of *taqwa* (9:8). In
general, when the Qur'an describes correct behavior stemming from true belief
or proper orientation toward ultimate reality, it uses the term *taqwa,* as in: "Cooperate with one another in virtue and *taqwa,* but do not cooperate in sin and
wrongdoing" (5:3). This verse then uses the term in its verbal form, indicating
its meaning of "taking refuge with" or "finding safety in": "And take refuge with
God; indeed, God is severe in punishment."

Taqwa, therefore, like other virtues in Islam, serves both to protect the individual from harm and to further God's cause; in the Islamic worldview, the two
goals are one. Correct belief, resulting in submission to the will of God, producing a conscience that guides behavior that promotes the well-being of the individual and, in the process, the well-being of society—these are the interrelated
virtues in Islam. But there is another virtue encouraged by the Qur'an that is
slightly more abstract in nature but also influences one's ability to fulfill the divine will. It is the pursuit of knowledge of one's surroundings. Knowledge of
God's will for humanity has its source in revelation; it is offered to humanity and
the virtuous response is acceptance of that knowledge on faith. But other kinds
of knowledge are also necessary for the fulfillment of God's will. The Qur'an
therefore continuously encourages believers to seek knowledge. We are told to
think and reflect upon the signs of God, which are everywhere, and to seek understanding. The Qur'an recounts numerous historical stories of people who
have been corrupt and greedy, so that people will learn from the examples.

> How many a town have we destroyed because it did wrong and was devas-
> tated with its roofs falling down to it foundations, its defunct wells and its de-
> serted palaces of stone reinforced with lead. Did not these people travel the
> earth in order to possess hearts to understand with and ears to hear with? It is
> not the eyes that become blind but the hearts in breasts. (22:46–47)

The history of peoples who came before us, therefore, is essential to our properly understanding God's will. We are told to ponder upon it so that we understand. People are told to travel the earth to see for themselves what happens to
those who reject the divine will:

> [God] helps whom he will, and he is powerful, merciful. The promise of God
> he does not break, but most people do not know. They know the externals of
> the life of the world and are heedless of the hereafter. Do they not think on
> their own? God created the heavens and the earth and what is between them

only in accordance with truth and for a fixed time. But many people do not
believe in the meeting with their lord. Have they not traveled the earth to see
the end of those before them? (30:6–10)

Even Prophet Muhammad is instructed to pray to God to "increase [his] knowledge" (20:115).

This kind of secular knowledge, meaning knowledge of the world in which
we live, is essential to being able to realize the will of God in our surroundings.
It is not considered sufficient for piety, obviously; *iman, islam,* and *taqwa* provide
the motivation and the orientation for fulfilling the purpose for which we were
created. But taking the initiative to properly understand our surroundings so as
to be able to do so is also necessary. Those who take upon themselves this responsibility are acting virtuously, as the current president of Iran recently
reflected:

> For how can we expect someone to solve a problem when he does not know
> that a problem exists? Here, moral rectitude will not suffice. Nor will knowl-
> edge by itself. A moral person who is a moving encyclopedia but lives outside
> his time, for whom the most pressing problems are for example the second
> and third Islamic centuries, cannot solve even the smallest of today's problems,
> for today's problems do not interest him.
>
> In contrast, the main quality of a [religious] intellectual is that she lives
> in her own time, taking on a social responsibility, her mind constantly cu-
> rious and restive about reality and human destiny. A [religious] intellectual
> is one who respects rationality and thinking and also knows the value of
> freedom. . . .
>
> The religious intellectual is one who loves humanity, understands its prob-
> lems, and feels a responsibility toward its destiny and respects human freedom.
> She feels that humans have a divine mission and wants freedom for them
> Whatever blocks the path to human growth and evolution, she deems as
> being against freedom.[2]

So some aspects of Islamic virtues have to do with proper recognition of and
orientation toward the infinite, accepting our own finitude. Other aspects of the
same virtues have to do with what Islam considers the inevitable response to development of those virtues: action in accordance with the divine will. Thus, Islamic virtues, even personal ones, manifest themselves publicly, in society. Those
aspects of Islamic virtue that are personal are concerned with eternal truths: the
existence of the one God, creator and judge of all humanity, and specific ways
in which God has instructed us to worship. Those aspects of Islamic virtue that
manifest themselves socially, however, may be quite dynamic, as we have seen in
the discussion of social virtue. The core of that dynamism is that circumstances
change; ways of implementing the divine will that are suitable in one situation
may not be suitable in other situations. It therefore becomes a requirement to

---

[2]Mohammad Khatami, *Islam, Liberty and Development* (Binghamton: Binghamton
University Institute of Global Cultural Studies, 1998), 77–78.

fulfill our divinely mandated *amanah* to seek knowledge of the world and our surroundings, even if, as the hadith says, the search takes us all the way to China. Or as another well-known saying has it: "To spend more time in learning is better than spending more time in prayer. . . . It is better to teach knowledge one hour in the night than to pray the whole night."[3]

HOW DOES THIS RELIGION DEFINE CHARACTER, GOOD AND BAD?

According to Islamic teaching, all human beings are born with potentially good character. All the hadith collections include reports that all children are born into *fitrah,* innate good character. This notion is based on a passage from Surat [chapter] al-Rum: "So set your face to the religion as a true practitioner, the nature with which God endowed human beings. There is no changing the creation of God. That is the right religion. Most people do not know" (30:31). It is believed, therefore, that human nature is created with the capacity to behave as God wills us to. The verse continues by outlining that behavior: "Turn to him and take refuge [show *taqwa*], establish prayer and do not be among those who associate [other things or beings with God]." In other words, serve God alone.

The teaching on *fitrah* assumes that all human beings are endowed by their creator with this good character, this ability to recognize God through his signs and to respond with humility and obedience. The teaching on family responsibilities—parents' responsibility to nurture their children, to train them and teach them the true religion—assumes that with proper care, that basically good human character will flourish. We saw above that the Qur'an also acknowledges human weakness such as our tendency to panic and lose faith in times of stress. That is why we are instructed to constantly reaffirm our faith and commitment through prayer throughout the day. And it is why the Qur'an reassures us repeatedly that we were not created without purpose; our efforts will indeed be rewarded and help is available when times are difficult, for God does not require from anyone what is beyond his or her strength to accomplish.

Nevertheless, the Qur'an also acknowledges that some people go astray. As we saw above, the Qur'an accounts for the existence of evil in the same way other monotheists do, through the story of the devil, Iblis, or Satan (Shaytan). It sometimes speaks of Satan in the plural, leading some commentators to assume the term simply stands for evil forces. For example, after stating that God sends angels to help guide people, the Qur'an says, "Similarly, we created for every prophet as an enemy satans [or evil ones] from among people and jinn" (6:113). In other statements, the Qur'an refers to Satan and Iblis as if they were individuals. For example, in the telling of the story of humanity's fall from grace in the garden, the Qur'an states that it was Satan who was the cause: "Satan caused

---

[3]Translated by Allama Sir Abdullah al-Mamun al-Suhrawardy, *The Sayings of Muhammad* (New York: Carol, 1990), 93.

them to fall from [the garden] and be expelled from where they had been, and we said to them, 'Go down as enemies of one another'" (2:37). The Qur'an also warns people again and again not to "follow in the footsteps of Satan," just as it makes it clear that "Satan in an enemy for people" (e.g., 2:169, 209; 12:6; 36:7). Such statements lead most commentators to believe that there are positive sources of evil lurking among us.

Whether Satan and/or Iblis are actually evil creatures or just symbolically represent the existence of evil, it is undeniable that some human beings commit evil acts. Regardless of the ultimate source of evil, two things are clear in the Qur'an. The first is that the individuals who commit the acts are themselves morally responsible for the consequences. As we discussed above, the Qur'an insists that human beings bear the ultimate responsibility for their actions. When they commit offenses, the Qur'an indicates this moral responsibility by saying that they have "wronged themselves." For example, in a passage from Surat Ibrahim describing the last judgment, it is predicted that Satan will reveal his strategy:

> They will all appear before God and the weak will say to the proud, "Indeed we were your followers. Cannot you help us at all against God's punishment?" They will say, "If God had guided us, indeed we would have guided you. It is the same for us if we are impatient or patient. There is no way out for us." And when the matter is decided, Satan will say, "God made a true promise to you but I promised you and failed you. And I had no power over you except that I called you and you obeyed me. So do not blame me, but blame yourselves. I cannot help you and you cannot help me. (14:22–23)

Second, the Qur'an contends that, in general, people are led astray and follow their baser instincts due to ignorance. After describing people who refuse to believe in revelation, the Qur'an says: "And even if we sent down angels to them and the dead spoke to them and we gathered together everything in front of their faces, they would not believe unless God wills. But most of them are ignorant" (6:112). The devil (Iblis, in the creation story) set for himself the task of leading human beings astray from the day he was ejected from paradise until the final judgment. The Qur'an describes God saying to Iblis upon the devil's refusal to acknowledge human beings' moral superiority: "Tempt whomever of them you can with your voice and send your horsemen and soldiers against them and participate with them in wealth and children and make promises to them. Satan promises them nothing except deceit" (17:65; cf. 15:40; 7:18).

Thus, the Qur'an describes most of the work of the devil (Satan or Iblis) as trickery, making things appear to be what they are not. This trickery is effective on some human beings because of their failure to think clearly, to read the signs—because of their ignorance. The Qur'an chastises "those who kill their children stupidly and without knowledge and who prohibit food God has given them by attributing false things to God. They have gotten lost and are not properly guided" (6:141). And it is not just the devil or devils who mislead human beings. The Qur'an mentions that misguided people also mistake poets for prophets, following them even though they spin yarns about things they have never done:

> Shall I tell you upon whom the satans come down? They come down upon
> every liar and sinner, repeating what they hear. And most of them are liars.
> And the poets, the misguided ones follow them. Do you not see how they
> wander around in every valley and that they say what they do not do?
> (26:222–227)

In this sense, people go astray through self-deception, by confusion in their
minds between their own selfish interests and desires and the true guidance that
is available to them through revelation: "But those who are unjust follow their
own desires without any knowledge" (30:30).

This understanding of evil as self-deception is reinforced in the Qur'an's description of the last judgement and punishment in the afterlife. When all human
beings are called before God, the ultimate judge, their veils of self-deception will
be removed from them and they will be faced with the reality of their behavior:

> When the sun is covered up and the stars hidden from view and the moun-
> tains move and when pregnant camels are abandoned and when the wild ani-
> mals are herded together and when the seas flow out and when people are
> united and when the infant girl buried alive will be asked for what sin she was
> slain and when the scrolls are unfurled and when the sky is pulled off and
> when hell is set fire and the garden is brought near, then every one will know
> what s/he has presented. (81:2–15)

No means of self-deception will be available to us. "You were heedless of this
but now we have torn your veil so your sight is clear today" (50:22). There will
be no one to hide behind because each one will "come to us all alone" (19:81).
And nothing will be hidden:

> [T]he day when the enemies of God will be gathered towards the fire and
> they will be driven on—until when they approach it, their own ears and eyes
> and skins will give evidence against them of what they were doing. And they
> will say to their skins, "Why have you testified against us?" and they will an-
> swer, "God who makes everything speak also caused us to speak. . . . You did
> not hide yourselves so that your ears and your eyes and your skins will not
> testify against you. No, you thought that God does not know much of what
> you do, and that which you thought about your lord has destroyed you and
> you have become among the lost." (41:20–24)

Our disposition in the afterlife, therefore, is ultimately our own responsibility. God guides us and is merciful; Satan or satans or Iblis or the devil represents
the sources of deception and the temptation we feel to substitute self-interest for
obedience and the well-being of the community. But it is we who either submit to the will of God or "wrong ourselves." At the final judgement our self-
deception will be exposed and our punishment will be the pain of facing the evil
we have thereby caused. The Qur'an speaks often of the fire into which sinners
will be cast. But it further suggests the torment sinners will feel at no longer
being able to deceive themselves:

> The agony of death shall come in truth [and it will be said to him], "Is this
> what you were trying to avoid?" And the trumpet shall be blown—that will

be the threatened day. And every person shall come forth along with a driver and a witness. [It shall be said to the evil ones,] "You were [sunk] in heedlessness of this, but We have removed from you your veil, so your sight today is keen." And his companion [angel] shall say, "Here is what I have ready [by way of testimony]." [It shall be said,] "Throw you two [the driver and the witness] into Hell every ungrateful rebel who withheld wealth [from the needy], a transgressor and a doubter [of the Revelation]; he who assumed another god besides God. Cast him into an intense punishment." His companion will say, "O our Lord! I did not beguile him but he [himself] was far afield in error. . . ." (50:19–26)[4]

Thus, people are basically good, but evil exists and it stems essentially from people's self-deception. They are created with a natural inclination toward good and the ability to recognize God and respond accordingly with submission and obedience. But through ignorance and self-deception they can bring perdition upon themselves by substituting their own personal whims for the eternal will of God.

BEYOND THE NORMAL VIRTUES: WHO IS THE EXTRAORDINARY PERSON?

Islam has a rich heritage of encouragement and respect for those who "bear witness" to God, not only in words but, more important, in deeds. The first duty of a Muslim, as we have seen, is to do so. The *shahadah* is not simply claiming to believe in God and Prophet Muhammad but commitment to give evidence of that belief in one's actions. Those who encounter severe difficulties in the effort to be true to that commitment, even having to pay for it with their lives, are called martyrs. The term for "martyr" in Arabic is *shahid,* a cognate of the term *shahadah,* and it means exactly what "martyr" means in English, coming from the Greek root meaning "to bear witness" of one's belief through actions.

The designation of martyr in general can apply to anyone who dies an untimely death as a believer, as expressed in the earliest surviving compendium of Islamic law:

Yahya related to me from Malik from Sumayy, the [client] of Abu Bakr ibn 'Abd ar-Rahman from Abu Salih from Abu Hurayra that the Messenger of Allah, may Allah bless him and grant him peace, said, . . . "Martyrs are five: the one killed by a plague, the one killed by a disease of the belly, the one who drowns, the one killed by a collapsing building and the martyr in the path of Allah."[5]

But it is the last category, those who die in the struggle to establish God's law on earth, who are most often referred to as martyrs and whose sacrifice brings

---

[4]Translated by Fazlur Rahman, *Major Themes of the Qur'an,* 118–119.

[5]Imam Malik ibn Anas, *Al-Muwatta of Imam Malik ibn Anas: The First Formulation of Islamic Law,* translated by Aisha Abdurrahman Bewley (London and New York: Kegan Paul International, 1989), 49.

highest respect. There are many reports of Prophet Muhammad praising such martyrs and encouraging his followers to become martyrs in battle by explaining the great reward they will receive. For example:

> Yahya related to me from Malik from Yahya ibn Sa'id that the Messenger of Allah, may Allah bless him and grant him peace, was stimulating people to do jihad, mentioning the Garden. One of [his followers from Medina] was eating some dates he had in his hand, and said, "Am I so desirous of this world that I should sit until I finish them?" He threw aside what was in his hand and took his sword and fought until he was slain.[6]

In fact, no greater glory can be accorded a Muslim than to be called a martyr in the path of God. God himself is described as encouraging martyrdom. As early legal scholar Malik ibn Anas related:

> Yahya related to me from Malik from Abu'z-Zinad from al-A'raj from Abu Hurayra that the Messenger of Allah, may Allah bless him and grant him peace, said, "Allah laughs at two men. One of them kills the other, but each of them will enter the Garden; one fights in the way of Allah and is killed, then Allah turns in forgiveness to the killer, so he fights (in the way of Allah) and also becomes a martyr."[7]

Included in these reports are the Prophet's own expressions of desire to die in battle. For example:

> Yahya related to me from Malik from Abu'z-Zinad from al-A'raj from Abu Hurayra that the Messenger of Allah, may Allah bless him and grant him peace, said, "By He in whose hand my self is! I would like to fight in the way of Allah and be killed, then be brought to life again so I could be killed, and then be brought to life again so I could be killed."
>
> Abu Hurayra said three times, "I testify to it by Allah!"[8]

Obviously, not everyone can become a martyr in battle to defend the Muslim community against attack or to spread God's law. Doing battle in this way is considered a duty only for enough people to make sure the job is done. Some scholars interpret that to mean that going to war is a duty only when the survival of the community depends upon it. But whether in self-defense or to spread the peace and security of Islam, war must be properly declared and conducted according to strict regulations that prohibit the attack of civilians, women, and children. Under those conditions, when war is necessary and fought fairly, it is sanctioned by God and those who fall in battle are promised rich reward:

> Yahya related to me from Malik from Yahya ibn Sa'id that Mu'adh ibn Jabal said, "There are two military expeditions. There is one military expedition in which valuables are spent, things are made easy for a fellow, the authorities are obeyed, and corruption is avoided. That military expedition is all good.

---

[6]Imam Malik, 182.

[7]Imam Malik, 180.

[8]Imam Malik, 180.

There is a military expedition in which valuables are not spent, things are not made easy, the authorities are not obeyed, and corruption is not avoided. The one who fights in that military expedition does not return with reward."[9]

For Shi'i Muslims, martyrdom is also an ideal type, based on a distinct historical legacy. The hero of Shi'i Islam is Imam Hussein, grandson of Prophet Muhammad. When Prophet Muhammad died, there was disagreement among the Muslim community regarding who should take up the leadership position vacated by the Prophet. The majority believed that no successor (in the literal sense of *khalifah* or caliph) had been designated, nor that the Prophet had established a new political system. They believed that Muhammad's prophetic mission was unique and that it ended with his death. They therefore thought that they should simply choose from among themselves the person they considered to be best qualified to lead in terms not only of administrative ability but also of wisdom and piety. They sought from among themselves the person they thought most nearly emulated the Prophet's way of doing things, that is, his sunnah. (They are therefore called Sunni Muslims.) Upon agreement of the majority, they chose the Prophet's close companion Abu Bakr. When he died they chose another companion, 'Umar, then 'Uthman, and then the Prophet's cousin and son-in-law 'Ali. A minority, however, believed all along that leadership of the community should stay within the Prophet's family. Since he died leaving no sons, the closest male relative was 'Ali. (This group was called the "faction" or *shi'ah* of 'Ali, which was shortened to *shi'ah*. In English we use the adjectival form, Shi'is or Shi'ites.) When 'Ali was chosen to be the fourth successor to Prophet Muhammad, it was on the basis of agreement among the community, rather than his family relationship to the Prophet. But the Shi'is had held that 'Ali was the only legitimate successor to the Prophet. As a result, they consider the first three caliphs to be usurpers and 'Ali to be the first true imam.

Within four years of 'Ali's assumption of the caliphate, organized opposition arose against him under the banner of a family that came to be called the Umayyads. When 'Ali chose arbitration as a way to end a battle between the two sides, some of his former supporters deserted him and accused him of compromise with oppressors, and he was assassinated. Thereafter, the majority accepted the Umayyads as legitimate caliphs, while 'Ali's son (with his wife Fatimah, Prophet Muhammad's daughter) Hassan was declared the rightful successor in Iraq. When he died, after retiring to Medina, he was declared a martyr on the assumption that he had been killed by his Umayyad opponents. His resistance to the Umayyads was considered exemplary.

Then Hassan's younger brother Hussein was declared the third imam. Hussein likewise refused to acknowledge the Umayyad caliph. In the year 680 C.E., Hussein and a group of his followers were massacred by Umayyad forces at Karbala, near Kufa (in Iraq). Hussein is therefore considered the quintessential martyr of Shi'i Islam. His battle against the Umayyads represents in Shi'i thought the heroic stand of the righteous minority against the powerful and self-serving majority. An ideal in Shi'i Islam, this martyrdom is commemorated annually

---

[9]Imam Malik, 182.

during the first ten days of the month of Muharram, and especially on the tenth day, known as 'Ashura', when plays depicting the drama are enacted, and to a lesser extent, forty days later.

Suffering even to the extent of giving one's life in the struggle for justice is therefore a dominant paradigm in Shi'i Islam. This point was expressed recently by Iranian President Khatami in a discussion of why religion is more popular in the Muslim world than in the Christian West, where religious leaders often colluded in oppression:

> People have always witnessed the fiery and bloodied face of religious revolutionaries who have risen to fight oppression and despotism. . . . Haven't most martyrs of truth been religious activists? Is it not the case that over the past hundred years religion has been the greatest champion of the fight against despotic agents of colonialism?[10]

However, martyrdom is not the only route to elevated status in Islam. There is a rich heritage as well of people who achieve extraordinary piety through prayer, learning, and meditation. This model is especially important in Islam's Sufi tradition, often called Islam's mystical tradition but more accurately described as its spiritualist or contemplative tradition. In fact, participation in the Sufi way is far more widespread than participation in military jihad. Sufism is a complex phenomenon, manifesting itself in ways ranging from simple piety and magnanimity to extraordinary asceticism and feats of spiritual discipline within specifically defined groups or "orders." Yet Sufis share in common the goal of internalizing the will of God, of becoming so imbued with grace that one overcomes all selfishness and acts solely through motivation to please God. Those who achieve this goal, though none would ever claim it for herself or himself, are sometimes known by the term *waliy* or "friend of God."[11] They are recognized within their communities for their outstanding acts of generosity and piety.

There is thus a range of designations for people who show extraordinary virtue in Islam, whether in charity and compassion, learning and wisdom, or courage and leadership. Such terms are often applied informally by the people most affected by their virtues, demonstrating the identifying characteristic of outstanding virtue in Islam. As discussed above, it is not a matter of mere ritual, "praying for show" or to gain glory. Essential to all virtuous acts in Islam is the intention; in fact, all essential rituals must begin with declaration of proper intention in order to be meritorious. Even the most generous gift, given without the intention to further God's will, is empty in the sight of God. By contrast, however, even the most invisible effort to dedicate one's life to the cause of God is considered part of the virtuous struggle. As the famous hadith puts it, valor in a just war is part of "the lesser jihad," while the daily effort to manifest true belief in righteous behavior is "the greater jihad."

---

[10]Khatami, 73.

[11]*Wilayah* (friendship/closeness to God) is a complex concept in Sufi thought, with a number of interpretations. For an introductory discussion, see Fazlur Rahman, *Islam* (Chicago and London: University of Chicago Press, 1979), 135ff.

COMMENTARIES

Judaism on Islam

by JACOB NEUSNER

Judaism concurs with Islam that man is created by God and is expected to do God's will. Man enjoys free will, for the exercise of which he is, therefore, responsible. Judaism's paradigm of man's relationship with God, which is the story of Adam and Eve in Eden, yields a doctrine congruent with that of Islam. Professor Sonn's description of the human condition—man is given moral freedom, for instance— could well serve for Judaism. That congruence extends even to a shared vocabulary, *nafs* in Arabic corresponding to *nefesh*, "soul," in Hebrew. Here too, in context *nefesh* would better be rendered, "self" or "person," just as in Islam.

"Charity" or *tsedakah* represents a principal virtue in Judaism as in Islam. But the imitation of God encompasses a variety of actions, all of them virtuous:

> R. Ishmael taught, "'This is my God and I will glorify him' (Ex. 15:2). But is it possible for a human being [directly] to glorify his creator? [No.]
>
> "Rather, 'I will glorify him' by means of [my performance of] religious duties. [Thus]: I shall make before God a glorious *lulav* (Lev. 23:39–40), *sukkah* (Lev. 23:42), *shofar* (Lev. 25:9), fringes (Num. 15:37–39), and phylacteries (Deut. 6:8)."
>
> [As an alternative interpretation of Ex. 15:2], Abba Saul says, "[The phrase 'I shall glorify him' (Ex. 15:2) means] 'I shall emulate him.' [Therefore], just as God is merciful and kind, so too you must be merciful and kind."
>
> Yerushalmi Peah 1:1 VI:A (trans. Roger Brooks)

In many ways, therefore, Judaism and Islam concur on basics, though each has its points of emphasis and proportion.

Personal virtue takes many forms but derives from a single source, expressed at B. Makkot, cited above: "Habakkuk further came and based them on one, as it is said, 'But the righteous shall live by his faith' (Habakkuk 2:4)." The Arabic and the Hebrew roots for "trust" once more intersect. An attitude of faith in God, meaning trust and reliance, forms the foundation of all virtue, and on that, Judaism and Islam concur. So too "bearing witness" in Islam and "sanctifying the name of God in public" in Judaism coincide: what one does attests to the state of one's faith.

While Judaism concurs with Islam that martyrdom represents the highest embodiment of exceptional virtue, it calls for martyrdom for only three causes. One must accept death rather than profane God's name in public through an act of idolatry, fornication, or murder. But there is another kind of virtue, which is renunciation, self-criticism, recognition of one's own faults and expressing regret for them. Here is a dramatic account of how a great sage acknowledged his own arrogance and atoned:

> There is the case of R. Simeon b. Eleazar, who was coming from the house of his master in Migdal Eder, riding on an ass and making his way along the sea

shore. He saw an unusually ugly man. He said to him, "Empty head! what a beast you are! Is it possible that everyone in your town is as ugly as you are?"

He said to him, "And what can I do about it? Go to the craftsman who made me and tell him, 'How ugly is that utensil that you have made!'"

When R. Simeon b. Eleazar realized that he had sinned, he got off his ass and prostrated himself before the man, saying to him, "I beg you to forgive me."

He said to him, "I shall not forgive you until you go to the craftsman who made me and tell him, 'How ugly is that utensil that you have made!'"

He ran after the man for three miles. The people of the town came out to meet him. They said toward him, "Peace be to you, my lord."

He said to them, "Whom do you call, 'my lord'?"

They said to him, "To the one who is going along after you."

He said to them, "If this is a 'my lord,' may there not be many more like him in Israel."

They said to him, "God forbid! and what has he done to you?"

He said to them, "Thus and so did he do to me."

They said to him, "Nonetheless, forgive him."

He said to them, "Lo, I forgive him, on the condition that he not make a habit of acting in that way."

On that same day R. Simeon entered the great study-house that was his and gave an exposition: "'One should always be as soft as a reed and not as tough as a cedar.'

"In the case of a reed, all the winds in the world can go on blowing against it but it sways with them, so that when the winds grow silent, it reverts and stands in its place. And what is the destiny of a reed? In the end a pen is cut from it with which to write a scroll of the Torah.

"But in the case of a cedar it will not stand in place, but when the south wind blows against it, it uproots the cedar and turns it over. And what is the destiny of a cedar? Foresters come and cut it down and use it to roof houses, and the rest they toss into the fire.

"On the basis of this fact they have said, 'One should always be as soft as a reed and not as tough as a cedar.'"

The Fathers according to Rabbi Nathan XLI:III.1

Simeon is a sage but not exemplary in his conduct, until he realized that he had sinned and so repented and atoned. He represents the highest form of virtue in Judaism: the proud man, the sage, who humbles himself and acknowledges his sin against God's creature. In this definition of matters, Judaism vastly differs from Islam and its martyrs in battle.

Christianity on Islam

by BRUCE CHILTON

Stewards or deputies have a distinctly mixed reputation within the New Testament. One, standing between the owner and the disappointing yield of a vineyard, promises preparatory work to assure productivity (Luke 13:6–9, the apparent allusion in the first paragraph of the treatment of this question from the point of view of Islam). More typically, however, stewards are corrupt and violent (Matthew 21:33–46; Mark 12:1–12; Luke 20:9–19). The crisis of any model of stewardship for an understanding of humanity's relationship to God is represented in Luke 16:1–8. There, the dishonesty of the steward is turned into a virtue, when he begins to forgive debts as his master, and heavenly Father, would have us all forgive sins. The undergirding logic of Christianity denies the adequacy of stewards as an analogy of our standing in relation to God. Stewards need to learn to become sons and daughters of God, enacting the divine will in defiance of any ordinary calcuation of profit and loss.

The capacity to choose to do that is taken to be inherently human within Christianity, as it is within Islam. There is no confusion of divine omniscience with determinism, because God's thorough knowledge of us in no sense obliges us to make the particular choices we do. There is also a profound agreement between the two religions in the insistence that people have always had the guidance they need to make informed decisions. God's invisible power and divinity have been palpable, cognitively available, in the evidence of creation, according to Paul (Romans 1:20); the truth of God is not only a form of words that one must hear in order to be able to consider, but part of the givenness of being human and being self-aware. That givenness, although it is radically spiritual in resurrected life, is also emphatically bodily: that is an axiom from the earliest witness to the resurrection (1 Corinthians 15:44) through the Apostles' Creed (in which the resurrection of the body for all is explicitly stipulated).

The embodiment of faith also pertains to the insistence, best articulated in the Letter of James, that faith and works belong together. No preaching can legitimately be proclaimed to the poor unless and until their misery is dealt with (James 2:1–7). Because the word of God, which is the object of faith, is creative and intervening, an authentic response to it cannot be characterized by passivity. That is the orientation that makes social activism the kind of imperative in Christianity that it is in Islam, as well.

A particular challenge in the study of Islam is that the Qur'an insists upon a theory of "the people of the book" in previous ages, to the effect that their failure was one of both belief and action. On a recent visit to Qumran, my bedouin guide informed me that, at that site, Jews worshipped the sun, moon, and stars, prior to the coming of the Prophet. Later, as his companion drove me to Masada, he asked me what my line of work was. When I told him, he allowed as how his reference to astrology at Qumran may have been a bit exaggerated. The difficulty here is cognate to the anti-Semitic tendencies within the New Testament. Is it necessary for believers to embrace the oppositional stance of their own Scriptures? I take it that the possibility of approving the faith and deeds of Jews and Sabians and Christians in Islam functions in much the same way as, in Paul's formulation, God's judgment is consequent on what people actually do—in accord with his will or not—not on their acceptance of specific forms of religion (Romans 2:12–16).

It is for that reason that the divine apportionment of good character, which is emphasized in the exposition, must also seem axiomatic from the perspective of Christianity. For that very reason, the illustration of the struggle for this character with military images, and examples of heroism in combat, may seem jarring to some. But Jesus also used going to war as an image of total commitment to divine sovereignty (Luke 14:31–33). Spiritual warfare is an appropriate metaphor for the acquisition of our true natures, provided it is clearly understood as metaphor.

Hinduism on Islam

by Brian K. Smith

Despite the radically different religious frameworks that distinguish Islam and Hinduism, there are a few interesting points of similarity when it comes to the topic of virtue. The first of these is the notion that human beings are created as they are for a purpose: "acceptance of one's purpose on earth . . . [is] not only correct belief but the route to security and well-being." In Islam, an omniscient God has given every community (and each individual within those communities) "sufficient guidance . . . to fulfill the divine will." Human failings are thus attributed either to wrong choices or to ignorance. In Hinduism, too, human beings are born into groups whose duties are set forth plainly. One either conforms to one's inborn nature, and pursues the "good," or one attempts to "swim upstream" against one's nature. Ignorance, in this sense, is usually not given as a reason for moral failures in Hinduism; it is hard to be ignorant about one's caste and the social expectations connected to birth into a particular caste.

Second, in both traditions there is no hard-and-fast line between social and personal virtue. Professor Sonn writes that "all virtue in Islam is social virtue," and mutatis mutandis, so too in Hinduism. In both traditions, given the value of the group (the community of believers in Islam, and the caste and sect in Hinduism), the individual's social and personal virtue are nearly one and the same. Finally, the mandate to "dedicate one's actions to God" in Islam finds its match in theistic Hinduism. The Bhagavad Gita's teachings regarding the fulfillment of one's duties with the "fruits" of actions offered up to Krishna seem to point in the same direction as Islam's teachings on conforming one's actions to God's will. In both cases, albeit from within very different contexts, these religions portray human virtue as the selfless engagement of action in the world regarded as a kind of sacrifice to God; and in both cases, it is "mindfulness of God" that is among the highest goals.

But what is called the "paradigmatic value" of Islam, social justice, cannot be said to be a heavily emphasized feature of traditional Hinduism. Be that as it may, in recent times social reformers have emerged in Hinduism and have, from within the tradition, offered visions of social justice that have and are redirecting Hindus from the excesses of caste and some of the more fatalistic features of the doctrines of karma and rebirth.

Buddhism on Islam

by Charles Hallisey

Buddhism and Islam both are aware of human limitation and weakness in the accounts of the life of virtue, but they differ markedly in their estimation of human potential. In the beginning and the end, humans are portrayed in Islam with imagery of being a servant. Humans *submit* to God, and the sincere recognition of this status is key to the life of virtue, the very means to turning to the resources we have to withstand the influence of our imperfections and to make correct choices for ourselves and others. In Buddhism, perfection is potentially possible for all beings, however imperfect they may be at the moment. We may be self-centered now, but we can still become of benefit to others; we may be impatient and quick to anger now, but we can still cultivate tolerance for the foibles of others through our own efforts; we are now in the midst of ignorance and this conditions all of our actions, but we can become wise and thus learn to act freely and effectively in the world. Moreover, perfection is what we owe ourselves, and just as the lotus flower rises above the stagnant, fetid water in which the plant grows to display untainted beauty that delights others, so we can reach a state of perfection that transcends all limitations that we currently experience. This state of perfection, in which we become of inexplicable value to others, is ultimately what we owe ourselves and no one else.

SUMMARY

Islamic scripture, the Qur'an, teaches that human beings were created as God's stewards on earth. Our job is to "establish justice," for a just society, healthy and balanced, is what God wants us to establish and maintain. The Qur'an further reveals that a just society is one whose overall well-being is measured by that of its weakest members—orphans, widows, the elderly, the marginalized—not by that of its powerful elites. We have been given guidance in the form of the Qur'an and the example of Prophet Muhammad (the Sunnah), as well as intelligence and freedom to make the choices required to fulfill our duties. Human beings will be judged by God according to the extent to which they worked to recreate in society the equality all human beings share in the eyes of their creator. Virtue, in the Islamic view, therefore begins with correct belief or faith (iman): accepting the existence of a single, omnipotent, just and merciful God who created us according to his plan. Integrally linked to correct belief is correct action. Islam teaches that those who truly believe in God will be motivated to do God's will by treating others as they would want to be treated. This entails being honest, dealing with others fairly, taking family and social responsibility, and being generous with those in need. The most generalized term for virtue in Islam is taqwa, "taking refuge" in God. It encompasses correct belief, resulting in submission to the will of God, that produces a conscience that guides behavior that promotes the well-being of both individuals and society.

GLOSSARY

amanah "trust"—the responsibility humans were entrusted with at creation; the purpose of human existence

'aqidah Islamic belief system or creed

fitrah   innate good character; Islam teaches that all people are born with innate good character

'ibadah   "servitude"; ideal relationship of believers to God

iman   faith

islam   "submission" to the will of God

khalifah   "successor" of Prophet Muhammad in political rule; more generally, "steward" or "vicegerent" of God; humans' role on earth

muslim   one who submits to the will of God; one who lives according to Islamic law

sadaqah   "charity"

shahadah   "bearing witness," vowing to demonstrate one's belief in God and the teachings of the Qur'an through correct practice and behavior. This is the first requirement ("pillar") for all Muslims.

shahid   martyr

taqwa   "piety" or "righteousness"; seeking refuge in God through obedience to the divine will

wilayah   "friendship" or closeness to God

DISCUSSION QUESTIONS

1.   What is the purpose of human existence in Islam?
2.   Does Islam teach predestination or does it teach that human beings have moral responsibility?
3.   What does Islam teach about basic human character (*fitrah*)?
4.   How will human beings be judged by God, according to Islamic teaching?
5.   How does the Qur'an explain the human tendency toward self-deception and destructive behavior?

 **INFOTRAC**

If you would like additional information related to the material discussed here, you can visit our Web site: http://www.wadsworth.com

4

Hinduism

BY BRIAN K. SMITH

CONVENTIONAL ANSWERS VERSUS THIS RELIGIOUS TRADITION: WHO ARE WE REALLY?

The nature of the self is one of the perennial and most important questions in the Hindu tradition. But as we shall see, the "self" can mean several different things. In Hinduism there is, first of all, a conceptualization of a self that is the product of our own actions; this self is also the agent of good or bad acts that will determine the nature of one's identity in the future. But, second, there is said to be a Self (called the atman) that is not bound up in ego, action, rebirth, and personal individuality—a changeless and eternal Self that is no different from the underlying essence of reality as a whole. Recognizing this transcendent Self as one's true identity and abandoning the lower or even false self that is the ego and that undergoes transmigration brings one to the state of liberation or freedom known as *moksha*.

In the earliest period of the Hindu tradition, the self was regarded as literally a construct or product of the sacrificial rituals one performed. "Man is born into a world made by himself," declares one text (Satapatha Brahmana 6.2.2.7), which is to say that one's identity in this world was the outcome of the sacrifices one offers. Conversely, the biologically given "self" was considered to be faulty and incomplete. One is conceived as an embryo in the mother's womb, but the biological self is at this stage more or less identical with the father, whose semen is a microcosmic double of himself:

> In a person, this one (i.e., the self) first becomes an embryo. That which is semen is the luminous power extracted from all the parts (of the man). In the self, truly, one bears another self. When he emits this into a woman, he then begets it. This is one's first birth.
>
> Aitareya Brahmana 2.4.1

The process of transforming this redundant self and creating a new and independent self is a matter of ritual work. Ritual action, or karma, creates a proper and independent human being out of the biological self (which, as we have seen, is without such transformation regarded as identical with the father's self). One type of such rituals are called the samskaras, rites of passage performed at critical junctures in the life of a child and youth. These life-cycle rituals are still performed by many Hindus today, especially those of the upper castes. Samskaras are rituals of ontological healing, construction, and perfection; they are aimed, as one scholar has written, not only at "the formal purification of the body but at sanctifying, impressing, refining and perfecting the entire individuality of the recipient."[1] Samskaras and other rituals thus create a true self out of the raw material of the biological self.

Among these ceremonies, the most important is the *upanayana,* a rite of initiation into the study of the sacred texts of the Veda and the performance of sacrificial rituals described in the Veda. It is regarded as a "second birth," a birth "out of the Veda" or "out of the sacrifice." A new self is created out of this ritual, one that is infused with all the rights and responsibilities of not only adulthood but membership into caste society. A boy born into a family of the so-called "twice-born" classes is, up until the *upanayana,* regarded as on a par with a member of the servant or Shudra class. As such, he is both considered to be totally irresponsible and prohibited from participation in Vedic ritual:

> They do not put any restrictions on the acts of (a child) before the initiation, for he is on the level with a Shudra before his birth through the Veda.
>
> Baudhayana Dharma Sutra 1.2.3.6

> No religious rite can be performed by (a boy) before the initiation, because he is on the level with a Shudra before his birth through the Veda.
>
> Vasistha Dharma Smriti 2.6

But this ritual of initiation—initiation into the study of the Veda under the tutelage of a guru, and also into caste society—did not simply create a generic "twice-born" human being, but rather created humans who were thought to be of different general types, members of particular social classes. The caste system of Hindu India assumes not only that individuals are born into a particular family and class (due, as we shall see, to the karma one carries from past lives) but also that people conform to their inborn nature by means of the activities they perform. Furthermore, the rituals performed upon children of the various classes help to create class-specific selves. Or as one text puts it, members of different castes are distinguished not only by different inborn natures but also by being constituted or made distinct through the ritual samskaras (Vasistha Dharma Sutra 4.1).

The notion that one's true self is, at least in part, ritually constructed has persisted throughout the history of Hinduism. The samskaras and other rituals continue to be practiced in order to both purify a biologically given (and therefore impure and faulty) self, and create a new and more viable self. But already by the time of the early Upanishads (ca. 700–800 B.C.E.) new conceptions about both the nature of the self and the relationship between personal identity and action arose. And these new ideas would alter the face of the Hindu religion irrevocably.

---

[1]Raj Bali Pandey, *Hindu Samskaras: Socio-Religious Study of the Hindu Sacraments,* 2nd ed. (New Delhi: Motilal Banarsidass, 1969), 17.

In the ancient sacrificial texts known collectively as the Veda, ritual action was thought to have important, indeed crucial, consequences for the contours of one's self. Ritual acts determined who you are now (your ritual resume being the index of your present identity), who you are becoming, and who you will be in the future. One of the revolutionary innovations of the Upanishads was to extend this cause–and–effect relationship of ritual action and self-identity to all action. From this time on, according to the so-called "law of karma" and re-birth, one's present self is regarded as the product of one's past actions (of all sorts, not just ritual actions), and one's future identity is shaped by one's present actions.

The law of karma presupposes that the self undergoes continual rebirth, reap-ing in lifetime after lifetime as the fruits of its own karma. Rebirth is often de-picted in terms of metaphors. Reincarnation is compared to the changing of clothes as the soul sheds one body for another: "As a man discards worn-out clothes to put on new and different ones, so the embodied self discards its worn out bodies to take on other new ones."[2] In the following, rebirth is portrayed as similar to a caterpillar moving from one blade of grass to another, or a weaver who weaves a "newer and more attractive" design out of her yarn:

> It is like this. As a caterpillar, when it comes to the tip of a blade of grass, reaches out to a new foothold and draws itself onto it, so does the self, after it has knocked down this body and rendered it unconscious, reaches out to a new foothold and draws itself onto it. It is like this. As a weaver, after she has removed the colored yarn, weaves a different design that is newer and more attractive, so the self, after it has knocked down this body and rendered it unconscious, makes for himself a different figure that is newer and more attractive. . . .[3]

One's rebirth is directed by the karmic record he or she carries from past lives. The self one has from birth, from this point of view, is the sum total of one's past karma, the product of the ethical behavior performed in past lives:

> What a man turns out to be depends on how he acts and on how he con-ducts himself. If his actions are good, he will turn into something good. If his actions are bad, he will turn into something bad. A man turns into something good by good action and into something bad by bad action.
>
> Brhadaranyaka Upanishad 4.4.5

The type of rebirth we receive is determined by our karma, which is created by our actions, but also by our desires. Bad or good, we are attached to our de-sires and our actions in this life and future lives; rebirth is the necessary end–result of such attachment and the karma thus produced. As the passage below indicates,

---

[2]Bhagavad Gita 2.22. This and all subsequent citations from this text are taken from Barbara Stoler Miller, translator, *The Bhagavad-Gita: Krishna's Counsel in Time of War* (New York: Bantam Books, 1986).

[3]Brhadaranyaka Upanishad 4.4.3–4. This and all other quotations from the Upanishads are found in Patrick Olivelle, *Upanisads: A New Translation* (New York and Oxford: Oxford University Press, 1996).

one is reborn as a being and in a place "to which his mind and character cling." We are reborn, in other words, in accordance to our desire, our action, and our attachments:

> A man who's attached goes with his action,
>> to that very place to which
>> his mind and character cling.
> Reaching the end of his action,
>> of whatever he has done in this world—
> From that world he returns
>> back to this world,
>> back to action.
>
> Brhadaranyaka Upanishad 4.4.6

One thus gets precisely the kind of self in future lives that one not only deserves but in some sense wants. For it is desire that lies at the origin of karma; one "turns out to be in accordance" with the karmic process set into motion originally by desire:

> And so people say: "A person here consists simply of desire." A man resolves in accordance with his desire, acts in accordance with his resolve, and turns out to be in accordance with his action.
>
> Brhadaranyaka Upanishad 4.4.5

Desire, resolve, and action (the components of karma) direct the course of an individual's future life both in this lifetime and in subsequent births.

Propelled by karma into one new life after another, the self is re-created in each new womb by means of a particular, karmically informed play of the three "qualities," "constituents," "strands," or "characteristics" of nature. These are (1) the quality of "lucidity," of lightness, purity, and goodness; (2) "energy," the quality of activity and passion; and (3) "darkness," the characteristic of inertia, sluggishness, and torpor. The selves of all beings, including humans, are composed of a mixture of these three qualities, with one or another predominating depending on the karma one carries with him or her from the past:

> Know that lucidity, energy, and darkness are the three qualities of the self, through which the great one pervades and endures in all these existences, without exception. Whenever one of these qualities entirely prevails in a body, it makes the particular quality predominant in the embodied (soul). Lucidity is traditionally regarded as knowledge, darkness as ignorance, and energy as passion and hate; this is their form, that enters and pervades all living beings.[4]

Individuals are thus shaped by one or another (or a combination of) these three qualities, depending on their karma. We will see below that these qualities of nature are also correlated with the social classes that make up the basis of the caste system; members of each class receive their innate characteristics at birth because of these qualities.

---

[4]Manu 12.24–26. This and all subsequent quotations are from Wendy Doniger with Brian K. Smith, *The Laws of Manu* (London: Penguin Books, 1991).

We have noted at the beginning of this chapter, however, that Hinduism recognizes two selves. One we have already identified: a self that is shaped by action and karma, that is reborn over and over again according to karma, and is molded by one or another of the qualities of nature that will prevail in an individual's makeup, again according to that individual's karmic record. But there is another, and more real, Self within every individual. A person is made up of what one text calls a "double spirit," one transient and the other eternal, supreme, and immutable:

> There is a double spirit of man
> in the world, transient and eternal—
> transient in all creatures,
> eternal at the summit of existence.
> Other is the supreme spirit of man,
> called the supreme self,
> the immutable lord who enters
> and sustains the three worlds.
>
> Bhagavad Gita 15.16–17

Or, as another text puts it, man's double nature is likened to two birds sitting on the same tree (i.e., the body). One bird is active, the producer of karma; the other merely "looks on," contented and inactive. It is this latter that is the true Self, the atman, the Lord:

> Two birds, companions and friends,
> nestle on the very same tree.
> One of them eats a tasty fig;
> the other, not eating, looks on.
> Stuck on the very same tree,
> one person grieves, deluded
> by her who is not the Lord;
> But when he sees the other,
> the contented Lord—and his majesty—
> his grief disappears.
>
> Mundaka Upanishad 3.1.1–2

The text continues by saying that when an individual recognizes the true Self, which is no other than the cosmic principle of unity called the *brahman*, he "attains the highest identity" and becomes liberated from all suffering, from all karma ("the good and bad") and from all subsequent rebirth:

> When the seer sees that Person,
> the golden-colored, the creator, the Lord,
> as the womb of *brahman*;
> Then, shaking off the good and the bad,
> the wise man becomes spotless,
> and attains the highest identity.
>
> Mundaka Upanishad 3.1.3

In other contexts, this higher Self is also distinguished from the lower self by means of its inactivity. The supreme Self is outside the realm of karma—it is without origin and without qualities; it is unchanging and "does not act." Furthermore, this Self is common to all creatures and is the principle of unity that underlies apparent diversity:

> He really sees who sees
> that all actions are performed
> by nature alone and that the self
> is not an actor.
> When he perceives the unity
> existing in separate creatures
> and how they expand from unity,
> he attains the infinite spirit.
> Beginningless, without qualities,
> the supreme self is unchanging;
> even abiding in a body, Arjuna,
> it does not act, nor is it defiled.
> Just as the all-pervading space
> remains unsullied in its subtlety,
> so the self in every body
> remains unsullied.
>
> Bhagavad Gita 13.29–32

The "subtle body" or essential Self or soul is called the *jiva* in the following text, and is the part of the individual that survives death. The *jiva,* said to be in the "form of a man the size of a thumb," experiences the consequences of karma but remains unaffected by karma. This Self is immortal and endures the dissolution of the body at death:

Earth, wind, sky, fire and water—these are the seed of the body of all who have bodies. The body made of these five elements is an artificial and impermanent thing which turns to ashes. The jiva has the form of a man the size of a thumb; this subtle body is taken on in order to experience (the fruits of karma). That subtle body does not turn to ashes even in the blazing fire in hell; it is not destroyed in water, even after a long time, nor by weapons, swords or missiles, nor by very sharp thorns or heated iron or stone, or by the embrace of a heated image, or even by a fall from a very high place. It is not burnt or broken.[5]

This true Self—"immense, unborn" and the "lord of all"—cannot be affected by virtue nor diminished by vice, for these after all are forms of activity and this Self transcends the world of karma and is wholly untouched by it:

---

[5]Visnudharmottara Purana (Bombay, no date) 116.1–12; 2.113–114. Translated in Wendy Doniger O'Flaherty, "Karma and Rebirth in the Vedas and Puranas," in *idem,* editor, *Karma and Rebirth in Classical Indian Traditions* (Berkeley and Los Angeles: University of California Press, 1980), 16.

This immense, unborn self . . . there, in that space within the heart, he lies—
the controller of all, the lord of all, the ruler of all! He does not become more
by good actions or in any way less by bad actions. He is the lord of all! He is
the ruler of creatures!

Brhadaranyaka Upanishad 4.4.22

Thus, while virtues of both social and individual sorts are to be practiced, and
vices to be avoided, such morality only affects the lower self, the self that wishes
to improve its karma in the hopes of a better rebirth. For those who have realized and thoroughly identified themselves with the higher Self, such ordinary
morality is irrelevant, as we shall see in the final section of this chapter.

WHAT ARE THE SOCIAL VIRTUES?

The social virtues in Hinduism pertain to the "lower" self—the self that produces and reaps karma of either good or bad, pleasant or unpleasant, types. What
we owe to our society in Hinduism is governed by a concept of absolutely critical importance to this religion: *dharma*. This term means "duty," "moral obligation," "religious law," or "principle," and guides both the public and private
life of the individual. Following one's dharma is in most texts regarded as the
supreme virtue—the secret to maximizing the accumulation of good karma for
the lower self as well as the principle of social order, interdependence, and mutual relations between the classes.

Dharma comes in two forms in Hinduism: "general" or "universal" dharma,
which is theoretically applicable to all Hindus regardless of their class or caste,
and "particular" dharma (*svadharma*, literally meaning "one's own dharma"),
which is duty and virtue tailored to one's individual circumstance. Social virtues
are included in both types of dharma. Lists of the traits and qualities associated
with "general" dharma include things like goodwill toward one's fellow men and
women, the importance of speaking the truth when conversing with others, not
stealing, maintaining forbearance and tolerance in one's dealings with others, and
being generous and giving to those in need and to those pursuing religious lives
that entail begging for alms. Especially important is the generally applicable duty
to practice nonviolence toward others. "A resolute, gentle, controlled, nonviolent man, who does not associate with people whose ways are cruel, wins
heaven through his control and generosity" (Manu 4.246).

The social virtues as they relate to particularized duty (*svadharma*) are guided
by the birth and circumstances of the individual and how the individual is to fit
into society. One's *svadharma* does not always conform in every respect to the
virtues adhering to general dharma. Creatures of all sorts, including human beings, are produced by nature with different natures, so to speak, and the doctrine
of *svadharma* requires the individual to follow his or her inborn nature, regardless as to whether or not this places one in conflict with general dharma. Some
are born with the ability to easily practice the social virtues demanded by general dharma—honesty, truthfulness, nonviolence, and so on. Others, however,
are born dishonest, violent, and so forth because of the "innate activity" the creator has assigned to different individuals:

And in order to distinguish innate activities, he (the creator god) distinguished right from wrong, and he yoked these creatures with the pairs, happiness and unhappiness and so forth. . . . And whatever innate activity the Lord yoked each (creature) to at first, that (creature) by himself engaged in that very activity as he was created again and again. Harmful or harmless, gentle or cruel, right or wrong, truthful or lying—the (activity) he gave to each (creature) in creation kept entering it by itself. Just as the seasons by themselves take on the distinctive signs of the seasons as they change, so embodied beings by themselves take on their innate activities, each his own.

Manu 1.26, 28–30

The "innate activity" assigned to every being is that person's *svadharma,* and an individual has the social obligation to follow the occupation and the personality characteristics distinctive to his or her birth. Each individual is born into a particular class or caste, and each of the classes from the time of creation are also sometimes understood in terms of the Hindu cosmological doctrine of the three *gunas* or elemental "constituents," "qualities," or "strands" of all creation. As the following text states, the work of the four principal classes of Hindu society is "apportioned by qualities born of their intrinsic being." Therefore, one achieves success and fulfills his social obligations by following his own nature and "his own action":

> There is no being on earth
> or among the gods in heaven
> free from the triad of qualities
> that are born of nature.
> The actions of priests, warriors,
> commoners, and servants
> are apportioned by qualities
> born of their intrinsic being.
> Tranquility, control, penance,
> purity, patience, and honesty,
> knowledge, judgment, and piety
> are intrinsic to the action of a priest.
> Heroism, fiery energy, resolve,
> skill, refusal to retreat in battle,
> charity, and majesty in conduct
> are intrinsic to the action of a warrior.
> Farming, herding cattle, and commerce
> are intrinsic to the action of a commoner;
> action that is essentially service
> is intrinsic to the servant.
> Each one achieves success
> by focusing on his own action;
> hear how one finds success
> by focusing on his own action.
> By his own action a man finds success,

> worshiping the source
> of all creatures' activity,
> the presence pervading all that is.
> Better to do one's own duty imperfectly
> than to do another man's well;
> doing action intrinsic to his being,
> a man avoids guilt.
> Arjuna, a man should not relinquish
> action he is born to, even if it is flawed. . . .
>
> Bhagavad Gita 18.40–48

The social virtues in this religion, then, refer primarily to remaining true to one's inborn nature and fulfilling one's duty by practicing the work and characteristic personality traits of one's class. Doing one's own dharma means assuming the duties that are proper to one's class or caste: "Your own duty done imperfectly is better than another man's done well. It is better to die in one's own duty; another man's duty is perilous" (*Bhagavad Gita* 3.35). Brahmins should practice virtues concerning purity and spirituality; a warrior's calling is to be heroic and brave; a commoner is to be industrious while a servant's highest social virtue is to serve humbly. Conversely, *adharma* or "evil" can refer to doing "another man's duty," or stepping outside the boundaries that were set for you by the class and caste in which you were born. The "confusion of classes, by means of which irreligion, that cuts away the roots, works for the destruction of everything" (Manu 8.353) and must be avoided.

WHAT IS PERSONAL VIRTUE?

If social virtue in this religion primarily revolves around conforming to the duties assigned to the class into which the individual was born, personal virtue concerns the way in which an individual performs his or her social duty. At one level, personal virtue means contentment with one's lot and the determination to fulfill the social duties assigned to one's class. One must eschew the duties of others, even when they sometimes seem preferable to one's own. If, for example, one is born a warrior one must fight, even if the violence one commits contravenes the virtue of nonviolence:

> Look to your own duty;
> do not tremble before it;
> nothing is better for a warrior
> than a battle of sacred duty.
> The doors of heaven open
> for warriors who rejoice
> to have a battle like this
> thrust on them by chance.
> If you fail to wage this war

of sacred duty,
you will abandon your own duty
and fame only to gain evil.
People will tell
of your undying shame,
and for a man of honor
shame is worse than death.
The great chariot warriors will think
you deserted in fear of battle;
you will be despised
by those who held you in esteem.
Your enemies will slander you,
scorning your skill
in so many unspeakable ways—
could any suffering be worse?
If you are killed, you win heaven;
if you triumph, you enjoy the earth;
therefore, Arjuna, stand up
and resolve to fight the battle!
Impartial to joy and suffering,
gain and loss, victory and defeat,
arm yourself for the battle,
lest you fall into evil.

Bhagavad Gita 2.31–38

As the end of this passage makes clear, personal virtue means not only contentment with one's duty but also carrying out one's social obligations with im-
partiality and equanimity. At another level, then, personal virtue concerns
detaching oneself from the world of desire, self-aggrandizement, greed, and am-
bition. One should remain disciplined and focused no matter what one is called
upon to do, and regard action as the impersonal play of nature's qualities (here
translated as "light, "activity," and "delusion"):

He does not dislike light
or activity or delusion;
when they cease to exist
he does not desire them.
He remains disinterested,
unmoved by qualities of nature;
he never wavers, knowing
that only qualities are in motion.
Self-reliant, impartial to suffering
and joy, to clay, stone, or gold,
the resolute man is the same
to foe and friend, to blame and praise.
The same in honor and disgrace,

to ally and enemy, a man
who abandons involvements
transcends the qualities of nature.

Bhagavad Gita 14.22–25

With this yoga-like attitude of detachment, the man of virtue does his duty without regard to the karmic "fruits" of such action. Indeed, if one succeeds in performing necessary action without desire, no karmic consequences follow at all, for as we have seen, karma is ultimately the product of desire. Desireless action is equatable to karma-less action, and when one ceases to produce karma one ceases to fuel the process of rebirth and thus nears final liberation or salvation:

What is action? What is inaction?
Even the poets were confused—
what I shall teach you of action
will free you from misfortune.
One should understand action,
understand wrong action,
and understand inaction too;
the way of action is obscure.
A man who sees inaction in action
and action in inaction
has understanding among men,
disciplined in all action he performs.
The wise say a man is learned
when his plans lack constructs of desire,
when his actions are burned
by the fire of knowledge.
Abandoning attachment to fruits
of action, always content, independent,
he does nothing at all
even when he engages in action.
He incurs no guilt if he has no hope,
restrains his thought and himself,
abandons possessions,
and performs actions with his body only.
Content with whatever comes by chance,
beyond dualities, free from envy,
impartial to failure and success,
he is not bound even when he acts.
When a man is unattached and free,
his reason deep in knowledge,
acting only in sacrifice,
his action is wholly dissolved.

Bhagavad Gita 4.16–23

Such a person of disciplined action, of desireless action, has perfected himself or herself—and attained the highest level of personal virtue—even while performing his or her social duty and perfecting the social virtues.

HOW DOES THIS RELIGION DEFINE CHARACTER, GOOD AND BAD?

In general, Hinduism defines "good character" as fulfilling oneself within the boundaries of one's inborn and inherent nature, including birth into a particular caste; "bad character" is demonstrated by one's rebellion against one's inborn nature. Thus the repeated injunction: it is better to do your own duty poorly than to do another's well. In fact, the more usual assumption is that it is more or less impossible for one to do another's duty well, for to do another's duty at all means that one is going against what Hindu texts regard as the natural order of things.

The crucial term *dharma* in Hinduism is both descriptive and normative— one *should* do what one's nature and character incline one to do. As one scholar has observed, in this religion the only wrong or "evil," and the sign of a bad character, is to strive against one's own innate nature:

> The nature of an individual is the source of his own dharma and that of the group to which he belongs; it is the nature of snakes to bite, of demons to deceive, of gods to give, of sages to control their senses, and so it is their dharma to do so. . . . The only wrong, the only "evil," is to strive against nature. . . . Thus the moral code (dharma) in India is nature, whereas in the west it usually consists of a conflict with nature.[6]

Good character here thus means "going with the grain," that is, enacting and realizing one's inherent nature. But different people are born with different abilities, and Hinduism certainly recognizes and embraces this fact. One of the possible indigenous terms for "character" in this religion would be *adhikara*— "predilection," "competency," "inherent ability," or "predisposition." What is entailed in this concept is the notion that different sorts of people are suited to different types of occupations, that they have different religious paths to follow, and that they are differently capable of different virtues. Good character, from this perspective, means recognizing, following, and maximizing one's innate predispositions.

The point is well illustrated by the following story—and the story within the story:

> Once upon a time there was a potter who badly cut his forehead when he fell down on some broken pots. The wound healed slowly and left an impressive scar. When a famine occurred, the potter and his family went to another region, where he was seen by a king who admired his size and assumed from

---

[6]Wendy Doniger O'Flaherty, *The Origins of Evil in Hindu Mythology* (Berkeley: University of California Press, 1976), 94–95.

his scar that he was a brave fighter. The king put the potter in charge of his army. Shortly thereafter the kingdom was attacked, and as the warriors were about to leave for battle the king happened to ask the potter how he had acquired his scar. When the potter told him, the king was angry and sought to get rid of him. The potter, however, pleaded with the king to be allowed to demonstrate his martial qualities. Thereupon the king told the potter this story:

> A lion while hunting once came upon a fox cub, but it was so small that he pitied it and brought it to his wife, who had two cubs of her own. The three cubs were nursed by the lioness and grew up together. One day, while playing together, they saw an elephant pass. The lion cubs, seeing the hereditary enemy, roared and lashed their tails and were going to attack. The fox was afraid, and dissuaded the lion cubs from doing such a foolhardy thing and ran home, followed by the other two cubs. They all told this incident to their mother, who got the fox cub aside, and told him who he really was, and said, "Son, you are brave, you have learned all there is to learn; you are handsome, but in your line big game is not killed. Go away before my sons realize who you are.

Having made his point, the king dismissed the potter. Potters are born to make pots. It is their nature, determined by their past actions. To pretend to be something one is not would be disastrous both for the potter and for the safety of the kingdom.[7]

Here, indeed, is as good a summary as any of what "good character" means in Hinduism: not pretending you are something you are not. Being yourself, fulfilling your inborn potential, realizing your innate proclivities—this is the way to live a virtuous life and be recognized as a person of "good character."

BEYOND THE NORMAL VIRTUES:
WHO IS THE EXTRAORDINARY PERSON?

Many of the various traditions that comprise Hinduism have assumed that a state of perfection or transcendence is attainable in this lifetime. For such perfected ones, ordinary morality no longer applies; indeed, in some conceptions of the "extraordinary person," such a one demonstrates his or her perfection through the disregard, or even the transgression of, ordinary morality. The liberated human being—however that notion is understood—is often thought to be beyond duality of all sorts, including the duality of "good" and "evil," or to be in a state of ecstatic grace that defies conventionality. From this point of view, the dictates of morality are mere constructs and part of the false world of apparent diversity and ordinary perception. For those who have, through the various means that distinguish the various traditions of Hinduism, attained liberation or

---

[7]David R. Kinsley, *Hinduism: A Cultural Perspective,* 2nd ed. (Englewood Cliffs, NJ: Prentice Hall, 1993), 157–158.

salvation in this life, a new kind of consciousness takes over and virtues, as well as vices, are understood quite differently.

One example of this type of "superhuman" is the so-called *jivan mukta,* "one who is liberated while living." This individual has fully realized his or her true nature as the true Self or atman and shed all illusion regarding the lower self or ego. Furthermore, he or she understands the true nature of reality; the illusory nature of differences and distinctions between things and beings is replaced by the consciousness of oneness and unity. Such a person also then sees through the illusion of change, of the process of birth, life, death, and rebirth Hinduism calls samsara. Freed from all such illusion and fully transformed by the acquisition of wisdom, knowledge, and true consciousness, the perfected man or woman lives in the world but is not of the world; he or she has become godlike:

> If a man knows, "I am *brahman*" in this way, he becomes the whole world.
> Not even the gods are able to prevent it, for he becomes their very self. So
> when a man venerates another deity, thinking, "He is one, and I am another,"
> he does not understand.
>
> Brhadaranyaka Upanishad 1.4.10

This godlike human is also capable of behavior others would find blame-worthy and sinful. In one of the classics of Hindu literature, the Bhagavad Gita, a warrior named Arjuna is faced with a painful and puzzling dilemma. Should he engage in his proper duty as a warrior when, as he sees looking over the bat-tlefield, his enemy consists of members of his own family? Arjuna is justifiably unclear as to what the right and virtuous path might be in this case, and turns to his companion and charioteer Krishna for advice. Krishna, who is also the Supreme Deity incarnate on earth, tells Arjuna that an enlightened man would not be confused by this apparent moral crisis. One who is liberated in this life would see the death of others, even the murder of one's own family members at one's own hand, to be illusory and without karmic consequence for the man of wisdom:

> You grieve for those beyond grief,
> and you speak words of insight;
> but learned men do not grieve
> for the dead or the living.
> Never have I not existed
> nor you, nor these kings;
> and never in the future
> shall we cease to exist.
> Just as the embodied self
> enters childhood, youth, and old age,
> so does it enter another body;
> this does not confound a steadfast man.
> Contacts with matter make us feel
> heat and cold, pleasure and pain.
> Arjuna, you must learn to endure

fleeting things—they come and go!
When these cannot torment a man
when suffering and joy are equal
for him and he has courage,
he is fit for immortality.
Nothing of nonbeing comes to be,
nor does being cease to exist;
the boundary between these two
is seen by men who see reality.
Indestructible is the presence
that pervades all this;
no one can destroy
this unchanging reality.
Our bodies are known to end,
but the embodied self is enduring,
indestructible, and immeasurable;
therefore, Arjuna, fight the battle!
He who thinks this self a killer
and he who thinks it killed,
both fail to understand;
it does not kill, nor is it killed.
It is not born,
it does not die;
having been,
it will never not be;
unborn, enduring,
constant, and primordial,
it is not killed
when the body is killed.
Arjuna, when a man knows the self
to be indestructible, enduring, unborn,
unchanging, how does he kill
or cause anyone to kill?

                    Bhagavad Gita 2.11–21

Arjuna is basically told here that a man of wisdom, who knows the true nature of the self and of reality, can even kill his own relatives without incurring sin: "When one is free of individuality," that is, when one understands the true Self to be not the ego, "and his understanding is untainted, even if he kills these people he does not kill and is not bound" (Bhagavad Gita 18.17). For one who has attained such an extraordinary consciousness and "untainted understanding," the world appears quite different:

Here a father is not a father, a mother is not a mother, worlds are not worlds, gods are not gods, and Vedas are not Vedas. Here a thief is not a thief, an abortionist is not an abortionist, an outcaste is not an outcaste, a pariah is not a pariah, a recluse is not a recluse, and an ascetic is not an ascetic. Neither the good nor the bad follow him, for he has now passed beyond all sorrows of the heart. Now, he does not see anything here; but although he does not see, he is quite capable of seeing, for it is impossible for the seer to lose his capacity to see, for it is indestructible. But there isn't a second reality here that he could see as something distinct and separate from himself.

Brhadaranyaka Upanishad 4.3.22–23

A second example of a figure who transcends morality is taken from the tradition within Hinduism known as Tantricism. Esoteric tantric groups, which came in both Hindu and Buddhist forms, claimed that the best way to achieve salvation was not to renounce the bonds that keep us enslaved in a world of desire and rebirth, but rather to confront them head-on. The tantric hero did just this under ritual conditions, engaging in practices that for the uninitiated would result in the most disastrous karmic ends. Through various meditative and ritual techniques, the tantric practitioner could "do whatever fools condemn" and rid himself "of passion by yet more passion":

> So, with all one's might, one should do
>   Whatever fools condemn,
> And, since one's mind is pure,
>   Dwell in union with one's divinity.
> The mystics, pure of mind
>   Dally with lovely girls,
> Infatuated with the poisonous flame of passion
>   That they may be set free from desire.
> By his meditations the sage . . .
>   draws out the venom (of snakebite) and drinks it.
> He makes his deity innocuous,
>   And is not affected by the poison. . . .
> When he has developed a mind of wisdom
>   And has set his heart on enlightenment
> There is nothing he may not do
>   To uproot the world (from his mind). . . .
> The mystic duly dwells
>   On the manifold merits of his divinity,
> He delights in thoughts of passion,
>   And by the enjoyment of passion is set free.
> What must we do? Where are to be found
>   The manifold potencies of being?
> A man who is poisoned may be cured
>   By another poison, the antidote.
> Water in the ear is removed by more water,
>   A thorn (in the skin) by another thorn.
> So wise men rid themselves of passion
>   By yet more passion.

As a washerman uses dirt
> To wash clean a garment,
So, with impurity,
> The wise man makes himself pure.[8]

Finally, let us turn to yet another case where Hinduism posits a religious or spiritual adept—the "extraordinary person"—who lies beyond the reach of ordinary morality. The saint within the devotional traditions of Hinduism neither has attained great wisdom that allows him or her to penetrate behind the illusion of good and evil, like the portrait of the man of wisdom Krishna painted for Arjuna, nor has intentionally engaged in apparently immoral activities in order to overcome and transcend them, like the tantric practitioner. Rather, it is his or her devotion that the saint to go beyond the normal confines of virtue and achieve salvation despite sin and failings.

The power of devotion and of the grace of God is such that virtue is in some ways beside the point. For as one text contends, even a "violent criminal" or "men born in the womb of evil" are capable of salvation if only they place their faith in God:

Men who worship me,
thinking solely of me,
always disciplined,
win the reward I secure. . . .
Whatever you do—what you take,
what you offer, what you give,
what penances you perform—
do as an offering to me, Arjuna.
You will be freed from the bonds of action,
from the fruit of fortune and misfortune;
armed with the discipline of renunciation,
your self liberated, you will join me.
I am impartial to all creatures,
and no one is hateful or dear to me;
but men devoted to me are in me,
and I am within them.
If he is devoted solely to me,
even a violent criminal
must be deemed a man of virtue,
for his resolve is right.
His spirit quickens to sacred duty,
and he finds eternal peace;

---

[8] *Cittavisuddhiprakarana*, 24–38. In Ainslie T. Embree, editor, *Sources of Indian Tradition*, vol. 1 (New York: Columbia University Press, 1988), 195, 196. This passage is taken from a text produced by a Buddhist tantric sect, but the sentiments expressed aptly convey the position of Hindu tantric ideology as well.

Arjuna, know that no one
devoted to me is lost.
If they rely on me, Arjuna,
women, commoners, men of low rank,
even men born in the womb of evil,
reach the highest way.
How easy it is then for holy priests
and devoted royal sages—
in this transient world of sorrow,
devote yourself to me!

Bhagavad Gita 9.22; 27–33

The mysterious and awesome power of devotion to save even the criminal, the evildoer, and those of low birth has had great appeal to the common folk of India. In some of its forms, the devotional movement seems to have attracted many low-caste followers and others who had been left out of or diminished by caste-oriented Hinduism. The movement's emphasis on simple devotion, humility, and the power of God's grace to redeem even the sinner had obvious appeal: "I am false, my heart is false, my love is false; but I, this sinner, can win Thee if I weep before Thee, O Lord. Thou who art sweet like honey, nectar, and the juice of sugarcane! Please bless me so that I might reach Thee."[9]

The power attributed to devotion and faith to overcome ordinary moral judgments and to short-circuit the karmic process is often said to be enormous—and inexplicable. In one Hindu myth, a demoness named Putana ("the Stinking One") who is described as a "devourer of children" takes on a pleasing form and visits the village where the infant god Krishna resided with his mother. Deceived about the demoness's true identity, the mother hands over her child to her: "Then the horrible one, taking him on her lap, gave the baby her breast, which had been smeared with a virulent poison. But the lord, pressing her breast hard with his hands, angrily drank out her life's breath with the milk." The demoness dies and resumes her true demonic form. But when her body is put on the funereal pyre, the villagers receive a shock, and the reader learns a lesson about the mysterious ways of God. For even though she had tried to poison Krishna, by the very act of maternally offering him her breast she "reached the heaven of good people":

The smoke that arose from Putana's body as it burnt was as sweet-smelling as aloe-wood, for her sins had been destroyed when she fed Krishna. Putana, a slayer of people and infants, a female Raksasa (demon), a drinker of blood, reached the heaven of good people because she had given her breast to Visnu—even though she did it because she wished to kill him. How much greater, then, is the reward of those who offer what is dearest to the highest Soul, Krisna, with faith and devotion, like his doting mothers? . . . Since they

---

[9] *Tiruccatakam* by Manikkavachakar, 90. In Embree, editor, *Sources of Indian Tradition*, 347.

always looked upon Krisna as their son, they will never again be doomed to rebirth that arises from ignorance.[10]

The ability of devotion to raise the devotee above the world of good and evil is a theme that runs through the works of devotional Hinduism. When it comes to the love of God, these texts seem to say, conventional morality and accepted customs have nothing to do with it. In songs, poems, and myths concerning Krishna and his playful dalliances with the cow-herder women known as the *gopis,* sexuality is placed in the service of an emotionalistic attachment to the divine. The *gopis,* often portrayed as married women, are lured by Krishna from their homes and husbands into the forest where they join the deity in ecstatic dance and sexually charged flirtations. Radha, one of the *gopis* herself, is depicted as the very incarnation of the longing for the elusive lover— which is no other than the longing for an inscrutable, apparently fickle and sometimes distant God. The evocation of "love in separation," which ratchets up the desire for the lover (i.e., God) to its highest levels, is sometimes complemented by the notion that the most powerful desire is that for one "who belongs to another." Illicit love on the part of the woman, in other words, is regarded in certain devotional traditions as a metaphor for a love of God that transcends the strictures of ordinary morality. Radha is in some traditions said to be a married woman who throws away her reputation out of an overweening desire for Krishna:

> I who body and soul
> am at your beck and call,
> was a girl of noble family.
> I took no thought for what would be said of me,
> I abandoned everything.[11]

Or, again, it is out of love for God that compels Radha to disobey her elders, ignore the strictures of duty or dharma, give up her honor, and defy the opinion of family and society. Because of her overweening and total devotion, Radha becomes like an outcast or hermit, "ruined" in the eyes of the world:

> At the first note of his flute
> down came the lion gate of reverence for elders,
> down came the door of *dharma,*
> my guarded treasure of modesty was lost,
> I was thrust to the ground as if by a thunderbolt . . .
> no more honor, my family
> lost to me,
> my home at Vraja

---

[10]From the *Bhagavata Purana* 10.6.1–20; 30–44. In Wendy Doniger O'Flaherty, translator, *Hindu Myths: A Sourcebook Translated from the Sanskrit* (Harmondsworth, Middlesex, England: Penguin Books, 1975), 214–217.

[11]Cited and translated in Edward Dimock and Denise Levertov, translators, *In Praise of Krishna: Songs from the Bengali* (Garden City, NY: Doubleday, 1967), 51.

lost to me. . . .
How can I describe his relentless flute,
which pulls virtuous women from their homes
and drags them by their hair to Shyam
as thirst and hunger pull the doe to the snare?
Chaste ladies forget their lords,
wise men forget their wisdom. . . .
My mind is not on housework.
Now I weep, now I laugh at the world's censure.
He draws me—to become
an outcast, a hermit woman in the woods!
He has bereft me of parents, brothers, sisters,
my good name. His flute
took my heart—
his flute, a thin bamboo trap enclosing me—
a cheap bamboo flute was Radha's ruin.[12]

Such devotion and its consequences were not simply the stuff of myth. The legend of the sixteenth-century Hindu female poet-saint Mirabai claims that, although married to a prince, she refused to consummate the union because of her devotion to Krishna. Despite the disapproval of both society and the royal family (the prince's mother is said to have tried to poison Mirabai), her erotic/spiritual attachment to God is described in heroic terms:

Mira unraveled the fetters of family;
    she sundered the chains of shame to sing
    of her mountain-lifting Lover and Lord.
Like a latter-day *gopi,* she showed the meaning
    of devotion in our devastated age.
She had no fear. Her impervious tongue
    intoned the triumphs of her artful Lord.
Villains thought it vile. They set out to kill her,
    but not even a hair on her head was harmed,
For the poison she took turned elixir in her throat.
    She cringed before none: she beat love's drum.[13]

Such examples of religious heroes and heroines abound in the Hindu tradition. For although Hinduism does indeed emphasize the practice of both personal and social virtues, ultimately most traditions within this religion hold out a goal that lies beyond conventional conceptions of duty or dharma. One might work toward liberation or salvation, however that state is conceived, by the practice of virtue and the performance of duty; but the ultimate attaining of that state

---

[12]Dimock and Levertov, 28–30.

[13]Nabhadas, *Bhaktamal,* cited and translated in John Stratton Hawley and Mark Juergensmeyer, *Songs of the Saints of India* (New York: Oxford University Press, 1988), 123.

also requires leaving such aids behind and ascending into spiritual territory where such moral guidelines become irrelevant.

COMMENTARIES

Judaism on Hinduism

by JACOB NEUSNER

The difficulty in forming a pertinent response in behalf of Judaism upon the Hindu conception of the person derives from a simple fact. Hindu doctrine begins with transmigration: "Recognizing this transcendent Self as one's true identity and abandoning the lower . . . self that is the ego and that undergoes transmigration brings one to the state of liberation or freedom." I cannot think of a single initiative in the whole of the classical Rabbinic statement of Judaism—from Scripture through the Talmud of Babylonia—that intersects with no fundamental a conception of Hindu religion. But, it goes without saying, that fact carries with it a profound response to the Hindu conception: the individual both endures on his own and forms part of a larger, enduring entity. Judaism proposes to show the way for the individual to endure, to attain eternal life. What the Hindu wishes to overcome the Israelite (defined within the framework of the faith) wants to perpetuate. Why is this the case? Because in the generative myth of Judaism, man is formed in God's image. Then the issue is, how is individuality, with its aspiration to eternity, legitimate? Should not everyone conform to a common pattern?

The Talmud of Babylonia's amplification of that point underscores the legitimacy of individuality:

Why was Adam created one and alone?
To show the grandeur of the king of the kings of kings, blessed be he.
For if a man mints many coins with one mold, all are alike.
But the Holy One, blessed be he, mints every man with the mold of the first man and not one of them is like another,
as it is said, "It is changed as clay under the seal, and all these things stand forth as in a garment" (Job 38:14).
It has been taught on Tannaite authority: R. Meir says, "The Omnipresent has varied a man in three ways: appearance, intelligence, and voice
intelligence, because of robbers and thieves, and appearance and voice, because of the possibilities of licentiousness."

Bavli tractate Sanhedrin 4:5 IV:I, V.I/38a

Individuation, here distinguishing one man from all others, as much as the Israelite from all Israel, serves the purpose of defining the private person as a moral category, a field of moral justice and judgment. Professor Smith states, "Individuals then are born into family and caste due to the karma one carries from past lives but also conform to their inborn nature, shaped by activities they perform."

Judaism takes a contrary position: while individuals are born into family and therefore caste, their own deeds, not their past, whether genealogical or supernatural, govern. The notion of lives continuous with one another ("past karma") and continual rebirth contrasts with the conception of individuality that governs: everyone is both like God and unlike everyone else.

When we come to the matter of dharma, "duty, moral obligation, religious law, principle," by contrast, we find that Judaism is right at home. The formulations of moral obligation in the Torah, oral and written, are very many, though coherent all together. Goodwill toward others, truth telling, not stealing, forbearance, and tolerance—these represent virtues espoused by the sages of the Torah. It would be hard to find a more congruent statement to Hindu virtue than a formulation such as the following:

> The master, Rabban Yohanan b. Zakkai] said to [his five disciples], "Go and see what is the straight path to which someone should stick."
>
> R. Eliezer says, "A generous spirit."
>
> R. Joshua says, "A good friend."
>
> R. Yosé says, "A good neighbor."
>
> R. Simeon says, "Foresight."
>
> R. Eleazar says, "Good will."
>
> He said to them, "I prefer the opinion of R. Eleazar b. Arakh, because in what he says is included everything you say."
>
> He said to them, "Go out and see what is the bad road, which someone should avoid."
>
> R. Eliezer says, "Envy."
>
> R. Joshua says, "A bad friend."
>
> R. Yosé says, "A bad neighbor."
>
> R. Simeon says, "Defaulting on a loan."
>
> (All the same is a loan owed to a human being and a loan owed to the Omnipresent, blessed be he, as it is said, The wicked borrows and does not pay back, but the righteous person deals graciously and hands over [what he owes] [Ps. 37:21].)
>
> R. Eleazar says, "Bad will."
>
> He said to them, "I prefer the opinion of R. Eleazar b. Arakh, because in what he says is included everything you say."
>
> Mishnah-Tractate Abot 2:9

At the level of practical virtue, Hindu and Judaic teachings intersect time and again. But there is a single primary duty in Judaism that takes priority over all else, contained in the statement of Yohanan ben Zakkai: "If you have learned much Torah, do not puff yourself up on that account, for it was for that purpose that you were created" (M. Abot 2:8). The Hindu focus on duty for whatever purpose would not concur. So too, "rebellion against one's inborn and inherent nature" of Hinduism contrasts with the counterpart, rebellion against God's will, as expressed in the Torah, within the definition of Judaism. So it appears that the points of contrast override the points of comparison and concurrence.

Christianity on Hinduism

by BRUCE CHILTON

The movement within one's caste in Hinduism, and particularly the description of that as a "second birth," is resonant with the Christian understanding that God begets us all over again "for a living hope through Christ Jesus' resurrection from the dead" (1 Peter 1:3). But, as we must expect by now (given our earlier comparisons), Christian rebirth is *out* of this world, apart from conventions of economy and caste, just as emphatically as Hindu rebirth is within this world's relations. Any acceptance of class within Christianity is instrumental, rather than ontological. That is, social conventions are strategically embraced (1 Peter 2:13–25), not authorized as being part of the order of creation or redemption. That is a profound difference with the cosmogonic view of Hinduism, where the language of transcendence is deliberately and carefully integrated within a divinely mandated ontology.

It is interesting, in this vein, that the best analogy to Hinduism's view of how actions result in bodily strengths or defects is provided by Origen's analysis of what happens when people are raised from the dead. In his argument, moral adjustments at that stage bring about bodily changes cognate with them. So the resurrection, not this life, finds the rewards and retributions that justice demands ("On First Principles" 10.8).[1] Looking now into what the Letter of James calls the law of freedom, and actually putting that law into effect, imbues the one who acts with the power and spirit of Jesus' teaching (James 1:25). For that very reason, Christianity does not and can not share the contention that the self (in any meaningful sense) is neither augmented by virtue nor diminished by vice. Although the heroic individualism of Enlightenment Protestant has been widely questioned as an authentically or necessarily Christian view, the fact remains that actions do directly impinge on who one is within the teaching of Jesus and the tradition that grew from that (Matthew 25:31–46). Even duty—and that indeed means dharma—cannot compete in the hierarchy of virtues with the realization by every person in baptism and thereafter of one's divine image and likeness. At just that point, Christianity and Hinduism are at odds, and should and must join in debate.

Within that debate, it seems clear that Hinduism can claim the force of nature, while Christianity is obliged to wrestle with the implications of claims of the transcendence of natural tendencies. Here, as in the question of work, Christian theology is not able to content itself with organic metaphors or arguments for straightforward integration. That is why the examples of Tantric Hinduism and Buddhism, with their emphasis on the use of human desire to achieve liberation, are alluring to the West (quite apart from their erotic side). The moment when convention may be cast aside, within an argument for the ontological valuation of class and status, is attractive to a consciousness that is sure that revolution is a good idea, quite apart from the particular conditions that might justify

---

[1]For a discussion, see Bruce D. Chilton and Jacob Neusner, editors, *Trading Places. The Intersecting Histories of Judaism and Christianity* (Cleveland: Pilgrim Press, 1996), 163–166.

it. Constantly and strategically, Christianity speaks of losing the self in order to discover it (Matthew 16:25; Mark 8:35; Luke 9:24), in a movement of self-transcendence paradoxically designed to strengthen the self. To a partial extent, this paradox may be explained by the simple acceptance of the terms of reference of Judaism, but a deeper explanation is required, and is readily available. Jesus' statement about losing and finding oneself appears in the context of vision. The self of which the Gospels speak as a substantial entity owes its substance, not to this world, but to the visionary practice in which one stands before the throne of God.

Islam on Hinduism

by TAMARA SONN

In Islam, the self is viewed holistically. The Qur'an uses the term *nafs* for the self and *ruh* for the soul or life force bestowed by the creator. Some mystical (Sufi) thinkers in Islam have distinguished the *ruh,* as the "higher" or spiritual self, from the *nafs,* the "lower" or physical self. In general, however, the Qur'an makes no such distinction. Physical and moral well-being are integrally connected, so much so that deprivation of physical needs is considered an evil that must be overcome. Feeding the hungry is an essentially moral act, as are caring for the sick and freeing the confined. The goal of Islamic life is creating a just society, which is defined as overcoming inequities in people's overall well-being. Furthermore, sexuality is an essential component of life, protected within marriage, for the fulfillment of the individuals involved and the nurturing of children. Any doubt about the holistic nature of the self in Islam should be dispelled by Islamic beliefs about the afterlife. The belief that only the soul survives death was rejected as heretical, in favor of the belief in the resurrection of the entire person—physical and spiritual together.

Buddhism on Hinduism

by CHARLES HALLISEY

Buddhist and Hindu reflections on what we owe ourselves in the life of virtue overlap to a considerable degree. This is not surprising given the historical interrelations the two traditions had in South Asia during formative periods for each. For example, Buddhist perspectives on the extraordinary person are similar to Hindu perspectives in giving the accomplished person a certain moral license to act outside conventional moral norms. For Buddhists, the qualities of compassion and wisdom, which have been cultivated to a maximal degree by a Buddha, give him a freedom to act in ways that might, in some circumstances, appear to be immoral by conventional standards. Buddhas can appear to lie, for example, in some circumstances out of an effort to be helpful to another.

What would strike a Buddhist observer as odd, and indeed troubling, in Hindu accounts of the life of virtue is the insistence on correlating virtue to social class. Buddhists mocked the Hindu notion that humans differed in essential ways and they would see accounts of virtue failing on their own terms. That is, if Hindus define "good character" as fulfilling oneself within the boundaries of one's inborn and inherent nature, then their accounts of the life of virtue fail because of their emphasis on secondary and arbitrary social conventions in place of what is really one's inborn nature. Moreover, Buddhists judged Hindu accounts of the life of virtue as being too-often inattentive to the inherent need to fulfill oneself by being of benefit to others, regardless of their social class.

SUMMARY

The life of virtue in Hinduism first presupposes knowledge of who we really are. The Hindu tradition identifies one's true Self as the philosophically and mystically discoverable essence of all reality, and contrasts it to a "lower" self that is continually reborn as a function of one's karma. The object of religious life for most Hindus is to produce good karma that will result in a better rebirth. The principal way of achieving this is to follow the social and personal virtues appropriate to one's class or caste and stage of life, and to do so with contentment, equanimity, and detachment. One's "character," good or bad, is largely defined by one's conformity to one's own appointed duty and the virtues related to it. For certain extraordinary human beings, and for practitioners of certain kinds of Hindu techniques for obtaining salvation, ordinary morality and virtue do not pertain. Ordinary conceptions of "good" and "bad" are transcended when one obtains true wisdom about the nature of the world, or in the course of pursuing special methods for rapid liberation, or as a result of one's overwhelming love of God.

GLOSSARY

Adharma   "unrighteousness" or "evil"; the opposite of dharma

Adhikara   "predilection," "competency," "inherent ability," or "predisposition." People born into different castes are said in Hinduism to be endowed by birth with differing *adhikaras*.

Arjuna   a warrior, one of the two main protagonists in the Bhagavad Gita

Atman   the true, changeless, and eternal "Self," distinct from the ego

Artha   "private gain" or "material or political advantage," "self-interest," "getting ahead in the world"; one of the "ends of life" in Hinduism, especially appropriate to the householder

Aryan   literally "noble one," the name the early Indo-European invaders of India gave to themselves

Bhagavad Gita   a key text of Hinduism that synthesizes some of the strands of the tradition around the concept of *bhakti*

Bhakti   literally "participation" in the divine being, or more commonly translated as "devotion" to God

Brahman   the macrocosmic principle of unity in the Hindu philosophy of monism; often equated to the *atman* or "Self"

Brahmins   "priests" or religious specialists, the highest of the classes or castes in the traditional Hindu social order

Dharma   a multivalent word that in Hinduism usually refers to "religious duty," determined by one's caste and stage of life

Gopis   "cowherder women," who figure prominently in the mythology of Krishna

Gunas   the three elemental "constituents," "qualities," or "strands" that alone or in combination underlie all things and beings in the universe: "goodness," "activity," and "inertia"

Guru   religious teacher

Jiva   "self" or "subtle body" of a person, sometimes used as a synonym for *atman*

Jivan mukta   "one who is liberated while living," a living human being who has attained liberation or freedom (moksha)

Kama   "sensual pleasure," one of the "ends of life" in Hinduism

Karma   "work," originally in the sense of "ritual activity" and later generalized to include all acts. In all senses of the word, karma refers also to actions that create the causes for experiences (pleasant and unpleasant) in the future.

Krishna   one of the chief deities of the Hindu pantheon and the central figure in the Bhagavad Gita

Kshatriyas   the warrior class of the traditional Hindu social order

Mirabai   sixteenth-century Hindu poet-saint, renown for her devotion to Krishna

Moksha   "freedom" or "liberation" from samsara, the ultimate goal of Hinduism

Prajapati   "lord of Creatures," a name for the creator god in Vedism

Purusa   "Cosmic Man," one name for the creator god of the Vedic pantheon

Putana   "The Stinking One," name of a demoness in Hindu mythology

Radha   one of the gopis or cowherder women in the mythology of Krishna, often portrayed as Krishna's consort

Raksasa   a demon

Rig Veda   the oldest text of the ancient Indian Vedas, which are regarded as sacred scripture by most Hindus

Samsara   the wheel of continual birth, life, death, and rebirth; in Hinduism and Buddhism it is also characterized, in general, by suffering

Samskaras   rites of passage

Shudras   "servants," the lowest class or caste in the traditional Hindu social order

Svadha   a ritual utterance in some Hindu ceremonies

Svadharma   one's "own duty"; dharma particularized to one's class or caste and stage of life

Tantricism   an esoteric tradition within Hinduism characterized by use of radical and unconventional methods to obtain liberation quickly

Upanayana the most important of the Hindu rites of passage, during which a young boy is initiated into the study of the Veda and receives the sacred thread symbolizing his "second birth"

Upanishads ancient texts in Hinduism that deal with philosophy and metaphysics

Vaishyas the commoners (merchants, agriculturalists, traders, etc.) of the traditional Hindu social order

Veda collective term for a group of ancient Indian texts regarded by most Hindus as sacred scripture

Vedism the earliest form of the Hindu tradition in India, centered on the performance and ideology surrounding the fire sacrifice

Yajnavalkya a religious teacher who figures prominently in some of the Upanishads

Yoga "discipline" of the mind and body, entailing detachment from the world of the senses

DISCUSSION QUESTIONS

1. How does ritual function in Hindusim to "create" the self-identity of Hindus? How does karma work to similarly determine one's identity?
2. Describe the differences between the "lower" self and the true, higher "Self" in Hinduism.
3. Identify and describe the highest social virtue in Hinduism.
4. How is personal virtue conceived and how is it related to social virtue?
5. What constitutes "good character" in Hinduism?
6. What kind of person can transgress ordinary morality in Hinduism?

INFOTRAC

If you would like additional information related to the material discussed here, you can visit our Web site: http://www.wadsworth.com

5

Buddhism

BY CHARLES HALLISEY

CONVENTIONAL ANSWERS VERSUS
THIS RELIGIOUS TRADITION:
WHO ARE WE REALLY?

To ask the question "what do we owe ourselves?" as part of any reflection about the contours of a life of virtue is to recognize that a relationship with oneself, cultivating and taking care of oneself, is as much a part of the ethical life as concerns about how to live with and for others.

Buddhists have consistently recognized this fundamental aspect of a life of virtue for more than twenty-five centuries, and they have expressed the results of their reflections in many ways. At one level, their various formulations of how one can best take care of oneself—how one can best cultivate a life of virtue that satisfies what one owes oneself—is just another example of the historical diversity of the Buddhist tradition. Buddhism spread from India, where it began in the life and teachings of Shakyamuni, "the Awakened One" (*buddha*), across all of Asia: to Central Asia, China, Korea, and Japan, to Tibet, and to Sri Lanka and Southeast Asia. In the twentieth century, Buddhist ideas, practices, values, and institutions have also found receptive audiences in Europe and the Americas. The manner in which the Buddhist heritage was "naturalized" in each new context explains the internal diversity of Buddhism: Buddhism changed the life of every community that appropriated its spiritual resources, but at the same time, the tradition was profoundly inflected by the broader cultures of these different communities. Historically, Buddhists have been relatively comfortable with a diversity of ideas and practices in their heritage, seeing it as a mark of the nature of Truth itself. A popular Buddhist parable tells the story of a group of blind men who tell each other what an elephant was like. Each had touched a different part of the elephant with his hands: one the hair of the tail, another the toenails, one the rough skin, another the soft tissue inside the trunk. Each generalized from the part of the elephant that he touched and asserted that the whole animal was like that. What they did not see, in their blindness, was that each of their explanations about the nature of an elephant was true in a relative way.

There is another reason for why it should be no surprise that conventional ideas about a person should vary from one Buddhist community to another, especially ideas about a person as a social being, as someone who finds herself or himself in a network of relations with others. Cultural assumptions and values about a person are always embodied in the practices of social life that constitute these networks of relations. These practices are what distinguish one culture from another: in one community, one shakes hands with another, in a second community, one bows to another. Even such a simple example allows us to recognize that such practices are not just differences that arbitrarily and accidentally distinguish one culture from another. When one bows to another, instead of shaking hands, the conception that one has of oneself, one's relationship with oneself, is shaped by that practice. To bow to another is to acknowledge that I am not equal to others, that others are my betters, whether in social standing, personal achievement, or moral worth; to shake hands is to deny the significance of human difference and to affirm that I am fundamentally equal to others.

In their reflections on the religious life, Buddhists have affirmed both human equality and human difference. They have, however, generally seen human equality as being of greater spiritual significance—all humans have the capacity of becoming awakened, regardless of their social location—but of lesser social significance. Human equality also seems to be of lesser significance for Buddhists for understanding what one owes to oneself. Buddhists have instead emphasized the importance of acknowledging human inequality for the life of virtue. For example, the second-century Indian Buddhist thinker, Nāgārjuna, said in a letter to a king that

> It is "presumptive pride" for one to presume
> that one is equal to someone who is better.
> If one presumes oneself to be
> even better than one's betters,
> then this is pride before pridefulness,
> thinking oneself to be even loftier than the lofty.
> It is excessively bad, like developing
> sores on top of your boils.[1]

Buddhists have consistently emphasized human difference in organizing their communities. These communities have historically been organized quite hierarchically, with standards of worth and prestige organizing the relations between monks and laypeople, men and women, old and young, powerful and oppressed. These hierarchies of worth are stressed to such a degree at times that it can appear that the worth of an individual per se is eclipsed. The following comment by Hajime Nakamura about Japanese culture could be applied to almost every Buddhist community with only minor modifications:

> Due to the stress on social proprieties in Japan another characteristic of its culture appears—the tendency of social relationships to supersede or take precedence over the individual. . . . When this type of thinking is predominant, consciousness of the individual as an entity appears always in the wider

---

[1]Nāgārjuna, *The Precious Garland,* translated by John and Sara McClintock (Boston: Wisdom, 1997), 74.

sphere of consciousness of social relationships, although the significance of the individual is still recognized.[2]

To understand the manner in which Buddhists recognize the significance of the individual, we should return to the parable of the blind men and the elephant noted above. Blindness is an image of ignorance in this parable, and we should note that the blind men's misperception of the elephant is not because they are completely wrong about the animal, but because they do not see the "big picture" that would put their partial perception into perspective. The same is true about conventional conceptions of a person. It is not that they are always wrong in and of themselves. They are wrong either because they fail to see "the big picture" or because they are connected to a delusional "big picture."

Buddhists are in surprising agreement about what this delusional big picture is: it is the wrong view that assumes—without supporting evidence—that there is a unitary and enduring personal entity, whether this is defined as a self or a soul.

> According to the teaching of the Buddha, the idea of the self is an imaginary, false belief which has no corresponding reality, and it produces harmful thoughts of "me" and "mine," selfish desire, craving, attachment, hatred, ill-will, conceit, pride, egoism, and other defilements, impurities and problems. It is the source of all the troubles in the world from personal conflicts to wars between nations. In short, to this false view can be traced all the evil in the world.[3]

If Buddhists agree about what a person is not—not stable, enduring, or unitary—they are in less agreement about what larger backdrop conceptions of a person should be placed.

One general backdrop is karma, the processes of moral cause and effect, in which one gets good for doing good and gets bad for doing bad. One's present nature is determined by the effects of one's previous actions. To quote Nāgārjuna again:

> Due to murder one is born with a short life-span;
> due to violence one encounters much torment;
> due to stealing one becomes impoverished;
> due to adultery one has enemies.
>
> By telling lies one becomes reviled;
> Through speaking divisively, one loses friends;
> due to speaking harshly, one hears unpleasant noises;
> From engaging in idle gossip, one's words will be disregarded.
>
> Covetousness destroys one's desired objects;
> maliciousness is said to bestow fear;
> wrong views lead to evil worldviews;
> imbibing liquor brings mental confusion.[4]

---

[2]Hajime Nakamura, *Ways of Thinking of Eastern Peoples*, 409, quoted in T. Kasulis, *Zen Action, Zen Person*, (Honolulu: University of Hawaii Press, 1981) 9.

[3]Walpola Rahula, *What the Buddha Taught*, (New York: Grove Press, 1974) 51.

[4]Nāgārjuna, 11.

The first line of these verses also makes it clear that the workings of karma assume that persons, like all beings, are reborn again. It is thus critical that one views one's present life as a person within the bigger picture of samsara, the cycle of birth and death in which beings repeatedly experience the suffering they produce for themselves because they misperceive their own nature and the nature of the world around them. In the words of the Buddha,

> Which is greater, the tears you have shed while transmigrating and wandering this long time—crying and weeping from being joined with what is displeasing, from being separated from what is pleasing—or the water in the four great oceans? . . .
>
> This is greater: The tears you have shed. . . . Why is that? From an inconceivable beginning . . . comes transmigration. A beginning point is not evident, although beings hindered by ignorance and fettered by craving are transmigrating and wandering on.[5]

Beings are generally ignorant about the larger cosmological processes that condition their own personal experience. Buddhists in different schools stress different cosmological processes as relevant for construing the big picture about a person. For some, it is merely the peculiar combination of substance, form, and mechanical processes that generate personal experience. This can be seen in the following dialogue between a king and a Buddhist monk about whether a person "really" exists. It opens with a question by the monk to the king about the nature of a chariot:

> "[P]lease explain to me what a chariot is. Is the pole the chariot? . . . Is the axle? . . . then the wheels, the framework, or the flagstaff, or the yoke, or the reins, or the goad-stick?" "No Reverend Sir." "Then is it the combination of pole, axle, wheels, framework, flagstaff, yoke, reins, and goad which is the 'chariot'?" "No, Reverend Sir." "Then is this 'chariot' outside the combination of pole, axle, wheels, framework, flagstaff, yoke, reins and goad?" "No, Reverend Sir." "Then, ask as I may, I can discover no chariot at all. Just a mere sound is this 'chariot.' But what is the real chariot? Your Majesty has told a lie [in saying that he came by chariot], has spoken a falsehood! There is no chariot! Your Majesty is the greatest king in the whole of India. Of whom then are you afraid, that you do not speak the truth? . . ."
>
> But king Milinda said to Nagasena: "I have not, Nagasena, spoken a falsehood. For it is in dependence on the pole, the axle, the wheels, the framework, the flagstaff, etc. that there takes place this denomination 'chariot,' this designation, this conceptual term, a current appellation and a mere name."
> "Your Majesty has spoken well about the chariot. It is just so with me. In dependence on the thirty-two parts of the body and the five [constituent elements of a person][6] there takes place this denomination 'Nagasena' [the monk], this designation, this conceptual term, a current appellation and a

[5]Samyutta Nikaya XV.3, translated by Thanissaro, *Wings to Awakening*, (Barre, MA: Dhamma Dana Publications, 1996) 45.

[6]They are body, feelings, perceptions, volitional dispositions, and consciousness.

mere name. In ultimate reality, however, this person cannot be apprehended. And this has been said by our sister [i.e., a Buddhist nun] Vajira when she was face to face with the Lord:

> "'Where all constituent parts are present,
> The word "a chariot" is applied.
> So likewise where [the five constituent parts of a person] are,
> The term a "being" commonly is used.'"[7]

What goes along with this conception of a person is a profound sense of the impermanence and mutability of persons and, as Daisaku Ikeda[8] says, "in Buddhism it is taught that one's mind fluctuates 840 million times a day. The alterations in one's life are, in other words, infinite. One's life is a succession of momentary instances of hot, cold, doubt, delight, sadness and other conditions."[9]

Such an image of the true nature of a person is obviously less than is conventionally supposed by notions of the individual. There are other Buddhist schemata about the nature of a person that make an individual much more than is conventionally supposed about an individual, and, as can be seen in the following passage by a British exponent of Soka Gakkai, this "more" is discerned by perceiving a person within another cosmological framework:[10]

> Imagine it is Monday morning. The alarm has just gone off, waking you from a deep and peaceful sleep. With a groan you drag yourself out of bed and pull yourself out of bed and pull the curtains. It is raining. You get dressed and go into the kitchen where you put the kettle on, feed the cat, then settle down to your own breakfast. You note corn flakes provides at least a quarter of an average adult's recommended daily intake of vitamins niacin, B1, B2, B6, B12 and D and, just then, hear the flap of the letterbox rattle. There are two letters—one from the electricity board, the other from the tax office. Fearing the worst, you decide to open the electricity bill first. In fact, it is outrageous. Deciding that those stupid bureaucrats at the electricity board must have made a mistake, you resolve to write them a stiff letter the minute you get to work. But then, it was a very cold winter and you did leave the heating on most of the night, most of the time. Your heart sinks. They might be right after all. And if they are, there goes your summer holiday. Feeling very depressed, you open the ominous brown letter from the Inland Revenue and— a tax rebate! More than enough to pay the electricity bill, right or wrong, and have plenty left over for the holiday. You whoop for joy and go off to work, oblivious of the pouring rain. . . .

---

[7]Edward Conze, *Buddhist Scriptures*, (New York: Penguin, 1977) 148–149.

[8]He is the leader of Soka Gakkai, a modern school of Buddhism with roots in the Nichiren tradition of Japan.

[9]Quoted in Richard Causton, *The Buddha in Daily Life,* (London: Rider, 1995) 38.

[10]It should be noted that Causton speaks more definitely about fundamental principles of Buddhism than is perhaps warranted, but even if his comments are not valid for all Buddhists, they are still an eloquent expression of an important Buddhist ethical orientation.

Apart from the tax rebate, perhaps, the passage above could be said to de-scribe a perfectly ordinary, average morning, one experienced (with varia-tions) by millions of people every day throughout the country. In the course of this short vignette, however, you have experienced nine of the Ten Worlds.

The Ten Worlds or Ten States of Life, an absolutely fundamental principle of Buddhism, teaches that everybody possesses ten basic inner states of being which we all experience moment to moment. Briefly these Ten Worlds are Hell, Hunger, Animality, Anger, Tranquillity, Rapture, Learning, Realization, Bodhisattva [a being that is on a course to Awakening], and Buddhahood. To explain a little further, Hell is the state of suffering; Hunger is the state of being under the sway of desires; Animality is the state of instinctive behav-iour; and Anger is the state of constant competition or conflict, in which one arrogantly tries to surpass others. . . . Tranquillity is the neutral state of peace and calm, and Rapture is the state of being temporarily overjoyed at the grati-fication of a desire. The six states from Hell to Rapture are called the Six Paths and arise spontaneously in our lives when prompted by external factors. In contrast, the four remaining worlds, called the Four Noble Paths, are char-acterized by the inner effort it takes to manifest them.[11]

The Six Paths, referred to by Causton, are also considered to be real states of rebirth: hell, hungry ghost, animal, titan, human, and god. Here this "objective" cosmology is portrayed as contained within a single person. The deep and peace-ful sleep with which the example opens is Tranquillity (but sleep itself is also an interesting comment on what conventional existence as a human is); not all sleep is Tranquillity because a nightmare could be Hell and a pleasant dream could be Rapture. Animality appears with the groan on waking. Facing the demands of the day is Hell, but Animality reappears with hunger. When the cat is fed the generosity of a bodhisattva is apparent. Reading about vitamins in corn flakes is Learning. The arrival of letters brings out Animality again, with fear, then fol-lowed by Anger ("those stupid bureaucrats"), and Hunger for the summer va-cation. Hell reappears with the memories of the cold winter, only to be followed with the Rapture brought by the tax rebate. What this larger cosmology helps us to see is that each of us is all of these Ten Worlds at every single moment, and all that changes is our shifting attention to various experiences.

The three examples of karma and rebirth, the analogy between a person and a chariot, and the Ten Worlds cosmology are very different from each other, but taking them together helps us to learn an important general lesson about Bud-dhist ethics: the moral life, both in terms of what we owe to others and what we owe to ourselves, always involves a proper understanding of oneself, one's true nature. Sadly for most of us, this understanding of our true nature, what may be the most important thing for us to know, is at odds with what we ordinarily think. It goes against the grain of unexamined, received ideas about the integrity of an individual's nature and experience that are conventionally held by both

---

[11]Causton, 35–36.

Buddhists and non–Buddhists. It is precisely these received ideas that prevent us from living ethically and cause us to experience suffering despite all of our best intentions.

WHAT ARE THE SOCIAL VIRTUES?

A distinction between social and personal virtues is not easily maintained in Buddhist ethics, both intrinsically and in terms of their benefits. The life of virtue inevitably benefits oneself and others and thus one owes it to oneself to live well with and for others. This can be seen in some verses by Nāgārjuna about the good qualities that a future Buddha (a bodhisattva) should cultivate, with the last verse referring to the workings of karma:

> In short, the good qualities that
> a bodhisattva should develop
> are generosity, morality, tolerance, heroic effort,
> concentration, wisdom, loving kindness, and so on.
>
> To be generous is to give up one's wealth,
> to be moral is to endeavor to help others;
> tolerance is the abandonment of anger;
> heroic effort is enthusiasm for virtue.
>
> Concentration is unafflicted one-pointedness [of mind];
> wisdom is definitively determining the truths' meaning.
> Loving kindness is a state of mind.
>
> From generosity comes wealth, happiness from morality.
> From tolerance comes beauty, splendor from heroic effort.
> Through meditation, one is peaceful, through understanding
> comes liberation. Compassion is what accomplishes all aims.[12]

Clearly, social virtues like generosity, morality, tolerance, and so forth, are about how we live with and for others. The fact that we live with others requires us, minimally, to avoid doing harm to those around us. For Buddhists, action is typed as bodily action, verbal action, and mental action, and thus avoiding harm to others must be realized in every aspect of a person. A standard set of five precepts for avoiding harm to others consists of refraining from killing, stealing, false speech, sexual misconduct, and the use of intoxicants.

Nāgārjuna, however, reminds us that "to be moral is to endeavor to help others" and that "what harms others are faults, what helps them are good qualities" and the life of virtue requires us to live for others, and not only with others. The idea that the life of virtue consists of a negative aspect—avoiding harm to others—and a positive aspect—doing good for others—can be seen in a fa-

---

[12]Nāgārjuna, 78, 67.

mous verse from the Dhammapada, a scriptural anthology of aphorisms attributed to the Buddha:

> Do no evil
> Do good
> Purify your own intentions:
> This is the teaching of the Buddhas.[13]

Basically, the life of living for others as well as of taking care of oneself is, for Buddhists, essentially defined by a single social virtue: undifferentiated delight in the happiness of others, and the pursuit of this delight motivates one to act on behalf of others. This can be seen in the following Pali text about loving-kindness (*metta*); it is from the Theravada Buddhist tradition of Sri Lanka and Southeast Asia. It begins with some attention to the personal virtues that are necessary supports for the social virtue of loving-kindness, and then goes on to give instructions for the cultivation of this particular virtue:

> He who is skilled in good and who wishes to attain that state of Calm should act (thus):
> He should be able, upright, perfectly upright, compliant, gentle, and humble.
> Contented, easily supported, with few duties, of simple livelihood, controlled in senses, discreet, not impudent, he should not be greedily attached to families.
> He should not commit any slight wrong such that other wise men might censure him. (Then he should cultivate his thoughts thus:)
> May all beings be happy and secure; may their minds be contented.
> Whatever living beings there may be—feeble or strong, long (or tall), stout, or medium, short, small, or large, seen or unseen, those dwelling far or near, those who are born and those who are yet to be born—may all beings, without exception, be happy minded!
> Let not one deceive another nor despise any person whatever in any place. In anger or ill-will let not one wish any harm to another.
> Just as a mother would protect her only child even at the risk of her own life, even so let one cultivate a boundless heart towards all beings.
> Let one's thoughts of boundless love pervade the whole world—above, below and across—without any obstruction, without any hatred, without any enmity.
> Whether one stands, walks, sits or lies down, as long as one is awake, one should maintain this mindfulness.[14]

Cultivating empathy, kindness, and compassion toward others is not an easy task because ignorance, desire, and self-interest are not easily uprooted. For such social virtues to develop, better conditions for their flourishing need to be produced. Attention to the "big picture" of a person, discussed in the previous section, is one way of producing these conditions.

---

[13]Quoted in Kasulis, 94.

[14]Walpola Rahula, *What the Buddha Taught*, 97–98.

WHAT IS PERSONAL VIRTUE?

Personal virtue is a necessary element in the conditions in which the social virtues can flourish. One must cultivate certain personal qualities in order to prevent one's *feelings* from obstructing one's *will* to be of benefit to others. Such debilitating feelings can be about others—for example, feeling that others do not deserve what I do for them—or about oneself—for example, feeling that I am not up to the task of what others need from me. Personal virtue is thus concerned with cultivating a critical detachment from the disturbing feelings of judgment and discouragement that inevitably arise in the life of virtue. This critical detachment has a variety of aspects, however, including humility; equanimity in the face of success and failure; flexibility about immediate courses of action depending on the circumstances; insight into the nature of the world; an ability to sacrifice proximate goods for the sake of a more valuable, but distant goal; and courage.

Humility is the attitude that enables one always to consider others as more important than oneself, no matter how they might treat one in turn. Its centrality in the life of virtue can be seen in the "Eight Verses for Training the Mind," a Tibetan text that the Dalai Lama has recommended as a useful part of a daily spiritual regimen of self-reflection. Note especially how the verses portray the humble person as one who is aware of the benefit that he or she receives from everyone and in particular from enemies; the latter are beneficial because they give us an opportunity to cultivate virtues that allow us to live well:

> Regarding all sentient beings
> As excelling even the wish-granting gem
> For accomplishing the highest aim,
> May I always hold them most dear.
>
> When in the company of others
> I shall always consider myself the lowest of all,
> And from the depth of my heart
> Hold them dear and supreme.
>
> Vigilant, the moment a delusion appears,
> Which endangers myself and others,
> I shall confront and avert it
> Without delay.
>
> When I see beings of wicked nature
> overwhelmed by negative actions and sufferings,
> I shall hold such rare ones dear,
> As if I have found a precious treasure.
>
> When others, out of envy, treat me with abuse,
> Insult me or the like,
> I shall accept defeat,
> and offer the victory to others.
>
> When someone I have benefited
> And in whom I have great hopes

Gives me terrible harm,
I shall regard him as my holy spiritual friend.

In short, both directly and indirectly, do I offer
Every benefit and happiness to all sentient beings, my mothers;
May I secretly take upon myself
All their harmful actions and suffering.

May they not be defiled by the concepts
Of the eight profane concerns.
And aware that all things are illusory,
May they, ungrasping, be freed from bondage.[15]

The eight profane concerns are gain and loss, high status and low status, praise and blame, and pleasure and blame. They are conditions that all humans encounter in the course of living in this world, the very conditions for our experience of things in this world. Payutto, a contemporary Thai Buddhist monastic writer, explains these eight worldly conditions in the following way:

Living in this world people must be affected by these [eight] things, and if they are not wise to them they will be dominated and dragged around by them. When they encounter the favorable side, which they like, they inflate, and when they meet the unfavorable side, which they do not like, they deflate. When they gain they swell, and when they lose they shrink.

To inflate is to become excited, to bubble, to get elated, to jump with excitement or get carried away.

To deflate is to shrivel up, to be saddened, to lose heart, or fall into depths of despair.

To swell is to swagger, to become conceited, to forget oneself, to become deluded, and this may extend to disparaging others or using wealth or power to oppress others.

To shrink is to lose one's strength or energy, and it may extend to disparaging oneself, to turning away from the virtuous way and neglecting goodness or one's own ideals.

Life in this world is like this. We must accept the truth that living in this world the [eight] worldly conditions are inevitable. Since we cannot escape them, we must encounter them and deal with them. We should not take them so seriously that we mistake them for personal belongings, but reflect on them, asking ourselves "How can we deal with them properly and live with them wisely?" If we are wise to them we will be able to deal with the worldly conditions well. We will be someone who neither inflates nor deflates, neither shrinks nor swells, and instead makes use of worldly conditions.[16]

Making use of the eight worldly conditions requires us to be flexible about the courses of action that we choose in different circumstances and to have an

---

[15]Renuka Singh, editor, *The Dalai Lama's Book of Daily Meditations* (London: Rider, 1998), xii–xiii.

[16]Quoted in Peter Skilling, editor and translator, *Beyond Worldly Conditions* (Bangkok: Fragile Palm Leaves, 1999), 99–100.

insight into the true nature of things. When good fortune occurs, whether as material success, social rank, praise from others, or pleasure, one should see that these conditions are temporary opportunities to benefit others. To quote Payutto again:

> The important point is that when we have wealth or possessions, rank, fame, and retinue, we are in a position to create a great deal of benefit and constructive action, so that our wealth and rank, for example, become instruments and opportunities for enriching our lives, for spreading benefit and happiness outwards on a broad scale in society, and helping to make the world into what the Buddha called . . . a world of love and kindness, a safe place free of exploitation, a place of peace. In this way we have a good relationship with our fellow human beings and receive true respect from them. The benefit on the initial level becomes a stepping-stone to a higher level of benefit.[17]

Conversely, unfavorable world conditions are opportunities to develop ourselves. They challenge us to develop qualities that allow us to persevere in the face of obstacles. Equally important, they provide us with an opportunity to develop a better understanding of the nature of the world insofar as all of the eight profane concerns are "impermanent, uncertain, and subject to change."[18]

Since the profane concerns are impermanent, uncertain, and subject to change, it is important for us to have something of a "long view" about the goals that we have for our life. In Buddhist terms, this long view is best understood as a life directed to the goal of enlightenment. Keeping one's eyes on this goal allows one to sacrifice proximate pleasures and goods for the sake of a future, but more valuable accomplishment. The personal virtue of being able to delay gratification is praised in everyone who is striving to become a Buddha. A future Buddha is entitled to be proud if he or she can say,

> [I aspire] after the great good, the perfect good, the sublime good, the pure good, the unchangeable good, the unprecedented good, the good that is a way of escape,[19] the transcendental good, the unique good, the beneficent good, the future good. (By being able to say) "There is no ease which I have not sacrificed to acquire that good, there is no ease in the transcendental world which I have not sacrificed to acquire that good; there is no suffering in the world which I have not grasped to acquire that good; there is no pleasure in the world which I have not sacrificed to acquire that good; there is not a beautiful thing in the world which I have not sacrificed to acquire that good; there is no sovereignty in the world which I have not sacrificed to acquire that good."[20]

An ability to keep one's eyes on the goal also requires the personal quality of courage, not just in the sense of bravery, but as a kind of self-confidence and perseverance that overcomes feelings of futility in the face of what is still to be done.

---

[17]Skilling, 102.

[18]Skilling, 101.

[19]escape from suffering and rebirth.

[20]J. J. Jones, translator, *The Mahavastu* (London: Pali Text Society, 1976), 261–262.

A story of one of the Buddha's previous lives shows how this is the case by analogy. The story is about someone guiding a caravan across a desert, a conventional image of the realm of rebirth in Buddhist literature. The leader had grown weary in the night and had fallen asleep. The oxen pulling the carts in the caravan turned themselves around and as a result, the effort of the night's traveling came only to the caravan being in exactly the same place from which it had begun; again, we can see that this is a detail suggestive of the exhausting pointlessness of ordinary life in the world.

> "Why this is where we camped yesterday," cried the people of the caravan. "All our wood and water is gone and we are lost." So saying, they unyoked their carts and made a camp and spread the awning overhead; then each man flung himself down in despair beneath his own cart. Thought the [future Buddha] to himself, "If I give in, every single one will perish." So he ranged to and fro while it was still early and cool, until he came upon a clump of kusa-grass. "This grass," thought he, "can only have grown up here thanks to the presence of water underneath." So he ordered a spade to be brought and a hole to be dug at that spot. Sixty cubits down they dug, till at that depth the spade struck on a rock, and everybody lost heart. But the future Buddha, feeling sure there must be water under that rock, descended into the hole and took his stand upon the rock. Stooping down, he applied his ear to it, and listened. Catching the sound of water flowing beneath, he came out and said to a serving-lad, "My boy, if *you* give in, we shall all perish. So take heart and courage. Go down into the hole with this iron sledge-hammer, and strike the rock."
>
> Obedient to his master's bidding, the lad, resolute where all others had lost heart, went down and struck the rock. The rock which had damned the stream, split asunder and fell in. Up rose the water in the hole till it was as high as a palm-tree; and everybody drank and bathed. Then they chopped up their spare axles and yokes and other surplus gear, cooked their rice and ate it, and fed their oxen. And as soon as the sun set, they hoisted a flag by the side of the well and traveled on to their destination.[21]

It is worth noting that the personal virtue of courage enables the leader to create the conditions for others in the caravan to take heart and to be successful in their own goals. Once again we see that it is not easy to keep personal virtue distinct from the social virtues.

HOW DOES THIS RELIGION DEFINE CHARACTER, GOOD AND BAD?

We can see a clear outline of Buddhist definitions of bad and good character in a sermon by the Buddha that is preserved in the Pali Canon used by the Theravadin schools of Sri Lanka and Southeast Asia:

---

[21]Robert Chalmers, translator, *The Jataka or Stories of the Buddha's Former Births* (Oxford: Pali Text Society, 1990), 10–11.

"Monks, I will teach you the unworthy man and the still more unworthy man. I will teach you the worthy man and the still more worthy man. Do ye listen to it carefully. Apply your minds and I will speak."

"Yes, lord," replied those monks to the Exalted One. The Exalted One said: "And of what sort, monks, is the unworthy man?

"Herein a certain person is one who takes life, steals, is a wrong-doer in sense-desires [i.e., sexual misconduct], is a liar, is given to the use of liquor fermented and distilled, causing negligence. This one is called 'the unworthy man.'

"And of what sort, monks, is the still more unworthy man? Herein a certain person is one who takes life and so forth, and further encourages another to do the same. This one is called 'the still more unworthy man.'

"And of what sort, monks, is the worthy man?

"Herein a certain person is one who abstains from taking life, from stealing and so forth. This one is called 'the worthy man.'

"And of what sort, monks, is the still more worthy man?

"Herein a certain person not only himself abstains from taking life and so forth, but also encourages another to abstain from so doing. This one is called 'the still more worthy man.'"[22]

This discussion of bad and good character is grounded in the set of five precepts that we have already noted in our discussion of the social virtues. They are expressions of the minimum that is required of us to avoid doing harm to others and to ourselves. In the context of character, however, two other points need to be emphasized. First, this brief discussion makes it clear that character is a matter of consistent behavior: "certain person . . . *is given to* . . . ," whether this behavior is good or bad. Second, this discussion introduces the idea that character is a matter of whether or not one benefits others in one's interactions with them.

This latter aspect of character manifests itself in other virtues that express one's openness to others, most notably in gratitude and kindness to others. In gratitude, mutuality structures one's inclination to benefit others. One acts to benefit others because one is aware of what they have done for you; the Sanskrit word for gratitude (*kṛtajña*), in fact, means "knowledge of what has been done." In kindness, one initiates acts on behalf of others even when they have done nothing for one or might otherwise have been undeserving of one's aid.

An allusion to the mutuality of a grateful openness to others is found in the "Eight Verses for Training the Mind" discussed above:

> In short, both directly and indirectly, do I offer
> Every benefit and happiness to all sentient beings, my mothers.[23]

By portraying all other sentient beings as one's mother—and this can be understood literally in the sense that in the innumerable previous lives that one has already experienced, all other sentient beings have been one's mother at one time

---

[22]F. L. Woodward, translator, *The Book of the Gradual Sayings (Anguttara Nikaya)*, Volume II (Oxford: Pali Text Society, 1992), 230–231.

[23]Singh, xiii.

or another—one is immediately encouraged to overcome one's indifference or hostility toward them by the gratitude one feels for the unsolicited aid that they gave to you, just as one feels love and gratitude toward one's mother in this present life. Gratitude depends on one's mindfulness of what another has done for you, as can be seen in Tsong Kha Pa's presentation of a meditation on all beings as one's mother; Tsong Kha Pa (1357–1419) is one of the great teachers in the Tibetan Buddhist tradition:

> Underlying the contemplation of all the beings as one's own mother, is the initial contemplation in regard to the mother of this life. One should think a single time, "I contemplate in front the clear image of my mother"; and should think, "The present time is not all: since beginningless life cycles the count of my mothers pass beyond all calculation. Thus in her time in the mother role she protected me against all harm, provided me with all benefit and happiness. In particular in this life also, the first thing I did was take a long period in her womb. Thereafter, in the time of rearing, my downy baby hair pressed against her warm flesh. Her ten fingers gave me recreation. She suckled me with the milk from her breast. With her mouth she fed me. My snivel she wiped from my mouth. Wiping away with her hand my filth, she succored me wearilessly by diverse means. Moreover, my own capacity falling short, she gave me food and drink in the time of hunger and thirst; clothes when I shivered, money when I was 'broke.'" Even when those necessities were not found easily, nevertheless, mixing with sin, suffering, and evil reports, she served, rearing me to the utmost of her ability." Wherein there are such things as disease and pain in a son, she thinks, "Better I die than my son die; better I be sick than my son be sick; better I suffer than my son suffer." She chooses this course sincerely; then provides the means of dispelling (those things, suffering, etc.).[24]

Such thoughts about the self-sacrifices of an idealized mother are meant to motivate reciprocal action on behalf of another. Like the other personal virtues discussed in the previous section, gratitude generates a consistency of behavior in the person of good character. This is because "For those who have helped them in the past, good people feel a sympathy that subsequent ill-treatment can do nothing to weaken. This comes of gratitude and ingrained patience."[25]

Lack of gratitude reveals the inconsistency and self-centeredness of a person of bad character. The following story about a previous life of the Buddha is a good example of Buddhist contempt for ingratitude. It is about a time when the future Buddha was born as a woodpecker and one day he happens to come upon a lion who is in pain because a bone from one of its prey had become caught in its teeth:

> When the woodpecker saw the lion so tormented by pain, it said, "Uncle, wherefore are you cast down?" The lion replied, "Nephew, I am tortured by

---

[24]Alex Wayman, translator, *Ethics of Tibet: Bodhisattva Section of Tsong-Kha-Pa's Lam Rim Chen Mo* (Albany: State University of New York Press, 1991), 47.

[25]Peter Khoroche, translator, *Once the Buddha Was a Monkey: Arya Sura's Jatakamala* (Chicago: University of Chicago Press, 1989), 153.

pain." "What sort of pain?" asked the woodpecker. When the lion told the whole story, the woodpecker said, "Uncle, I will treat your case. As you are the lion and king of all four-footed beasts, and can be of service, therefore you must from time to time be of service to me." The lion replied, "I will act in accordance with your words."

The woodpecker extracts the bone from the lion's teeth while he is asleep and shows it to him when he awakes.

The king of beasts was greatly astonished and said, "O nephew, as I wish to recompense you for this service, come to me from time to time in order that I may be of use to you." The woodpecker replied, "Good, I will do so," and flew away.

At another time, while the king of beasts was devouring flesh, the wood-pecker who had been seized by a falcon and had only just escaped death, appeared before the king of beasts in a state of suffering from hunger. Having described its need, it said to the lion, "O uncle, I am tormented with hunger, so give me a piece of flesh." The lion replied. . . . "Are not you, who passed between my teeth, thankful for remaining alive?"

The woodpecker answered . . .

"Profitless are forms seen in dreams and accumulations flung into the ocean. Profitless are intercourse with a bad man, and benefits conferred on the ungrateful."[26]

In the Buddhist traditions, an empathetic openness to others that helps others without expecting any reciprocation is more astonishing and more admirable than the mutuality that structures patterns of grateful behavior. Santideva, a medieval Indian author, says in his *Entering the Path of Enlightenment*: "Truly, whoever reciprocates for a service rendered is highly praised; but what can be said of a [future Buddha] who is not concerned with his own good?"[27]

BEYOND THE NORMAL VIRTUES: WHO IS THE EXTRAORDINARY PERSON?

It is Buddhas and the great future Buddhas who are the preeminent persons in the Buddhist traditions, and they are so extraordinary that they are beyond comparison. As one medieval Japanese text puts it, "In all the heavens and all the realms of earth below, there is nothing like the Buddha; nor in all the worlds in the Ten Directions is there anyone comparable to him."[28]

---

[26]F. Anton Von Schiefner, translator, *Tibetan Tales* (Gurgaon, India: Vintage Books, 1991), 311–312.

[27]Marion Matics, translator, *Entering the Path of Enlightenment* (New York: Macmillan, 1970), 146.

[28]Edward Kamens, translator, *The Three Jewels* (Ann Arbor: Center for Japanese Studies, University of Michigan, 1988), 103.

Future Buddhas (bodhisattvas) are cultivating the virtues that a Buddha already possesses to a maximal degree. These include all of the social and personal virtues that we have been considering, and they are summarized in a list of six or ten "perfections"; these perfections were mentioned in the verses from Nāgārjuna's *The Precious Garland,* which we looked at in our consideration of the social virtues. Buddhas possess to a maximal degree the qualities of generosity, morality, tolerance, heroic effort, concentration, and wisdom according to the list of six; when the list consists of ten items, other qualities such as "skill-in-means" (*upaya*), resolution, strength, and knowledge may be added, as in one formulation, or truth, renunciation, loving-kindness, and equanimity, in another.

Buddhas are different from the rest with respect to the degree to which they have cultivated the social and personal virtues intrinsic to the good life. They are also different from the rest of us in their wisdom, and in this they appear to be different kinds of beings than we are. Their insight into the true nature of reality, which is portrayed as omniscience, allows them to behave more freely than us and in ways that are more effective than others. Buddhas and future Buddhas are also beings that others can rely upon with confidence. *The Perfection of Wisdom in 8000 Lines,* an influential Indian Mahayana text, describes by analogy a future Buddha in ways that display his accomplishment and heroic nature. Note how it emphasizes both his effectiveness in action on behalf of himself and others and his experience of joy and self-satisfaction in his actions:

> [The Lord said:] Suppose that there were a most excellent hero, very vigorous, of high social position, handsome, attractive and most fair to behold, of many virtues, in possession of all the finest virtues, of those virtues which spring from the very height of sovereignty, morality, learning, renunciation and so on. He is judicious, able to express himself, to formulate his views clearly, to substantiate his claims; one who always knows the suitable time, place and situation for everything. In archery he has gone as far as one can go, he is successful in warding off all manner of attack, most skilled in all arts, and foremost, through his fine achievements, in all crafts. . . . Any work he might undertake he manages to complete, he speaks methodically, shares his great riches with the many, honours what should be honoured. . . . Would such a person feel ever-increasing joy and zest?
>
> [A disciple:] He would, O Lord.
>
> [The Lord:] Now suppose, further, that this person, so greatly accomplished, should have taken his family with him on a journey, his mother and father, his sons and daughters. By some circumstance they find themselves in a great, wild forest. The foolish ones among them feel fright, terror and hair-raising fear. He, however, would fearlessly say to his family: "Do not be afraid! I shall soon take you safely and securely out of this terrible and frightening forest. I shall soon set you free. If then more and more hostile and inimical forces should rise up against him in that forest, would this heroic man decide to abandon his family, and to take himself alone out of that terrible and frightening forest—he who is not one to draw back, who is endowed

with all the force of firmness and vigour, who is wise, exceedingly tender and compassionate, courageous and a master of many resources.

[The disciple:] No, O Lord, For that person, who does not abandon his family, has at his disposal powerful resources, both within and without. On his side forces will arise in that wild forest which are quite a match for the hostile and inimical forces, and they will stand up for him and protect. Those enemies and adversaries of his, who look for a weak spot, who seek for a weak spot, will not gain any hold over him. He is competent to deal with the situation, and is able, unhurt and uninjured, soon to take out of that forest, both his family and himself, and securely and safely will they reach a village, city or market town.

[The Lord:] Just so, is it with a future Buddha who is full of pity and concerned with the welfare of all beings, who dwells in friendliness, compassion, sympathetic joy and even-mindedness.[29]

We can see in such an account that one becomes a being of inexplicable value when one is able to act effectively on behalf of others. In short, we owe it to ourselves to be of benefit to others.

COMMENTARIES

Judaism on Buddhism

by JACOB NEUSNER

The Judaic counterpart to the Buddhist conception of karma—"one's present nature is determined by the effects of one's previous actions"—may be located in the conception of a common humanity, in which each generation bears the burden imposed by its predecessors. A common heritage shaped by the earlier for the later generations may be seen to correspond, for the collectivity, humanity, to the karmic idea. Adam and Eve's actions in Eden determined the fate of humanity for ages to come; but that is a statement on the human condition, not on individuals' particular fates. Here is an account of why old age, suffering, and sickness affect humanity. It is on account of the decision of the patriarchs, Abraham, Isaac, and Jacob:

> "When Isaac was old, and his eyes were dim, so that he could not see, he called Esau his older son, and said to him, 'My son,' and he answered, 'Here I am'" (Gen. 27:1):
>
> Said R. Judah bar Simon, "Abraham sought [the physical traits of] old age [so that from one's appearance, people would know that he was old]. He said before him, 'Lord of all ages, when a man and his son come in somewhere, no one knows whom to honor. If you crown a man with the traits of old age, people will know whom to honor.'

---

[29]Quoted in Edward Conze, *Buddhist Texts through the Ages* (New York: Harper Torchbooks, 1964), 128–129.

"Said to him the Holy One, blessed be he, 'By your life, this is a good thing that you have asked for, and it will begin with you.'

"From the beginning of the book of Genesis to this passage, there is no reference to old age. But when Abraham our father came along, the traits of old age were given to him, as it is said, 'And Abraham was old' (Gen. 24:1).

"Isaac asked God for suffering. He said before him, 'Lord of the age, if someone dies without suffering, the measure of strict justice is stretched out against him. But if you bring suffering on him, the measure of strict justice will not be stretched out against him. [Suffering will help counter the man's sins, and the measure of strict justice will be mitigated through suffering by the measure of mercy.]'

"Said to him the Holy One, blessed be he, 'By your life, this is a good thing that you have asked for, and it will begin with you.'

"From the beginning of the book of Genesis to this passage, there is no reference to suffering. But when Isaac came along, suffering was given to him: 'his eyes were dim.'

"Jacob asked for sickness. He said before him, 'Lord of all ages, if a person dies without illness, he will not settle his affairs for his children. If he is sick for two or three days, he will settle his affairs with his children.'

"Said to him the Holy One, blessed be he, 'By your life, this is a good thing that you have asked for, and it will begin with you.'

"That is in line with this verse: 'And someone said to Joseph, "Behold, your father is sick"' (Gen. 48:1)."

Genesis Rabbah LXV:IX.1

In the sense that the condition of humanity in the here and now carries forward the decisions and actions of prior generations, Judaism can attempt to approach the conception of karma. But that, as we see, is collective, not individual. When it comes to an understanding of one's true nature, matters prove equally tentative. But the social virtues, as we have come to expect, prove to correspond: generosity, morality, loving-kindness, and the rest for Buddhism and Judaism match quite neatly. Like Buddhism, Judaism will see various levels of virtue and of vice. Here is an account of the types of thievery that people practice:

There are seven kinds of thieves.

The first among all of them is the one who deceives people.

He who presses his fellow to come as his guest but does not intend to receive him properly.

He who overwhelms him with gifts and knows concerning him that he will not accept them.

He who opens for someone jars of wine which already had been sold to a storekeeper.

He who falsifies measures.

He who pads the scales.

He who mixes up seeds of St. John's bread in seeds of fenugreek, and vinegar in oil.

And not only so, but they hold him culpable as if he [supposed he] were able to deceive the Most High and fool [Him].

He who deceives people is called a thief, and it is said, "So Absalom stole the hearts of the men of Israel" (2 Sam. 15:6).

Who is the greater? The thief or the one who is the victim? One must say it is the one who is the victim, who was well aware that he was the victim of thievery but who kept silent.

Tosefta Baba Qamma 7:8

Here we see the counterpart to the division of action into the categories of bodily action, verbal action, and mental action. Time and again, we observe, religions differ fundamentally and yet concur on practical matters of ethical conduct.

Christianity on Buddhism
by BRUCE CHILTON

Christianity's reflection on what it means by "self," which comparison with Hinduism demands, is only emphasized further when Buddhism is brought into the discussion. The bifurcation between the capacity to be awakened and the hierarchy of social conventions, which Buddhism is described as sanctioning, has perplexed Christian thinkers. One reason for the dynamism and ferment characteristic of societies influenced by Christianity is that the dialectic between salvation and social structure has really never been agreed. In this case, the relative immaturity of the religious system has turned out to encourage the appearance of what is commonly called progress and what is obviously (on any reading) a powerful influence.

The breakdown of the self, whenever it is subject to even cursory analysis, is a profound point of intersection between Buddhism and Christianity. The volatility and instability of the human subject, precisely from its own point of view, was vividly documented by Paul (Romans 7:15–23):

> For what I achieve, I do not know; for what I want, this I do not perform, but what I hate, this I do. But if I do that which I do not want, I agree with the law, that it is beautiful. But now it is no longer I that achieves, but sin dwelling in me. Because I know that good does not dwell in me, that is in my flesh, because to want lies in me, but to perform what is beautiful does not, because I do not do the good I want, but the bad I do not want, this I perform. But if what I do not want, this I do, I am no longer achieving, but the sin dwelling in me. Then I find that while the law to do the beautiful is in my wanting, the evil lies in me. For I consent with the law of God according to the inner person, but I observe another law in my members, at war with the law of my mind and leading me captive by the law of sin which is in my members.

This radical analysis is not only a typical feature of Christian spirituality, but it also characterizes much existentialist and postmodern interpretation, in that the loss of a sense of the legitimacy of self may appear to license a self-indulgent attitude toward the nonself. Again, the appeal of Tantra in the West referred to in "Christianity on Hinduism" might be relevant to this point.

But exactly at this juncture, Paul (and the Christian tradition as a whole) moves in quite a different direction. Paul refers to the pain of his position and articulates a response in a single breath, although it is obscured in traditional interpretations (Romans 7:24–25): "I am a miserable person. Who will deliver me from the body of this death? But there is grace in God through Christ Jesus our Lord!" "Grace" for Paul is a salvific force, because it provides the insight of one's being in the presence of God. The self that is the object of salvation is not a function of social forces at all, but what is achieved in the moment of baptism, when one dies to the dissolution of sin and is raised to the life of Christ (Romans 6:3–11).

So Christianity, with Buddhism, finds itself at odds with received ideas about the nature of the human self, but then urges an alternative definition. If the resurrected life, which is already a force within our experience, may be known in ethical terms, then our attitude toward ourselves and others ought radically to be revised. The appropriate orientation is teleological, in the direction of the goal we are pursing. Curiously, at just the moment when the difference with Buddhism seems most palpable, Christianity catalogs virtues (and implicit virtues) that would be at home in Buddhist sources (Mark 7:18–23):

> And he says to them, So, are you senseless, too? Don't you apprehend that everything outside proceeding into the person is not able to defile one, because it does not proceed into the heart of one, but into the belly, and proceeds out into the latrine? [Making all foods clean.] But he was saying that: What proceeds out from the person, that defiles the person. Because from within, from the heart of humanity, bad intentions proceed out: sexual abuses, thefts, killings, adulteries, greeds, malices, deceit, indecency, evil eye, cursing, arrogance, foolishness. All these evils proceed out from within and defile the person.

The reality of the false self that defiles, of the pure self that God embraces, is an irreducible aspect of the Christian vision.

Islam on Buddhism

by Tamara Sonn

Islam and Buddhism are fundamentally in accord in their beliefs in human moral equality. Both traditions see all people, not just a select group, as capable of achieving the ultimate goal. Their views on what the ultimate goal is, however, are widely divergent. Unlike Buddhism, Islam holds firmly to the notion of a unique self, created by God and destined for eternal life, after the present life. The self is not an illusion, nor are there multiple rebirths. Nor is our "true nature" much of a mystery in Islam. We are human, meaning we have a great inherent dignity as servants of the one God, created with divine purpose, yet we are also weak and prone to despair. Nevertheless, the person of faith knows God is always receptive to human prayers, the source of eternal guidance. Therefore, time need not be spent in great self-contemplation. It is better spent in efforts to understand the world, to know the sources of injustice and the ways to reverse it. The next step is simply to work against injustice and oppression, confident in divine guidance. For suffering does not result from ideas; in the Islamic view, suffering comes from oppression and inaction in the face of it. Still, there is some concurrence on virtue between Buddhism and Islam. Both traditions teach that helping others is essentially moral. Islam stresses more active efforts than does Buddhism; the latter teaches that we should do good and do no harm, while the former calls for doing good and prohibiting evil. Yet Islam does recognize that not all can actively intervene in evil (Qur'an 3:111, 9:71). A famous oral report (hadith) therefore allows those who cannot help "with the hand" to do so "with the voice;" those who can do neither should be content with doing so "with the heart."

Hinduism on Buddhism

by BRIAN K. SMITH

Buddhism and Hinduism have, in general, many shared doctrines: the belief in karma and transmigration; the supposition that karma and rebirth are driven by desire; the conceptualization of worldly existence as characterized by suffering and illusion; and the ideal of the cessation of suffering and rebirth in the attainment of a radically different perception of reality: *nirvana* or "awakening" and *moksha* (freedom and liberation). And both tend to affirm hierarchical orders in opposition to the egalitarian ideals of the modern West and, to a certain degree, of Western religions.

It is with these similarities in mind that we turn to the principal difference when it comes to the teachings of each religion on virtue. For Buddhism, hierarchical thinking is counterbalanced by the notion that "all humans have the capacity of becoming awakened, regardless of their social location." And for Buddhism, the religious life dedicated to such an awakening can be adopted not only by anyone but at any time in the life cycle. Hindu thinkers reacted to such teachings by formulating the *varnashrama* system, the foundation of caste differences and the structuring of life into stages, each with its own mandates and virtues. Under this system, first, human beings of different sorts are thought to have different spiritual capacities. While some may be born into stations where the ultimate goal might fruitfully be pursued, others do not have (in this life, at least) the inborn capabilities to do so. For them there are different paths that, if successfully completed, will ensure a better rebirth in the future—and eventually a birth from which the final goal may be attained. Second, even for those with such innate spiritual capacities, the mainstream Hindu view encourages them to stay in the world (and practice worldly virtues) until old age.

There have been alternatives and exceptions to this schema within the history of Hinduism. Some of the devotional sects have embraced a kind of spiritual egalitarianism and taught that even the socially despised are equal in the eyes of God. Some have even suggested that those accustomed to servitude in social life are better able to render proper service, with humility, to God. And in the past as today, not all Hindu renunciants wait until old age to renounce the world and dedicate their lives to liberation. Generally speaking, however, the spiritual equality that Buddhism assumes—and the generality with which that tradition speaks of personal and social virtues—is contrasted to the specificity with which Hinduism refracts the very concept of virtue.

SUMMARY

For Buddhists, we owe it to ourselves to be of benefit to others, and thus the life of virtue inevitably benefits both oneself and others. False notions about who we are as human beings often prevent us from seeing this, but even when we do, there are feelings that can obstruct our intent to help others. The life of virtue then is a process of self-transformation that ends in happiness for ourselves and others.

GLOSSARY

Aggañña-sutta   "The Discourse on What is Primary," an account in Pali, pre-served by Theravāda Buddhists, that explains the origins of human social life

bodhisattva   a being who is cultivating the virtues and capabilities necessary to become a Buddha

Buddha   an awakened one who is able to freely aid others because of his true understanding of reality

chanda   [Pali] the acceptable desire for well-being; contrasted with *tanhā*, greed for pleasure

dhamma, dharma   the true nature of the world that was taught by the Buddha, refers to both reality itself and to the Buddha's teaching

karma   [Sanskrit] a law of moral cause and effect by which good actions produce good results, especially good rebirths, and bad actions produce undesirable results

Nāgārjuna   a second century Indian Buddhist philosopher, one of the most influential thinkers in the Buddhist tradition

samsara   [Sanskrit] the cycle of birth and death in which beings are reborn in varying conditions of well-being or torment

sangha   [Pali] the Buddhist monastic order

Soka Gakkai   a new Buddhist lay association which originated in Japan in this century and which is now found around the world

śresthi   [Sanskrit] a person of great wealth

tanhā   [Pali] the self-destructive greed for pleasure

Vinaya   the code of behavior for Buddhist monks

DISCUSSION QUESTIONS

1. What personal virtues are necessary for the successful cultivation of social virtues? Why are they necessary?

2. What is the true nature of a human being in Buddhist thought? How are these conceptions at odds with what people ordinarily think about themselves?

3. Why is gratitude important in the Buddhist vision of the life of virtue? How is gratitude connected to Buddhist conceptions of rebirth?

4. How does the Buddhist understanding of the moral life always involve a proper understanding of one's true nature?

5. What is the place of karma in the life of virtue?

6. How is the moral behavior of a Buddha different from ordinary people?

 **INFOTRAC**

If you would like additional information related to the material discussed here, you can visit our Web site: http://www.wadsworth.com

A P P E N D I X

Where Do We Find the Authoritative Statements of the Religious Traditions?

When we represent the views of the religions treated here, we rely upon and cite at some length the classical and authoritative sources of those traditions. The writings on which we base our accounts are the ones that the generality of the faithful of the respective traditions acknowledge as authoritative. That is to say, whatever other writings groups of the faithful of those religious traditions may value, the ones on which we draw exercise authority for all of the faithful within the large and diverse religious tradition at hand.

We recognize that many diverse writings and viewpoints are encompassed by each tradition treated here. For all of them trace long histories, played out over vast spaces and many centuries. Surely over time people formed conflicting opinions on the basis of diverse experience. And in today's world, the faithful of Judaism, Christianity, Islam, Buddhism, and Hinduism divide into competing, often conflicting groups. Reform and Orthodox Jews differ on important religious questions, as do Protestant, Catholic, Orthodox, and Mormon Christians, Sunni and Shi'ite Muslims, Theravada and Mahayana Buddhists, and Vaishnava and Shaivite Hindus. Not only so, but individual practitioners of the great religious traditions accept the faith but also pick and choose and form their own ideals in dialogue with the received ones. But all those who practice (a) Judaism refer to the Torah, all who practice (a) Christianity build upon the Bible, all Muslims base themselves on the Qur'an and the Sunna of Prophet Muhammed, all Hindus acknowledge the authority of the Vedas, and all Buddhists see their authoritative texts as "Buddha-speech." So in portraying the Judaic, Christian, Muslim, Hindu, and Buddhist views on the issues we address, we refer specifically to documents or doctrines to which all of the faithful of Judaism, Christianity, Islam, Hinduism, and Buddhism, respectively, will refer and affirm. Whatever writings may find a hearing in the diverse systems of the families of

Judaism, Christianity, Islam, Hinduism, and Buddhism, the sources cited here will enjoy authoritative standing in their respective traditions. That is what we mean when we call them "classical."

JUDAISM

Like Christianity, Judaism begins in the writings of ancient Israel and appeals to the Hebrew Scriptures that the world knows as "the Old Testament" and Judaism calls "the Written Torah." But Judaism appeals also to oral traditions called "the Oral Torah." So, like Christianity, Judaism values additional writings. To state the matter in simple language: the New Testament is to the Old Testament as the Oral Torah is to the Written Torah. What is the meaning of this key word, "Torah"?

The word covers a number of matters. "The Torah" refers first of all to the Pentateuch, the Five Books of Moses, Genesis, Exodus, Leviticus, Numbers, and Deuteronomy. These are inscribed in a scroll, read aloud in synagogue worship, carefully protected as a holy object: "the Torah." So by "the Torah" Judaism means, the object, the holy scroll that sets forth the Pentateuch. But the Torah is comprised, further, by the remainder of the Hebrew Scriptures, the prophets and the writings. The prophets are the books of Joshua, Judges, Samuel, Kings, Isaiah, Jeremiah, and Ezekiel, as well as the twelve smaller collections. The writings encompass Psalms, Proverbs, Chronicles, Job, the Five Scrolls (Lamentations, Esther, Ruth, Song of Songs, a.k.a. Song of Solomon, and Qoheleth, a.k.a. Ecclesiastes). All together, if we take the first letters of the three words—Torah, Nebi'im, and Ketubim—the Torah (Pentateuch), Prophets (Hebrew: Nebi'im), and Writings (Hebrew: Ketubim) yield the Hebrew neologism for the Old Testament, TaNaKH.

But since Judaism, like Christianity, values further traditions as divinely revealed at Sinai, by "the Torah," more writings are encompassed. Specifically, classical Judaism, which took shape in the first seven centuries of the common era (= A.D.), by "the Oral Torah" means traditions revealed by God to Moses at Sinai—oral traditions right along with the Written Torah (Genesis through Deuteronomy). These other traditions were preserved orally, in a process of oral formulation and oral transmission, from Sinai through prophets and elders, masters and disciples, until they were finally reduced to written form in a set of documents that reached closure from ca. 200 to ca. 600 C.E. (= A.D.). All together, these documents are classified as "the Oral Torah," meaning the repositories of the oral tradition of Sinai.

What are the documents that initially comprise "the Oral Torah"? The first and most important of them is the Mishnah, a law code of a deeply philosophical character, closed at 200. The code quickly attracted commentators, who analyzed its contents and clarified and applied its rules. The work of the commentators was put together and written down. It reaches us in two Talmuds, that is, two distinct traditions of explanation of the Mishnah, the Talmud of the Land of Israel, which reached a conclusion at ca. 400 C.E. in what was then Roman-ruled Palestine, and the Talmud of Babylonia, finished at ca. 600 C.E. in Iranian-ruled Babylonia (approximately the area of central Iraq today).

Once the work of explaining the Mishnah got under way, the same approaches to the reading of the received tradition led the Judaic sages to provide the Hebrew Scriptures with compilations setting forth extensive explanation and amplification. This work of rereading Scripture in light of contemporary questions was called "Midrash," from the Hebrew word *darash,* meaning search. In the formative age of the Judaism based on the written and the oral traditions of Sinai, a number of compilations of readings of scriptural books were completed. In particular, books of the Written Torah that are read in synagogue services received systematic exposition. To the book of Genesis was attached Genesis Rabbah (the amplification of Genesis); so too to Leviticus, Leviticus Rabbah; to Exodus came a work amplifying the normative rules of Exodus, called Mekhilta Attributed to R. Ishmael; to Leviticus another legal commentary, Sifra; to Numbers and Deuteronomy legal commentaries called Sifré to Numbers and Sifré to Deuteronomy. Four of the Five Scrolls—Ruth, Esther, Song of Songs, and Lamentations—were systematically reread. In medieval times, other compilations addressed the books of the Written Torah neglected in the formative age.

These are the sources utilized in the account of Judaism's positions on the practical issues addressed in these pages. Most Judaic religious systems we know today—Reform, Orthodox, Conservative, Reconstructionist, New Age, and the like—value other writings in addition, but all share in common the Torah, oral and written, that took shape in ancient times, differing on its authority and its meaning. And, needless to say, other writings, authoritative for one Judaism or another, take up the same topics. But most Judaisms would concur on the pertinence of the sources cited here, even though each Judaic religious system will assign its own weight to the classical sources and will, further, add to the list of authoritative writings further documents of its own choosing. So "Judaism" here is represented by its formative and normative writings.

CHRISTIANITY

The Scriptures of Israel have always been valued within the Church, both in Hebrew and in the Greek translation used in the Mediterranean world. (The Greek rendering is called the "Septuagint," after the seventy translators who were said to have produced it.) Those were the only Scriptures of the Church in its primitive phase, when the New Testament was being composed. In their meetings of prayer and worship, followers of Jesus saw the Scriptures of Israel "fulfilled" by their faith: their conviction was that the same Spirit of God that was active in the prophets was, through Christ, available to them.

The New Testament was produced in primitive communities of Christians to prepare people for baptism, to order worship, to resolve disputes, to encourage faith, and like purposes. As a whole, it is a collective document of primitive

Christianity. Its purpose is to call out and order true Israel in response to the triumphant news of Jesus' preaching, activity, death, and resurrection. The New Testament provides the means of accessing the Spirit spoken of in the Scriptures of Israel. Once the New Testament was formed, it was natural to refer to the Scriptures of Israel as the "Old Testament."

The Old Testament is classic for Christians, because it represents the ways in which God's Spirit might be known. At the same time, the New Testament is normative: it sets out how we actually appropriate the Spirit of God, which is also the spirit of Christ. That is why the Bible as a whole is accorded a place of absolute privilege in the Christian tradition: it is the literary source from which we know both how the Spirit of God has been known and how we can appropriate it.

Early Christianity (between the second and the fourth centuries C.E.) designates the period during which the Church founded theology on the basis of the Scriptures. Although Christians were under extreme—sometimes violent—pressure from the Roman Empire, Early Christianity was a time of unique creativity. From thinkers as different from one another as Bishop Irenaeus in France and Origen, the speculative teacher active first in Egypt and then in Palestine, a common Christian philosophy began to emerge. Early Christianity might also be called a "Catholic" phase, in the sense that it was a quest for a "general" or "universal" account of the phase, but that designation may lead to confusion with Roman Catholicism at a later stage, and is avoided here.

After the Roman Empire itself embraced Christianity in the fourth century, the Church was in a position to articulate its understanding of the faith formally by means of common standards. During this period of Orthodox Christianity, correct norms of worship, baptism, creeds, biblical texts, and doctrines were established. From Augustine in the West to Gregory of Nyssa in the East, Christianity for the first and only time in its history approached being truly ecumenical.

The collapse of Rome under the barbarian invasions in the West broke the unity of the Church. Although the East remained wedded to the forms of Orthodoxy (and does so to this day), the West developed its own structure of governance and its own theology, especially after Charlemagne was crowned as emperor of the Romans by Pope Leo III on Christmas day in 800 C.E.

To severe arguments regarding political jurisdiction, East and West added doctrinal divisions. The pope was condemned by a synod in Constantinople in 876 for failing to prevent a change in the wording of the Nicene Creed that had become accepted in the West. A papal legate in 1054 excommunicated the patriarch of Constantinople. But even those acts pale in comparison with what happened in 1204: European Crusaders on their way to Jerusalem sacked and pillaged Constantinople itself.

European Christianity flourished during the Middle Ages, and Scholastic theology was a result of that success. The Scholastics were organized on the basis of educational centers, Thomas Aquinas at the University of Paris during the thirteenth century being the best example. During the periods of Early Christianity and Orthodoxy, theologies as well as forms of discipline of worship were developed for the first time. Scholastic theology was rather in the position of systematizing these developments for the usage of the West. At the same time, Scholastic theologians also rose to the challenge of explaining Christian faith in the terms of the new philosophical movements they came into contact with.

The Reformation, between the sixteenth and the eighteenth centuries, challenged the very idea of a single system of Christianity. Martin Luther imagined that each region might settle on its own form of religion, while in England the settlement was on a national basis and in Jean Calvin's Geneva the elders of the city made that determination. But in all its variety, the Reformation insisted that the Bible and worship should be put into the language of the people, and that their governance should be consistent with their faith.

From the eighteenth century until the present, Christianity in its modern form has been wrestling with the consequences of the rise of rationalism and science. The results have been diverse and surprising. They include Protestant Fundamentalism, a claim that the Bible articulates certain "fundamentals" that govern human existence, and the Roman Catholic idea of papal infallibility, the claim that the pope may speak the truth of the Church without error. In both cases, the attempt is made to establish an axiom of reason that reason itself may not challenge. But modern Christianity also includes a vigorous acceptance of the primacy of individual judgment in the life of communities: examples include the Confessing Church in Germany, which opposed the Third Reich, and the current movement of Liberation Theology in Central and South America.

Today, Christians may use many combinations of the sort of sources named here to articulate their beliefs, and the resulting pattern is likely to be as distinctive as what has been produced in the past.

ISLAM

The absolute foundation of Islam is the Qur'an (which used to be spelled phonetically as "Koran"), Islam's sacred Scripture. The Qur'an is believed to be the literal word of God, revealed through Prophet Muhammad, in the early seventh century C.E. in Arabia. (The Arabic word *qur'an* means "recitation.") Muhammad is called the prophet of Islam, but he is not considered its founder. In fact, he is called the last prophet of Islam, the "seal of the prophets" (Qur'an, Sura [chapter] 33:40). He is believed to be the one chosen by God to deliver the full and final message of God to humanity. Islam's beginnings are believed to be primordial; the Qur'an tells of a sacred trust assumed by humanity that guided their very creation. God created human beings specifically to carry out the divine will of creating a just society. (The Arabic word *islam* means "submission"—to the will of God.) The Qur'an then names a number of prophets, beginning with Adam and including many known to Jews and Christians, though not necessarily as prophets (Noah, Abraham, Moses, and Jesus, for example). It also includes others unknown to the earlier scriptural traditions, such as Shu'aib, Salih, and Hud. All the prophets have brought essentially the same message, although some communities have allowed their scriptures to be corrupted. The scripture revealed through Prophet Muhammad is considered the most complete. It provides the necessary correctives to misinterpretations of earlier messages, and the guidance required for effectively carrying out the will of God on earth.

But the Qur'an is not a law book. Of its 114 verses, only a few deal with specific legislation, such as those prohibiting female infanticide, prostitution, usury, and gambling; those imposing dietary restrictions (the prohibition of alcohol and pork); and those specifying family law on issues such as inheritance, dower, and arbitration in divorce. The majority of the Qur'an's verses deal with theological teachings, such as the oneness of God, and moral themes, establishing general standards for virtue and justice. What is more, they were revealed gradually, over some twenty-two years. Over that period, many of the themes developed, some made more specific, some exemplified by the Prophet's words and example.

Those words and examples, though not part of the Qur'an itself, are considered essential to full understanding of Scripture, since the Qur'an itself said repeatedly that Prophet Muhammad set the best example of how to follow its teachings. Collectively known as the Sunna ("way" or normative practice; also spelled Sunnah) of the Prophet, reports (*ahadith*; sing.: *hadith*) of these examples were originally transmitted orally from one generation to another. But by the second century after the Prophet's death in 632 C.E., scholars began to recognize the need to record these reports. They collected as many individual reports as possible, then carefully screened them for authenticity, organized, and codified them. By the third century after the Prophet (late ninth/early tenth century C.E.), there were six major collections of hadith reports for Sunni Muslims. (Shi'i or Shi'ite Muslims, a minority who differ with the Sunni Muslims on issues of community leadership, compiled other collections of hadith reports, and by the eleventh century C.E. had identified three major books of Sunna.) Two of the Sunni collections (those of ninth-century scholars Muhammad al-Bukhari and Muslim ibn Hajjaj al-Nisabur) were designated by the majority of scholars at the time as most authoritative.

The hadith collections, and especially those of al-Bukhari and Muslim, are the basis of commentaries purporting to amplify the meaning of Qur'anic verses (*tafsir*), and provide essential precedents in Islamic legislation (*fiqh*). Islamic law (collectively known as Shari'a; also spelled Shari'ah) is the basis of Islamic life—personal and collective. There are four major schools of Islamic law for Sunni Muslims, and another for Shi'i Muslims. Other, smaller groups of Muslims rely on other formulations of normative behavior. But all Muslims agree that the sources for knowledge of normative behavior are the Qur'an and the Sunna of the Prophet. They are, therefore, the sources used in the treatment of issues presented in this volume.

HINDUISM

The principal texts of Hinduism in which ethics in general, and the ethics of practical matters such as family life, work, and personal virtue, in particular, are covered are those that deal with *dharma,* meaning "duty" or "law." Some references to this topic already appear in the various texts collectively known as the Vedas (ca. 1200 B.C.E.–400 B.C.E.), especially in the philosophical and mystical treatises known as the Upanishads. The works that concentrate on dharma, however, are the somewhat later Dharmashastras and Dharmasutras, some of which have been collected and translated by Georg Buhler under the title *The Sacred Laws of the Aryas* (reprint ed., Delhi: Motilal Banarsidass, 1975). Among these dharma texts, the most important and comprehensive is the Manusmriti; this work has recently been translated by Wendy Doniger with Brian K. Smith as *The Laws of Manu* (Harmondsworth, Middlesex, England: Penguin Books, 1991). These texts on dharma have been regarded and used by Hindus for many centuries as the authoritative guidelines for personal and social duties of an ethical nature.

References to ethics may also be drawn from texts called the Puranas, encyclopedic and sectarian compilations composed during a long period between 200 C.E. and 1700 C.E. Another source for ethical instruction is two epics of the Hindu tradition, the Mahabharata and the Ramayana, both of them compiled between 300 B.C.E. and 300 C.E. The two epics serve as the foundations for Hindu culture and religion; their characters, stories, and plotlines are familiar to nearly everyone in India and are extremely important popular sources for ethical guidance.

Of especial importance is a text enfolded within the Mahabharata and preserved separately: the Bhagavad Gita. The Gita consists of a dialogue between a warrior named Arjuna and his charioteer, the Lord Krishna. In the course of the work, Krishna instructs Arjuna as to how to best perform his duty, or dharma, especially in circumstances where the right thing to do is not always obvious. The Gita has been translated into English many times, most recently by Barbara Stoler Miller as *The Bhagavad-Gita: Krishna's Counsel in Time of War* (New York, Bantam Books, 1986).

BUDDHISM

Buddhism begins with Gautama, the Awakened One (*buddha*), who lived and taught in India in about the fifth century before the common era; scholars frequently give 563–483 B.C.E. as the dates of his life, but they are not certain. Buddhism spread subsequently to many lands in Asia, from India to Sri Lanka and Southeast Asia, and from India to Central Asia and then to China, Korea, and Japan, always developing and adapting as it spread; more recently, it has been embraced and transformed in Europe and the Americas. In this process, its authoritative ideas, practices, experiences, and values have been multiplied in almost every way imaginable, and the modern historian sees Buddhist authoritative literature as a record of that grand process. The resulting diversity of Buddhist life has been so exuberant that we do well to speak of Buddhism in the plural—Buddhist traditions—for this helps us to remember that the basic premise of this series applies to Buddhism alone; the point can be made by altering just slightly the statement made by Jacob Neusner in the preface, "even where [different parts of a religion] appear to resemble one another, they turn out to be different" and thus we have to be careful against being misled by failing to recognize that "what looks alike . . . may upon closer examination prove quite different, and difference may well obscure the meaning of points of concurrence."

When approached with the yardstick of the relatively simple canons of authoritative literature in Islam, Judaism, and Christianity, Buddhists may appear to accept an extraordinarily wide variety of texts as containing authoritative statements. All Buddhists do not accept the same texts, however, and there is no single canon on which all Buddhist religious systems build. In fact, there are very few individual texts that can be found in every Buddhist tradition, not even those statements that a modern historian would take as the record of the teaching of Gautama Buddha, the founder of Buddhism. Moreover, the size of individual canons accepted by particular traditions—whether these are defined on sectarian grounds (for example, Zen Buddhism) or cultural grounds (for example, Tibetan Buddhism)—can be huge in their own right, and we might think of them more as a library than as a "canon" or "scripture." The Chinese Buddhist canon, to take one impressive example, is almost one hundred thousand pages long. It goes without saying that the contents of these many texts are varied, and frequently contradictory.

To give an account of the literature that has been authoritative for Buddhists would be to give an account only of difference, and this would obscure some important points of concurrence among Buddhists. We still need to generalize about *Buddhism* out of the study of many *Buddhisms*. One generalization we should keep in mind is that Buddhists have not seen their own history as simply as the modern historian portrays it. Even as all Buddhists have acknowledged the importance of Gautama Buddha, in their honor and devotion to him especially, no Buddhists have seen the Truth that he taught as beginning with him as an individual. He taught Truth, to be sure, but he only rediscovered it. Truth has been known and taught by others too. Consequently, the record of Gautama's teachings is not the only place where one should expect statements of Truth. There have been other awakened persons, other Buddhas, and there will be more in the future; indeed, Truth is directly available to us now.

This observation is key for understanding where the contemporary Buddhist and the academic student of religion both can look for authoritative statements on the topics addressed by this series. We turn to *buddhavacana*—"Buddha-speech"—but it is important to remember that this does not name the record of the teachings of Gautama Buddha, nor was it ever only that in the eyes of Buddhists. The basic point we should keep in mind is best expressed in an old Buddhist aphorism: "what Buddha taught is well-said," but it is equally true to say that "what is well-said Buddha taught."

Buddha-speech comes in a number of genres, some concerned with monastic life, others with philosophy, but for the purposes of this series the most important genre will be *sutra*. This is a generic name given to an account of an occasion on which a Buddha taught. Most *sutras* are attributed to Gautama Buddha, although a modern historian would be skeptical about any claims that the *historical* Gautama Buddha actually taught some of the most influential ones, such as the *Lotus Sutra* (Saddharmapundarika) and the *Sutra on the Land of Bliss* (Sukhavativyuha), to name two texts that have been very important in East Asian Buddhism.

Another generalization about Buddha-speech draws our attention to another source of authoritative statements. Buddha-speech contains two kinds of sentences: some that have obvious meanings that do not require interpretation or elaboration in order to be understood, and others, that do require their meaning "to be drawn out." The latter kind of sentence thus requires commentary for proper understanding, and the commentaries by learned or spiritually accomplished teachers on Buddha-speech are as authoritative as sources of valid and useful knowledge as Buddha-speech itself. Buddhist sectarian differences can stem from disagreements over what counts as Buddha-speech as well as from disagreements over how to understand a text or statement about which there is concurrence that it is Buddha-speech. In this series, we will turn then both to Buddha-speech and to commentaries to find authoritative statements that address the practical issues of everyday life taken up by each volume.